The Last Puritans

The
Last Puritans

Mainline Protestants and the Power of the Past

MARGARET BENDROTH

The University of North Carolina Press *Chapel Hill*

Published with the assistance of the Anniversary Fund of the University of North Carolina Press.

© 2015 The University of North Carolina Press
All rights reserved
Designed by Alyssa D'Avanzo
Set in Calluna by codeMantra

Manufactured in the United States of America

Cover illustration: Pilgrim Tableau (Courtesy of Congregational Library)

Library of Congress Cataloging-in-Publication Data
Bendroth, Margaret Lamberts, 1954–
The last Puritans : mainline Protestants and the power of the past / Margaret Bendroth. — 1st [edition].
    pages cm
Includes bibliographical references and index.
ISBN 978-1-4696-2400-6 (pbk : alk. paper) —
ISBN 978-1-4696-2401-3 (ebook)
1. Congregational churches—United States—History. 2. Protestantism—United States—History. 3. United States—Church history. I. Title.
BX7137.B46 2015
285.8′73—dc23
2015010504

Contents

Illustrations

Acknowledgments

Many thoughtful and patient people contributed to this book. The librarians and archivists at the Congregational Library—Claudette Newhall, Jessica Steytler, Sari Mauro especially—were enormously helpful at all times, including all my many odd searches and off-the-wall queries. Ed Cade at the United Church of Christ archives also pointed me to just the right collections at just the right time. Daryl Ireland was an invaluable research assistant as well. The following friends and colleagues at the Boston Area Religious Historians seminar provided detailed and perceptive comments and critiques of several chapters: Jon Roberts, David Hempton, Patricia Appelbaum, Randall Stephens, Heather Curtis, Roberta Wollons, Cliff Putney, Chris Beneke, and Linford Fisher. Thanks also to John Turner, Barbara Brown Zikmund, and Jeff Cooper for reading early drafts and to David Hollinger and Ken Minkema for astute suggestions and well-timed encouragement.

The Louisville Institute provided a Project Grant in 2010, which allowed me to get the most out of the sabbatical provided by the American Congregational Association, including quiet time away and travel to archives. I am also very grateful to Elaine Maisner, at the University of North Carolina Press, who has been the careful, judicious, and encouraging editor that every writer wishes for.

My personal debts have piled high over the years it has taken to finish this book. I am grateful to the staff of the Congregational Library and the board members of the American Congregational Association for their commitment to what has turned out to be a very long scholarly task. Friends and colleagues—theologians, musicians, bicycle enthusiasts—have contributed in immeasurable ways. And as always, I treasure my husband, Norman, and our children, Nathan and Anna, for being my wonderful—and always surprising—family.

The Last Puritans

Introduction

Congregationalists are the oldest and, in many ways, the most anonymous American Protestants. They appear early and often in the opening chapters of American history, as main characters in the unfolding drama of Plymouth Rock and Massachusetts Bay, the Revolutionary War and the first steps toward political democracy. Many famous writers and thinkers—from Harriet Beecher Stowe and Emily Dickinson to John Dewey, W. E. B. DuBois, and even Mary Baker Eddy and Walt Disney—grew up Congregationalist. A Congregationalist minister's daughter, Kathrine Lee Bates, wrote "America the Beautiful." Yet despite an obvious gift for long-term survival, they are surprisingly unknown today. Not only would the average American have a difficult time recognizing a Congregationalist on the street, but many historians of American religion would be hard-pressed to say what has happened to them since the Civil War.

This book addresses this anonymity problem—it is a history of Congregationalism from the early nineteenth century to the present—and it adds a twist. The following pages deal not just with what happened to this denomination, though that is a story worth telling; they contain a larger story about religious faith and the fate of religious institutions in modern American culture. More specifically, it is one about the role of the past in mainline Protestant churches, those mostly northern, mostly moderate to liberal white denominations that until late in the twentieth century dominated American life.[1]

Of all religious groups today, mainline Protestants seem the most deracinated, the least bound by historic Christianity. Whereas conservative evangelicals pride themselves on standing without apology for "the faith once delivered," mainline churches seem to alter ancient creeds, liturgies, and baptismal formulas at will, readily accommodating their beliefs and behaviors to modern sensibilities. Even in churches with centuries of denominational history, tradition has become fully negotiable, as one researcher put it, "a resource or a commodity" to be used, or not used, as each individual pursues a separate spiritual quest.[2]

No wonder these churches have declined, critics charge. Americans today want certainty, a "strong" religion faithful to Christian history and tradition.[3] Mainliners have been "so careful not to offend," as historian Randall Balmer writes, "so intent on blurring theological and denominational distinctives that they stand for nothing at all."[4] The decline in numbers and influence is certainly startling—according to the General Social Survey, mainline churches dropped from almost 30 percent of the American religious marketplace in the early 1970s to 13 percent in 2008—and it is much debated. Once the undisputed cultural establishment, northern Presbyterians, Methodists, Baptists, Lutherans, Episcopalians, and Congregationalists are fast becoming a religious minority, dwarfed by rising numbers of evangelicals and Pentecostals and, even more worrying- to church officials by the "unchurched" and unbelieving. While in the 1950s only a tiny fraction of Americans claimed no religious affiliation of any kind, roughly 16 percent of American adults and a quarter of young adults ages eighteen to twenty-nine do so today. There are as many explanations for mainline decline as there are solutions for remedying it, most tending to agree on a fundamental need for cultural backbone.[5]

If we focus only on loss, however, we miss the larger story. Though the mainline churches do not have anything close to the membership and financial stability of their heyday, they can claim considerable success in the long run: American culture today has absorbed the social values of these old-line denominations—tolerance, freedom of thought, and respect for differences—at a deeper level than it has the polarizing rhetoric of culture warriors.[6] According to one of the most recent and influential studies of American religion, Robert Putnam and David Campbell's *American Grace*, the vast majority of Americans are "increasingly likely to work with, live alongside, and marry people of other religions—or people with no religion at all." The "true believers," those who are convinced that they are right and everyone else is wrong, are a small and declining minority. To an overwhelming extent, Americans today have learned how to hold their own religious beliefs without disparaging those of others.[7]

The picture may be surprising, but this is largely because we have focused so long on the politicized voices at either end of the ideological spectrum, the fundamentalists of various persuasions. As a result, the middle ground is relatively uncharted; though the history of fundamentalists and evangelicals has been told many times and well, the same is not true of the mainline. We have few if any historical works about twentieth-century Presbyterians or Methodists or Baptists or

Congregationalists; their leaders, institutions, and ideals, especially in the years after World War 1, are something of a mystery, or they are dismissed as thoughtless capitulation to modern culture. As a result, we miss an important story about Protestants who were both theologically grounded and socially aware, "self-interrogating" and ecumenically minded, Protestants who, to a large degree, made the religious diversity of contemporary American society possible.[8]

In other words, the best interpreter of contemporary mainline Protestantism is history rather than statistics. At the very least, we need to know more of what happened, especially in the mid- to late twentieth century, within a larger perspective and in closer, contextualized detail. This means developing a more nuanced understanding of those years, especially as they were experienced by laypeople. Somehow these ordinary people managed challenges to the historicity of the Bible and the exclusivity of Christianity that brought many scholars and intellectuals to grief. Somehow they kept going to church and considering themselves religious believers.

One of this book's core arguments is that mainline Protestants are not simply failed evangelicals, traditionless and compromised, but people with a particular historical burden, distinct from that of newer twentieth-century denominations and religious organizations. The "spiritual crisis" of the late nineteenth and twentieth centuries did not mean just "cultural acquiescence and enthusiastic historicism," as Kathryn Lofton writes. It was a time for coming to terms with the authority of the past—an opportunity to renegotiate old obligations to their spiritual ancestors. The result was a modern piety, a respectful but ironic distance from the past, an understanding of history and historical context that contributed to a practical ethic of tolerance and equanimity.[9]

The compromise was complex and ongoing. Religious traditions by their nature imply the existence of social and spiritual communities with limits and lines that must not be crossed. They are, as historian Jaroslav Pelikan has written, the "perennial themes and key metaphors" that frame a common life.[10] If you decide not to baptize adults, you cannot really call yourself a Baptist; if you disavow John Wesley, bottom line, you are not a Methodist. Not all American Protestants drew the lines this brightly—Congregationalists, as we will see, resisted perhaps the most strongly of all—but in the nineteenth century, an era of Protestant hegemony and unbounded faith in progress, blurry edges were not a problem. What would become the mainline denominations operated within a loose "evangelical consensus," emphasizing their commonalities in public and their idiosyncrasies in private. In fact, splitting hairs over fine points of polity or doctrine was decidedly counterproductive; those who chose to were happily sent packing to found new sects or denominations.

The anxieties of the twentieth century changed all this, bringing old invisible lines into sudden sharp relief. The religious history of the era is as much about fortress building as it is about ecumenical cooperation: even if we exclude the fundamentalist-modernist debates of the 1920s, this urbane and presumably secular age saw far more debate about what it meant to be a Baptist or a Presbyterian or a Congregationalist—or, for that matter, a Roman Catholic or a Jew or an evangelical—than any earlier time. In fact, as sociologist Robert Wuthnow explains, this combative new awareness is a "feature of modern religion." As theological certainties begin to fail and old cultural identities fade, says Wuthnow, symbolic cultural boundaries take their place, and the ongoing task of religious groups is to define and police them.[11] The criteria for defining who is in and who is out can vary widely—and are based on a broad list of "languages, rituals, artifacts, creeds, practices, [and] narratives"—but the purpose is the same. When the public power of religion declines and doctrinal religious identities can no longer be taken for granted, symbolic boundaries became indispensable tools.[12]

In the mid- to late twentieth century, then, many religious battles turned inward. Some debates about boundary lines were more productive than others, and some groups were more adept at using controversy to separate insiders from outsiders. The rise of the Religious Right in the 1980s is a prime example, with "hot button" issues like abortion and homosexuality, the inerrancy of the Bible, and the role of women used as a means of sorting true believers from false. But conservatives were not the only ones who argued about boundaries. Many of the mainline churches, as we will see, had been dealing with divisive questions of identity since the 1930s, as the unprecedented scope and scale of the Great Depression pushed old assumptions about Methodist or Baptist or Congregational boundary lines to the limit. Despite their long histories and time-tested skills at consensus building, many of the old denominations saw their traditional symbols of public unity—the rite of baptism and the wording of creeds, as well as long-standing myths about their founders—become the focus of internecine and sometimes even ruinous combat. These symbolic battles could be complex and subtle. What might look like a run-of-the-mill insider dispute about church names or a new hymnal might also be an attempt to deal with a long and complicated historical legacy.

Congregationalists are especially apt for this kind of story. To begin with, from the early nineteenth century onward, they have played a major role in shaping American culture, exerting an influence well beyond their relatively modest numbers. Jonathan Edwards and Horace Bushnell forged the path of American Protestant theology and were followed by a generation of "new theologians," men like Theodore Munger, Lyman Abbott, and Henry Ward Beecher, who helped define and spread Protestant liberalism. Lewis Tappan, Joshua Leavitt, and Simeon Jocelyn helped free the African captives on the *Amistad*; Washington Gladden was a leader of the Social Gospel movement; and Francis Clark, a Congregational minister in Maine, founded the Christian Endeavor movement, one of the largest and most influential organizations for young people, reaching millions worldwide by the early 1900s. Charles Sheldon, a Congregational minister from Topeka, Kansas, asked the memorable question "What Would Jesus Do?" in his book *In His Steps*, which even to this day continues to sell millions of copies. In 1909, Cyrus Scofield, a Congregational minister from Texas, published the Scofield Reference Bible, which went on to become a staple of fundamentalist Bible interpretation.

Congregationalists also founded important American institutions, though they rarely attached their denominational name to them. Many of today's leading colleges and universities had Congregational founders, from Harvard and Yale to the University of California, Berkeley. Through the American Board of Commissioners for Foreign Missions, the missionary society Congregationalists helped found in 1810, they also established schools around the world; many of them, like Robert College in Istanbul, the American School in Beirut, and the Inanda Seminary in South Africa, are still alive and flourishing. The American Missionary Society, also a Congregationalist organization, founded some of the most prominent schools and colleges for African Americans in the South, including Fisk, Tougaloo, Talladega, and the Hampton Institute; Congregationalists also helped found Howard University in Washington, D.C.

Moreover, of all the mainline Protestant denominations, Congregationalists have the longest and in many ways the most dramatic narrative of change: today most of the heirs of New England Puritanism are part of the United Church of Christ (UCC), a mainline Protestant denomination perched near the far left end of the theological and political spectrum.[13] They were also heirs of a tradition with a strong narrative bent, founded by Puritans and Pilgrims who believed they were agents of God's plan in human history. Up to recent times Congregationalists wielded their unusually heavy burden of history with passion and creativity. From the mid-nineteenth until surprisingly late in the twentieth century, they made regular visits back to Plymouth Rock, searching their history for answers to questions about Congregational identity and practice: Would the Pilgrim fathers, who established the principle of local church independence, have approved of state associations of churches? Would they have approved of a national denominational structure—or, later, a denominational agency with the power to make decisions on behalf of everyone else? Then there was the final question, whether it was possible for independent Congregational churches to merge with another denomination. This was the rock on which Congregational unity, always tenuous, would ultimately founder.

In some respects, by focusing on just one denomination, this book takes up an old approach to American religious history. The back shelves of libraries are full of these volumes with their slow parade of bureaucratic achievements, theological disputes, and semifamous people. Many of those same plot devices will figure in this book, at least partly to introduce readers to a virtually unknown story, especially as Congregationalism unfolded in the twentieth century. The effort is worth the trouble: Congregationalists were a group well positioned for important cultural work, having inherited both a solid intellectual tradition and a decentralized polity that encouraged wide-ranging discussions between laypeople and their leaders. Their story allows us to see, as other more hierarchical denominations do not, where theology and elite opinion intersect with the hopes and worries of ordinary people.

By definition, the "Congregational Way" came without a manual, only the conviction that relying too much on standard procedures would hinder the leading of the Holy Spirit and the word of scripture. And so a robust conversation about church practice began as soon as the Puritans reached New England in the 1630s, as laypeople and pastors hammered out answers to questions about requirements for church membership, standards for the ordination of clergy, and rules about administering baptism. Within the safe confines of New England, where the Congregational churches enjoyed exclusive state support well into the nineteenth century, temporary uncertainties were rarely a problem. Their common identity was so obvious and well established that it never came up for discussion. In fact, up through the mid-nineteenth century, most local churches rarely even referred to themselves as Congregational, if they used the word at all.

History began to weigh more heavily in the early nineteenth century, however, and in ways Congregationalists did not foresee or welcome. The end of state support found them woefully ill prepared for the rigors of denominational competition in the open religious marketplace, especially with their Unitarian and Presbyterian cousins. It was during this time that Congregationalists first staked their claim to the Pilgrim and Puritan heritage, building a common identity around their New England ancestry.[14] The connection to those seventeenth-century refugees proved an enduring source of pride, establishing them as the most democratic, orthodox, and—without a trace of irony—the most persecuted of all Protestants.

In the years up to and following the Civil War, the deepest tensions among Congregationalists were not theological or philosophical but regional. Even difficult questions about the ordination of women and the role of female evangelists, issues roiling all of the other Protestant denominations for most of the nineteenth century, rarely troubled Congregational unity, as each local church could decide who to call as pastor. This is not to say that gender was a nonissue—after all, it was the Pilgrim fathers, not mothers, who became the focus of denominational loyalty. But by the 1850s, an ideological fault line had grown up between New England and the churches in the "West," then primarily Ohio, Illinois, Michigan, and Wisconsin.

Congregationalists met as a national body in 1865, an unprecedented step but one they hoped would settle some of those festering disagreements. The Boston Council failed on both counts—debates about polity and belief would continue for the next hundred years, in fact—but it became an opportunity to bond once more around their Pilgrim past, this time literally on the graves of the Pilgrim fathers as they adopted a common statement of faith on Plymouth's Burial Hill. Yet as the post–Civil War years unfolded, Congregationalists again found themselves running to catch up with other more centralized Protestant denominations and their growing array of Sunday schools and publishing houses and missionary societies. They faced the realization that their much-prized historical tradition of local independence was a liability: somehow they would have to come to terms with their Pilgrim and Puritan inheritance. In the late nineteenth and early twentieth centuries, that task took on many different dimensions. While Congregational historians and church leaders debated the specifics of seventeenth-century polity, laypeople began to enjoy their history in an ever-growing variety of ways: in Congregational clubs and historical societies, novels and plays, pageants and pilgrimages.

This separation of past and present, I argue, allowed history-bound groups like the Congregationalists to embrace change. It did not so much destroy as mitigate the authority of Puritans and Pilgrims, providing permission for laypeople and pastors to accept unsettling changes in American belief and behavior and to avoid the increasingly rigid Biblicism characteristic of fundamentalists and conservative evangelicals. By the early twentieth century, in other words, Congregational laypeople understood that Adam and Eve were a "Hebrew myth" in the same way that they had replaced their traditionally plain meetinghouses with imposing Gothic cathedrals, stained glass, choir stalls, and organ music—in other words, everything their Pilgrim and Puritan ancestors had fought to eradicate. For the average American, those medieval churches might have been an homage to a vanished premodern age when religion was safe and serene; for Congregationalists, they symbolized just the opposite, freedom from both the stern theology and the aesthetic convictions of their ancestors. Tolerance for ambiguity was certainly not unique to Congregationalists, but it does explain their passion for wider Protestant unity. They had learned to hold their denominational pride loosely, convinced that their traditions were the best but not necessarily better than those of others.

It was not until the mid-twentieth century that Congregationalists began to fight among themselves about their history. This time the debate was about the denomination's core concerns for social action and ecumenism, about creating a Council for Social Action and then forming a merger with the Evangelical and Reformed Church, with both sides firmly convinced they were on the side of historical continuity. The controversy arose in the 1930s and then persisted for so many years—in many ways it is still continuing—because past precedent no longer smoothed over disagreements. Where they had once brought the denomination together, the Pilgrim fathers now divided it into angry camps.

Is it any wonder that history would be a problem in the United Church of Christ? Of all the mainline denominations, it is the most unmoored from the past: Presbyterians and Methodists, Baptists, Lutherans, and Episcopalians can all point to a founder and a respectably lengthy chronology. The UCC, however, does not really claim the legacy of William Brewster or John Winthrop. It is emphatically oriented to the present, a stance that has allowed the denomination to take the lead on social issues of race, gender, and sexuality but has also meant regular searching for a clear and distinct identity.

The UCC is far from unique, however. As a brand-new denomination entering the maelstrom of the 1960s already saddled with an ambivalent relationship to its past, the UCC's story is a particularly dramatic and telling one. But one would be hard-pressed to find Protestants of any type who believe that the past offers unfiltered wisdom for people in the present. Even conservative evangelicals, the "traditionalists" in the world of American religion, are not really interested in preserving history, except perhaps in spiritualized versions, altered beyond recognition for use in the culture wars.[15]

The past is a problem for all of us, of course: freedom from tradition, the ability to choose and carry out our personal destinies, these are the cores value of modern secularism. Our world, with its ever-changing urban landscapes and endless array of new and improved products, is one in which, as Karl Marx once said, "all that is solid melts into air." And so in its largest sense this story about Congregationalists is not just about one group of American Protestants, or even about religion. It is about the challenges we all face as modern people looking for footholds in an always changing world.[16]

CHAPTER ONE

Protestant Saints

The Power of Congregational Memory

"We had no ushers in those days, but I remember a Sunday morning when everybody would have been glad if there had been someone on whom to lay the blame." When Geraldine Taylor recounted this story for the members of her Medina, Ohio, Congregational Church in 1909, she was likely the oldest person in the room, still living in the house her parents had built in 1844.

She knew how to tell a good story. One Sunday morning, one of the town's "business men," Taylor related—he was "not a church member but his mother was and he was quite a regular attendant"—marched down the aisle, his children in single file behind him. This gentleman always came with a cane, "and as there was no carpeting on the floor [it] made considerable noise." When he reached his usual seat, the thumping came to an abrupt halt. "It seems," said Mrs. Taylor, "that . . . his mother and two other ladies [were] in his pew." In rapid order, the businessman pulled the pew door open and "rapped on the floor with his cane two or three times." Whether from surprise or indignation, the ladies stayed in their seats. "So," Mrs. Taylor said, "he shut the door, turned the button and walked out again, with his cane thumping on the floor and his children filing after." When the offended gentleman reached the church entryway, he turned and announced to the stunned congregation, "It is very well for people to keep their own places." Apparently, this was enough; satisfied that he had made his point in a dignified manner, the businessman returned the next Sunday and "did not let it interfere with his regular attendance."[1]

Geraldine Taylor's Medina church is a good place to begin thinking about early nineteenth-century Congregationalists and the ways they forged relationships with the past. After all, religious life for all American Protestants during that time, whether in Ohio, New England, or elsewhere, was profoundly local. As much as we may want to explain American religion in terms of denominational growth and stands on national social issues like slavery, women's rights, and temperance, these do not by any means tell us the whole story. For most people, religion took place in small-town churches like the one in Medina, where families lived together for generations, more or less learning to tolerate each other's peculiarities. "Love was understood, once for all, to be the basis on which their life was built," as Harriet Beecher Stowe wrote in her iconic portrait of small-town New England in *The Minister's Wooing*, "and after that, the less said, the better."[2] We can easily imagine the public rift between mother and son in Geraldine Taylor's story quietly resolved in a pointed conversation around the dining room table, and then folded into the lore of the town's history.[3]

More than that, in small-town churches like those of Medina, the past was real. As this chapter shows, early nineteenth-century church people talked about their ancestors in surprisingly immediate ways, as people with a continuing interest in the work of the living and a moral claim on them. This sense of personal connection is the beginning point for measuring all the changes that followed, the emerging sense of history and time that this book describes. It demonstrates, as we will see, the continuing power of old Puritan ideals within nineteenth-century Congregational churches, especially a faith in God as the author of time and the directing force behind human history. Deference to ancestors was not just a nod to Yankee traditionalism but rested on a deep sense of obligation forged between people and families over time.

LOCAL CHURCH TRADITIONS

The early nineteenth century was a lively time in American history, socially as well as religiously. Even small-town Congregationalists were not immune from change. To be sure, the iconic "white towns" of antebellum New England and its Midwest diaspora were famous for their neoclassical clapboard homes and towering church steeples; they seem the quintessential image of quiet stability and order. In retrospect, however, those picture postcard towns were themselves the product of economic and social change. The early to mid-nineteenth century was a dynamic era for American small towns, fueled by an orgy of canal and road building that linked rural communities together into a growing national economy. From Rhode Island to New Hampshire, textile mills began to appear, supplied by the emerging "Cotton Kingdom" in the southern states and employing ever-larger numbers of Irish immigrants.[4]

The "White Village" from John Warner Barber, *Historical, Poetical, and Pictorial Scenes* (New Haven, 1851)

In New England, the infusion of wealth gave community life a new vigor, buoyed by a rising regional pride in the Yankee ethic of hard work and innovation. Towns that had gradually dispersed over time began to centralize. Storekeepers, artisans, lawyers, and doctors set up shop in town centers, and weedy meetinghouse lots were cleaned up and enclosed with picturesque stone fences. Neatly pruned cemeteries replaced wild and untended burying grounds, often scattered with unmarked graves. Churches, businesses, and homes were all painted a pristine white—the most expensive shade at the time—and formed a clean visual whole, all of them with matching dark shutters and clapboard shingles.[5]

The same aura of order and stability emanated from the Congregational churches gracing town squares from Massachusetts and Connecticut to the emerging Midwest. For two centuries Congregationalism was the established faith of New England, and those churches seemed all but immune to time and change. Massachusetts was the last state to end tax support for its Congregational establishment, in 1833—fifteen years after Connecticut in 1818—but a change in the law books did not necessarily mean the end of social privilege. When other denominations moved into town, they had to identify themselves as Baptist or Methodist or Presbyterian, but the Congregational church was simply the "First Church" of Wenham or Townsend or Ipswich. No denominational label was necessary; everyone just knew.

The close ties between Congregational churches and their local communities were the result of clear theological intent. Unlike most other Protestants of the time, Congregationalists did not answer to a higher earthly authority—whether a national synod or a conference or an assembly—and did not envision themselves as part of some larger whole. Each individual congregation stood theologically complete on its own, with the spiritual right to choose its own officers and settle its own disputes.[6] From the mid-seventeenth century onward, the founding document of every Congregational church was a written covenant, an agreement that bound the people to each other and the entire church to God. That covenant was to be, as Maine pastor Thomas Upham advised in 1829, "express and recorded," the product of lengthy prayer and fasting.[7]

The one point of unity among Congregationalists was the Cambridge Platform, a constitution for New England's churches issued in 1648. In many ways, the Platform was an artifact of its time, written to defend the Commonwealth against charges of lax orthodoxy from England and to align the churches more closely with the civil authorities of Massachusetts Bay. It gave seventeenth-century laypeople clear directives to curb any aspirations for power among the clergy. But it also laid out what came to be called the "permanent principles" of Congregationalism: the autonomy of the local congregation, the mutual dependence of churches for advice and counsel, and the limited authority of the clergy. Printed out, presented to each local church, voted upon, and then ratified by the General Court in 1649, the Platform was undeniably important—but the extent of its authority was unclear even in the mid-seventeenth century. As the years passed, some Congregationalists revered it as a procedural guidebook, while others took it to be mostly a description of the Congregational Way in practice. Nevertheless, the Cambridge Platform stood for many years as a symbol of New England's orthodoxy and order— though as later generations would discover, it was an ambiguous and unwieldy tool.[8]

In fact, by the early nineteenth century, there was considerable theological turmoil within those glistening white clapboard walls. This was a time of dramatic change in American religious belief and practice and in the history of Christianity itself. For the first time anywhere religion was fully voluntary: instead of depending on tax receipts and automatic membership of everyone in the vicinity, churches would have to establish a case for the loyalty and support of their members—or risk losing them to a competitor. In the long run, voluntary religion was a good thing. It spurred unprecedented growth and entrepreneurial energy, as churches had to attract new converts and find new sources of income. In the short run, however, the older Protestant churches found themselves scrambling to adjust to practicalities they had never faced before. As we will see, Congregational churches would find this a difficult challenge: in many ways, the entire narrative of this book is of their ongoing struggle to master the rules of the religious marketplace.

Still, within an era of change, Congregational church life maintained old and familiar rhythms and a deep respect for the past. In fact, the slightly brittle formality in Mrs. Taylor's story tells us something about the importance of continuities even in a relatively new frontier settlement. No doubt this particular story stuck in her mind because even as a child she recognized the truth it told about her religious upbringing. The insistence that "people keep their own places" was not a bizarre demand or a laughable breach of decorum. It was simply an exaggerated instance of a general rule that no one felt the need to name. Though the practice of buying or renting family pews was slowly dying out, people still expected, as they do today, to sit in the same spot every Sunday morning. The average churchgoer did not find it agreeable to "sit promiscuously," as one authority on church etiquette explained. Allowing each family to "go to the house of God secure of the seat they are to occupy" would avoid the "care and embarrassment" of searching for an empty seat in front of everyone.[9] Even outside the confines of New England, the Medina church still followed the principle of "keeping one's own place."

Outsiders, including many historians, have often interpreted this residual formalism as complacency, betraying a lack of spiritual passion. Others have even suspected an element of snobbery, especially toward the rough-and-tumble world of Methodists and Baptists. While these younger churches were expanding exponentially in the years after the American Revolution and for most of the nineteenth century, so the argument goes, Congregationalists remained mostly huddled in New England, with far fewer churches in the West and South. Elitists all, according to this view, they were saddled with clergy "of genteel origin" who preferred to publish their sermons rather than bellow them out to the common folk; Congregationalists simply could not match the fervor of other "upstart sects." Indeed, the original faith of the Puritan fathers "had been so accommodated that it no longer could inspire or sanctify."[10]

The realities of local church life were more complicated, of course. Formalism was not just a way of imposing rank and privilege—it was an expression of powerful and unspoken continuities between the church and community and between the present and the past.

This was an attitude that nineteenth-century Congregationalists came by honestly, a product of their own peculiar religious heritage. From their Puritan roots they inherited not just a set of doctrinal precepts but a "lush culture of print" and a robust practice of theological storytelling. "From the colonial era through the nineteenth century," historian Joseph Conforti writes, "New Englanders were America's most prolific producers of historical works."[11] In a tradition traceable from John Foxe's *Acts and Monuments* (popularly known as *Foxe's Book of Martyrs*, published in 1563) to William Bradford's *History of Plimouth Plantation* (completed in 1651) and Thomas Prince's *Chronological History of New England* (1736), narrative was the dominant language of faith. The other crowning achievement of the Puritan narrative tradition is Cotton Mather's *Magnalia Christi Americana* (1702), a "seven-vault archive," as Mather's biographer has written, "of fact, reminiscence, document, verse, and legend." By its size alone, the *Magnalia* declared in no uncertain terms that, despite difficult political times in New England, God's providential care continued.[12]

In Puritan New England, narratives of the past served a variety of spiritual purposes. They offered moral lessons, testimony to God's care, or warnings about disobedience, all rooted in a firm confidence in divine providence. As Bradford explained, history allowed children to "see with what difficulties their fathers wrestled in going through these things in their first beginnings, and how God brought them along notwithstanding all their weaknesses and infirmities."[13] The Puritans who arrived in the mid-seventeenth century saw themselves not as refugees but as actors in a divine plan. The Geneva Bibles they carried with them opened with a picture of the Israelites standing on the shores of the Red Sea, gazing toward the Promised Land. "God hath dealt with us as with the people of Israel," wrote Peter Bulkeley in 1651; "we are brought out of fat land into the wilderness." And so their voyage to the New World was in many ways a reenactment: they were leaving England just as the Israelites had once fled from Egyptian slavery.[14]

History provided both hope and judgment. In sermon after fast-day sermon, New England's Puritans heard about the superior virtues of their ancestors and the risks their descendants ran through continued disobedience. Stories of the past, rolled into stirring jeremiads, served as corporate warnings to the Commonwealth itself, especially as the city on a hill began to falter after the first generation of settlers had passed. But at the same time these stories affirmed that New England was a special place with a special destiny. "The power of the jeremiad," writes Andrew Murphy, "always lay, in part, in the way it expressed *both* a sense of chosenness *and* a deep anxiety about the prospects of continued blessing."[15]

The Puritan view of the past was not historical, however, at least not in the sense we understand that word today. The point was not development and change over time, the gradual accumulation of differences between "then" and "now," but the continuing power of beginnings. Puritans looked backward onto a sacred past, a mythic "strong time" when God was specially present and active in the world. This "primitive time," when biblical figures like Abraham and Isaac, Jesus and Saint Paul still walked the earth and the sacred texts were still being written, was not over and done, forever inaccessible to the present, but still morally relevant. In important ways, the past overlapped with the present, providing spiritual power and insight. God's people were to "live ancient lives," in Boston pastor John Cotton's wonderful phrase, making an imaginative return to the biblical age for guidance and finding there "the crucial bearings for their own continuing venture through history."[16]

The great theologian Jonathan Edwards, witnessing the signs and wonders of the Great Awakening a century after Cotton, also turned to narrative as a way of understanding God's purposes. As historian Avihu Zakai has argued, Edwards's history of the New England revivals was an answer to the Enlightenment's increasingly secular view of time, making it "blind to God's providence and indifferent to God's redemptive activity." In fact, *Edwards's History of the Work of Redemption* (1739), unfinished at his death, was to be his ultimate work, summing up his theology in a grand narrative of divine activity, from the Garden of Eden to the millennial culmination.[17] The continuing power of the narrative tradition forged by Edwards and his Puritan forebears derived not from its grand scale, however, but from its attention to detail. Divine providence, from John Winthrop to Cotton Mather to Jonathan Edwards, was to be found in small events and small places. In fact, Edwards's musings on history began after an incident in his church in Northampton, a "little revival" of religion that seemingly came out of nowhere in 1734–35.

Nineteenth-century Congregational churches, therefore, inherited a narrative tradition that gave profound moral and spiritual significance to the histories of local churches, as unique testimonies to God's work in the world. Even the most mundane church fight or building project could be evidence of God's providential care. "Our own history, as a church and congregation, may be . . . like that of a thousand others in New England," as Taunton pastor Mortimer Blake admitted to his congregation in 1862; "still, it has an inner soul of its own."[18] Even good record keeping was a godly task. A church's "record of names, and dates, and events, and statistics," said a Newburyport pastor in 1859, showed the world "the way in which the Lord her God has led her."[19]

NINETEENTH-CENTURY JEREMIADS

Puritan churches did not mark anniversaries or celebrate milestones—this was an innovation of the early nineteenth century, as churches responded to a growing enthusiasm for the past in American culture at large. For their first half century as a nation, Americans paid little attention to preserving old records and provided little instruction in history in public schools. In practical terms, they did not have all that much history to teach, but the spirit of the day was decidedly unsentimental. Founding documents disappeared, and old buildings, including the home of Benjamin Franklin and George Washington's presidential mansion, were torn down without regret. In 1837, the fiftieth anniversary of the Constitutional Convention went by mostly unnoticed. But the early nineteenth century was also a time of growing national pride, and history became its primary mode of expression. By the time of the Civil War, Americans could boast an array of monuments commemorating historical events, a lengthening shelf of patriotic historical accounts, and national rituals around the celebration of the Fourth of July.[20]

The early nineteenth century was a time of general and growing fascination with historical narrative, in fact. This was the age of Edward Gibbon and Leopold von Ranke, when the study of history—understood less and less as divine providence and more and more as the mechanisms of change and transformation over time—began to take root in universities across Europe. History was an engine of modern nationalism, creating a "common dramatic frame" for people living through the aftermath of the French Revolution and the rise of nation states. Vivid and heavily footnoted stories about the past created emotional ties to geographic amalgams like Germany, Great Britain, and Italy, abstract and "imagined communities" of people united around a shared sense of citizenship. In the United States, history also became a primary tool of national pride and self-confidence, of a "manifest destiny" to take Western civilization across an untamed continent to the shores of the Pacific Ocean. The great theme of historian George Bancroft's major work, *The History of the Colonization of the United States*, was, as he said, "to explain the origin of our country and to follow the steps by which a favoring Providence called our institutions into being."[21]

By the 1840s and 1850s, local churches were uplifting the past as well, celebrating anniversaries and milestones within a format that would remain tried and true for many generations. The main event was a lengthy morning worship service, headlined by an equally lengthy and detailed "Historical Discourse" by the pastor. Afterward church members met for a more informal celebration, involving homemade food, greetings and remembrances from dignitaries, and then more poems, hymns, and reminiscences by church members.

Historical discourses were as varied as the pulpit skills of individual pastors, some dull, others pithy, and a few even warm and humorous. All followed a similar pattern and purpose, however. These were sermons narrating significant events in the life of the congregation, usually laced with biblical texts and florid tributes to past ministers, deacons, and founding church members. To a man, pastors believed that the past was both authoritative and powerful. "To review the past, to call to remembrance the various scenes through which we have been led," a Marlborough, Massachusetts, minister declared, "is both instructive and profitable." "This is the way to know God," said another, "by meditating on the past, present and future. And of all knowledge this is the most valuable to our well being."[22] It did not hurt that meditating on history encouraged greater awareness of life's brevity and the inevitability of death. "The very streets in which you walk today," as Great Barrington pastor Calvin Durfee admonished his flock, "were once traversed by those who have long since gone the way of the earth. As you survey the past can you resist the impression that you, too, are rapidly hastening through those scenes which have borne your fathers to the tomb?"[23]

Most of the historical discourses followed the trajectory of a classic Puritan jeremiad, laying out the virtues of the past, the sins of the present, and a hope for the future. This was not a time to flatter the congregation or to list its accomplishments: many described times of conflict and discouragement, some that would have been within memory of listeners. In Jamestown, New York, for example, a sermon featured a lengthy account of open battle between Congregationalists and Presbyterians, punctuated by public accusations, angry departures, and, at one point, the hurling of a Presbyterian church manual. The pastor stressed that these episodes did not reflect poorly on the present-day congregation but provided an opportunity, as he said, to "appreciate our feebleness" and recognize the hand of God in whatever success the church enjoyed. As "one of the small communities brought into existence by the providential dealings of our Heavenly Father," he reminded them, "we have assembled to-day, in memory of our planting, to honor those who under God assisted in laying these foundations [and] to profit by the lessons which our history teaches."[24]

The virtues of the ancestors often stood in sharp contrast to the shortcomings of their descendants. In 1857, the members of the East Windsor, Connecticut, church were reminded that in olden days, stormy weather never posed an obstacle to faithful church attendance. "The soaking rain and the driving storm of snow were matters of little account with the hardy ancestors of this settlement," their pastor admonished. Going to church was an "indispensable duty," and "it was no uncommon thing for neighbors to question each other if for one or two Sabbaths any were absent from their place. Alas!" he sighed, "that the good habit should ever have been laid aside."[25] "It is a serious thing, my brethren, for us to belong to a church, whose founders and members of former generations were such as we know ours to have been," a Leominister pastor warned in 1843. "How strict were they in observing the Sabbath! How constant in their attendance at the sanctuary! How faithful in maintaining family prayer, and in giving daily instruction from the Scriptures to their households, as well as in all the other duties of family religion!"[26]

Yet on the whole these nineteenth-century jeremiads were a far milder version of anything the Puritan ancestors had witnessed. The fundamental point was the importance of keeping faith with previous generations, especially the founders. "Our ancestors toiled and suffered, withstood the enemy of the forest, and repelled the invaders of their rights, threw off the chains of servitude, and fought for independence, not merely for themselves," a Haverhill, Massachusetts, pastor reminded his people, "but for us."[27] "We have received a rich inheritance from our fathers," a Rhode Island pastor agreed, "in the prayers they offered, the principles they adopted, the system of truth they embraced, the rules and regulations they observed." It is up to us "whether we secure the respect and gratitude of those who come after us. With all the advantage of the light of past experience, the study of history, the page of divine Providence, can we so recreate in our high trust, so unmindful of our obligations, so false to our covenant vows, as to desert this standard, forsake our principles, and abandon our ground?" "Around these altars where our father worshipped, standing on the spot where holy men sang and prayed," he said, "we pledge ourselves to rally under the standard of evangelical truth, and by divine grace, will maintain the integrity of our creed, and perform the conditions of our covenant."[28] The fundamental message of all historical discourses was faithfulness, and their "altar call," such as it was, urged rededication to the original vision of the founding generations.

In general, the ancestors were proud and pleased of their descendants, still deeply interested in their success. "Could the early members of this church have been able to look down the long vista of a hundred years," said a Connecticut pastor, "how would their hearts have swelled with joy and exultation!"[29] But that did not mean that their descendants could not disappoint them. In 1840, at the 200th anniversary of the church in Quincy, Massachusetts, Reverend William Lunt conjured up the daunting image of all the former pastors being called from their resting places, "in yonder burying ground," and marching "in ghostly procession up this aisle to this altar." "What think ye would be the lessons that would be uttered by those ministers of Christ?" Lunt demanded. "Would they not say to you; Preserve the institutions which we, in our day, exhorted men to honor. Desert not the sanctuary of your fathers. . . . If you must renounce our dogmas, do not, O do not renounce our principles . . . or fall from a life of piety and Christian righteousness."[30] Warning his congregation against spiritual laxity, Leominster pastor Rufus Stebbins likewise invoked the "spirits of our fathers." "Who can say," he declared, "but they hover over us?"[31] The "congregation of the dead," as one pastor described it, was both present and demanding. And the message was clear: "Do for others," he declared, "what your fathers have done for you."[32]

CONSTRUCTING LOCAL MEMORY

With these admonitions ringing in their ears, church members went out to a celebration designed and organized by a planning committee of laypeople, usually without direct pastoral supervision. Here was another opportunity to put a nineteenth-century stamp on an old Puritan tradition, not so much secularizing a religious observance as it was expanding the sacred beyond the traditional boundaries of sermon and church service. This phase of the festivities in particular reflected the power of human, homemade bonds in a church culture no longer defined by the laws of the land.

Many church anniversaries were essentially family reunions, occasions for inviting former pastors, local dignitaries, and scattered friends and family back to old and familiar haunts. Consequently, the afternoon festivities often took a light-hearted tone, featuring tables of food, rafts of floral decorations, and strings of greetings and accolades. In fact, the entire celebration had a simple, cozy feel to it, usually featuring a poem or two by a literary laywoman or an original hymn commemorating the occasion.[33]

Summer anniversaries were celebrated as family picnics. In 1860, after their Sunday morning service, the congregation in Norwich, Connecticut, reconvened in a nearby grove, led there by a procession of Sabbath school children and a marching band. On a beautiful July afternoon, they sat on a craggy hillside—a "terraced amphitheater of nature's construction"—and enjoyed presentations by "musicians, juvenile singers, and speakers" and a view of a table "tastefully ornamented with floral decorations, and richly loaded with refreshments."[34] Winter gatherings also featured elaborate decorations. Meeting in the winter of 1851, the North Church in Weymouth, Massachusetts, celebrated the twenty-fifth anniversary of its pastor's service with an indoor party described as a "Family Festival." The chapel was decked with greens, and vases of flowers framed the pulpit. Behind it, in letters "wrought of evergreen," was a tribute to "Our Pastor, from 1838 to 1863," and wreathed portraits of former ministers on either side, framed in gilt.[35] Not to be outdone, the church in Westminster, Massachusetts, decorated the entire church with evergreens and covered the pulpit with "wreaths, crosses, and bouquets." Suitable mottoes greeted the guests as they arrived: "On the right hand wall, as you entered the audience room," the *Boston Journal* reported, "was the motto 'Present,' and the date, '1868'; and on the opposite wall, 'Past,' and '1742'; and before you, over and back of the pulpit, was the word 'Future,'" all "linked together with evergreen festooning."[36]

Sacred objects also played a role in the proceedings, an innovation that would not have pleased their iconoclastic Puritan ancestors. In Templeton, Edwin Adams, the junior pastor, brought the original church covenant to the pulpit, waving it before the congregation at the climax of his sermon. "Precious relic!" he declared. "May it be safely preserved many centuries more!"[37] And in the small western Massachusetts town of Charlemont, the pastor held out a piece of wood from the "Old Pulpit," built in

1788 and discovered stowed away in an outbuilding. "O, how engraven on my memory is every color and angle in that old pulpit," he said, "on which the eye of my childhood looked in years of long sermons." This was no dead object: in fact, the aged pastor had no doubt that the entire pulpit was now "gone up to heaven," taking its place "around the throne of the Redeemer."[38]

Most anniversary celebrations culminated with a time of personal reminiscences from older members. Many of these also ended up in commemorative books, carefully transcribed and reprinted. Although often quirky and amusing, these recollections were uniformly cast in the warm glow of love and deference, echoing in more intimate language the moral message of the pastor's historical discourse. "In looking back on my childhood and to the people who to me were fathers of this church," a Pittsfield, Massachusetts, deacon declared, "I cannot help surrounding them with a sort of halo of goodness and uprightness." In 1866, a member of the Jamestown, New York, church turned to his aged Sunday school superintendent on the platform and spoke with obvious emotion. "I can never forget that stormy night, so many years ago," he said, "when, three lads, myself the youngest, sat around you in church, while you expounded to them the third chapter of John's gospel."[39]

The twenty-fifth anniversary of the Winslow Street Church in Taunton, Massachusetts, in 1862, is a particularly good example of the power of congregational memory. The quarter-century milestone was not all that much by New England standards, but it was a great occasion for the town of Taunton. The local paper reported that the town hall was "transformed into a mammoth tea-table" and the pillars draped with evergreens. For the four hundred people gathered there, the evening was a potent mixture of hilarity, music, and pious memory. The congregation had the pulpit from its first building, as well as the Bible of John Reed, the man who had founded the Sunday school, and put both on display for the anniversary service in 1862, placing them in the spot normally reserved for the town ballot box. "They cannot speak, but they are here present," one member commented, "with a moving tale to tell." The reminiscences followed suit. One elderly member of the Taunton church still remembered very clearly the congregation's beginning in "John Reed's School Room," the site of that first Sunday school. Others joined him in powerful reminiscences of "our Mount of Beatitudes" in that small sacred space. "*Churches which are true to themselves and to Christ, never die,*" another old friend exhorted.

In honor of the occasion, one of the church women, Mrs. Hodges Reed—apparently married into John Reed's family—read aloud her poem entitled "Past-Present." "There's no dead Past," she said, "except for those Who in life's web were only shoddy," spending too much time "with capon, turtle, soup, and toddy." Those with eyes to see, however, could recognize "the savor / Of good deeds done, of good words spoken, / Their line by centuries unbroken." In that sense, said Mrs. Reed, Saint Paul was "now more alive than ever" and "Moses still lives, although his grave / Remains unfound in Moab's valley, / Ready to lead the finally rally." "Good words and deeds can never die" was Mrs. Hodge's simple lesson. Though bodies might be hidden "a short space from mortal eye," they were absent only in physical form and that temporarily. A series of toasts followed, included one lifted to the entire congregation, praising its members for their piety, which once "irradiated the darkness of Heathenism," "pierced the night of the Middle Ages," and "shone around the heads of our Pilgrim Fathers."[40]

That evening in Taunton, and in many other church celebrations like it, time was not just the straight horizontal line we imagine in the present. The old saints of past congregations were not just "back there" and forever inaccessible but formed a complex and continuing bond with their heirs in the present. As firmly orthodox Protestants, Congregationalists did not pray to the dead or expect help from saints—these were Roman Catholic practices that their Puritan ancestors had decisively rejected.[41] Nevertheless, their nineteenth-century descendants resisted the idea that the dead were therefore irrelevant to the living. "What connection, if any, departed spirits have with this world, we know not," Braintree pastor Richard Storrs told a group of mourners in 1847. "Whether they are ministering spirits to their surviving friends, or are employed on errands of love to other parts of the universe, we have not light enough to determine." There was no doubt, however, that they were busy "furthering the great designs of God, and carrying out into execution his vast purposes of benevolence." Andover Seminary professor Leonard Woods went further, imagining the dead as God's busy servants, spreading out across the universe. "It seems to me," he said, "that the saints in heaven will be as much more active than they ever were in this world, as they are more holy, and more benevolent, and endured with higher powers. They will be full of action, because they will be full of love."[42]

It is tempting to label these speculations as one step removed from Roman Catholic theologies of sainthood, from those people that historian Peter Brown has called the "invisible friends" of medieval Christians. This is not to deny that Puritans and their religious descendants were sincere in denouncing the use of relics or the practice of saints' processions and holy days; New England's calendar was as bare and unembellished as the plain wood church buildings that dotted the landscape. The Protestant saints of nineteenth-century Congregational churches manifested an old tradition deeply rooted in Puritan piety as well as a common human urge to chart one's place in the world through "ideal relationships with ideal figures."[43]

A CHANGING LANDSCAPE

But the realities of secular life were equally strong, as even the citizens of Taunton would find out in the years after their anniversary celebration. Organized in 1637 as part of the original Pilgrim settlement in southeastern Massachusetts, by the mid-nineteenth century the town was a busy crossroads of textile mills and railroads. The citizens had learned to transform the iron they found in nearby bogs into stoves, tacks, and locomotives and to take part in a growing national market economy. From a rural economy where work followed the episodic rhythms of the seasons, they learned to live in an economic marketplace in which time was ordered and disciplined by clocks, watches, and factory schedules. In industrializing America, the hours of the day could be bought and sold, divided up and meted out like any other commodity.[44]

Congregationalists also began to locate themselves within a growing mound of numbers and statistics. Joseph Clark was the first to write a history oriented toward facts and evidence, a decade-by-decade accounting of the churches in Massachusetts that was published in 1858. This was the work of some twenty years, begun in 1839 when Clark was secretary of the Massachusetts Home Missionary Society and faced with the task of serving some eighty "feeble" churches. "I found a necessity laid upon me to investigate the causes of their weaknesses," Clark explained, and he began to "look into the *sources* of their troubles, the better to relieve them." Before long, the editors of the *Congregationalist* were pressing him to write a series of articles on the history of the Unitarian controversy, at least in part to counter the story being told by the Unitarian *Christian Register*. "It was evident," said Clark, "that some of the remoter causes of that schism lay so far back" that it became necessary to "trace the stream down from its source," beginning with the first churches formed in New England.

Clark was by nature a statistician, happiest with a pen and pencil in hand, but he also realized the practical and spiritual value of all his numbers and dates. He urged his readers to recommit themselves to serving "the Redeemer's cause"; his "honest aim" was only to point them toward the "old paths, where is the good way"; and his book was a "finger-board at the entrance of each devious path," providing both warning and hope.[45] But the statistical picture he created was not all that encouraging. According to Clark's research, by the late 1850s, Congregationalists comprised only a third of all the church bodies in the state—490 out of 1,625. Close behind were Methodists (277), Baptists (266), and Unitarians (170).[46]

Subsequent efforts by the *Congregational Quarterly* to keep these statistics up to date met with continual resistance from local churches, who criticized it as a "useless outlay, and an uninteresting occupancy of columns which ought to be better filled." This was a cause of some frustration to editor Isaac Langworthy, who launched a lengthy scold in 1862. "Look at these figures," he said, "and see if they do not reveal culpable *indifference.*" Some churches refused to send in statistics; others sent only round numbers that suggested a wild guess more than an accurate count; other accounts were late or partial. "Can such persons have any proper estimate of the importance of, at least, an annual and careful looking over the church records to find whether the number of Christ's friends is increasing or diminishing?" Congregationalists needed to realize that the forces arrayed against them were "sleepless, vigilant, [and] persistent." "A professed trust in God, with the powder wet," said Langworthy, "cannot amount to much." What the denomination needed was "aggression," keeping up with "the advancing line of God's providence." "Say not that our modesty, or timidity, or cares, or hopes that others will do it, hold us back. The mandate from the throne is to 'go forward.'"[47]

This message would be repeated many times over the following decades: Congregational churches needed to find new ways to work together if they were to survive, much less flourish in the new order. This was a tall order for churches with few institutional ties and a long tradition of independence. But the times demanded it, and the Pilgrim fathers would play a vital role in showing the way forward.

CHAPTER TWO

Sons of the Pilgrim Fathers

How Congregationalists Claimed Their History

For much of the early nineteenth century, Plymouth Rock was the pride of New England but not much anywhere else. Since the Revolutionary War, the town's citizens had been celebrating the anniversary of the Pilgrims' arrival on 22 December 1620 with toasts and parades, revelry to which the local clergy added lengthy sermons and church services. Over time, Forefathers' Day, as it came to be called, grew into an annual local event following the easily recognizable form of a church anniversary celebration, a combination of fun and moral reflection. By the time of the bicentennial in 1820, the practice had begun to spread among Congregational churches, usually in the form of a sermon on the superior virtues of New England's ancestors. It would take some doing, however, for the Pilgrims to have much currency west of the Hudson River or south of Connecticut.[1]

In fact, the early years of the nineteenth century saw a growing sense of alienation between New England and the rest of the United States. An economic embargo imposed against the British before the War of 1812 took a terrible toll on the region's thriving export business as well as its cultural pride. New England's political fortunes hit rock bottom in the years after 1815, when its old Federalist leaders muttered openly about secession, threatening to take the region out of the United States entirely. They could see the balance of political power shifting to the South and West, with the nation's leadership changing hands from the cultured sons of New England to rough-hewn men from faraway places like Kentucky and Tennessee. The Louisiana Purchase, the completion of the Erie Canal in 1825, and the end of hostilities with Great Britain made possible a large-scale population shift across the Appalachian Mountains and into the opening western territories. While the rest of the country began to imagine a new national destiny in the West, New England's confidence in its own providential role took a tumble.[2]

The region's dwindling cultural stock took a turn for the better in 1820, thanks to the oratorical gifts of Massachusetts senator Daniel Webster.

In his now-famous speech given at the Pilgrim bicentennial, Webster transformed Plymouth Rock from a local into a national symbol, the true touchstone of American patriotism. At that sacred spot, he said, all Americans—not just New Englanders—could "hold communion at once with our ancestors and our posterity." Far more than just a landing place for a bedraggled band of English refugees, it was the spiritual point of departure for all Americans past, present, and future. "Two thousand miles, westward from the rock where their fathers landed," Webster declared, "may now be found the sons of the Pilgrims, cultivating smiling fields, rearing towns and villages," and stretching out to the shores of the Pacific.[3]

Webster's speech marked a cultural turning point, when American patriotism became fixed to New England's history. The tradition endures today, of course, in the crowds that flock to Boston's eighteenth-century tourist sites along the Freedom Trail and in the political protest movement identified with the Boston Tea Party of 1773. It also lives in the popular association of the Pilgrims with American democracy, as the Mayflower Compact, a shipboard agreement that the settlers themselves soon forgot, became the forerunner to the American Constitution, and their autumnal feast, part of an ongoing Puritan practice of fasting and thanksgiving, became one of the most important national holidays. And the Pilgrims themselves became "founders of a secular apostolic succession," leading figures in an open-ended narrative of American progress.[4]

But the memorialization of the Pilgrim fathers was not just a cultural milestone; it was also a religious event, and a contentious one at that. In fact, some of the people listening to Webster's speech in Plymouth's First Church would have been mulling over the irony of his presence there. Two centuries after its founding in 1620, the church was locked in an angry divide between liberal and orthodox factions, so intractable that the latter group left to form a new congregation, Plymouth's Third Church. But the trouble did not end there: as we will see, the two churches had been arguing over the Pilgrim heritage for many years before 1820. And just months before the Pilgrim bicentennial, the First Church liberals had gone out of their way to renounce in public every tenet of the founders' Calvinist convictions.[5]

The fact that Webster spoke from the First Church pulpit, in an adamantly liberal congregation, was at least as symbolically important as his enshrining of the Pilgrim fathers. How could Webster praise New England's spiritual forebears in a church that, to orthodox sensibilities, had explicitly rejected their core convictions?

In the middle decades of the nineteenth century, and after considerable struggle and conflict, Congregationalists made the Pilgrim fathers their own. This meant, first of all, wresting the memory from their denominational competitors, their Unitarian and Presbyterian cousins. But it also meant something more: as Congregationalists took ownership of the Pilgrim story, local memories preserved in small church communities would begin to reside within a much longer past, populated by men and women who were, in a strict sense, outsiders to the inner circle of memory. The individual historic events recorded in local Congregational churches began to join together into extended episodes, taking on grander meaning as they did. Building this larger narrative was a complicated task, but the result was powerful: the more consciously Congregationalists rooted themselves in the past, the more they were able to contemplate their future.

And so in one sense this chapter describes an easily recognizable process, a scattered group of churches beginning to unite under a collective memory, as common stories of the past forged a single group identity in the present. The psychology behind it is fairly simple, too: we could say that Congregationalists resolved their sense of threat, in this case with some of their closest Protestant neighbors, by uniting under a symbol of cultural prestige. In a broad sense, the Pilgrim fathers helped New England's established churches move beyond Puritan folkways and survive in an increasingly market-driven religious culture.[6]

But then there is the matter of the Pilgrim fathers themselves. The first English settlers were not simply role models or patriotic symbols to their Congregationalist descendants. They were family patriarchs, exemplifying masculine virtues and demanding unquestioning loyalty from their children. As Northampton pastor John Mitchell warned, abandoning the true faith would make present-day Congregationalists "degenerate as sons and Christians."[7] But we should not press the gendered metaphor too far. In a much larger sense, the patriarchal figures of speech were less about power than they were about connection: the Pilgrim fathers gave their descendants a clear line of heredity and a family name—not an inconsiderable need for a group with few institutional ties. Congregationalists would never really master the aggressive language of masculine bluster; more important in the end were the historic and spiritual bonds that held disparate people and churches together. In fact, the deeper question behind their claim to a Pilgrim heritage is about history, and the primary focus in this chapter is how early nineteenth-century Congregationalists understood and used their connections to the past.

Regionalism plays a powerful role in this story. This was, of course, the age of rising sectional awareness, of growing economic and cultural competition—and ultimately animosity—between the industrial North, the slave-owning South, and the emerging West. These geographic divisions affected all of the Protestant denominations in the early nineteenth century, some more than others and in different ways. Baptists and Methodists would divide into northern and southern factions over slavery; other groups, like the Mormons and Disciples of Christ, took their identity as frontier faiths. Congregationalists were no different. The western expansion of their churches, never as widespread as that of other Protestants but accelerating in the first half of the nineteenth century, was on the one hand a confirmation of the Pilgrim legacy and on the other a test of its practical value. Seventeenth-century church polity was a hard sell for churches struggling with challenges foreign to New England Congregationalism: sectarian competition, criticism for lax doctrine, intense and sometimes violent debates about slavery, and, of course, life as a religious minority. The glory days of Puritanism would have little purchase on western soil, where, as an Iowa clergyman said, "the carefully written and able sermons" beloved by New England churches would have a western audience "sleep[ing] soundly."[8]

The first part of this chapter deals with fairly familiar territory in American religious history, the acrimonious split between Trinitarian and Unitarian Congregationalists. In the course of this debate, the orthodox would stake their claim to the Pilgrim fathers and begin to build their common identity on that foundation. But it was among the churches of the Western Reserve of Ohio, New York, Michigan, Illinois, and Iowa—not those of Boston and beyond—where the most important questions would emerge, not just about the logistics of church polity but about continuity. What exactly did the churches of the nineteenth century owe to those long-dead religious refugees?

Congregationalists were not the only ones asking this question. The larger setting for this chapter is an opening conversation within American society about the power of the past, about the limits and extent of human freedom. It was a preeminent question for a newly forming democracy, lingering in the hearts and minds of immigrants leaving the Old World to seek fortunes in the New, and fueling passionate debates about slavery and women's rights. Not surprisingly, perhaps, in the early nineteenth century this question unfolded theologically, in long and complex disputes about divine providence and human sin.

By disposition and training, Congregationalists played a leading role: these were, after all, issues deeply encoded in their theological tradition. The Puritan system, drawn from Augustine and Calvin and embodied in the Westminster Confession and the Cambridge Synod of 1648, was an argument for continuity. Sin was not an individual choice, or even a series of choices, but "original," a fixed inheritance from the first human pair. The "federal theory," as it was called, placed all of humanity under the penalty for Adam and Eve's long-ago transgression in the Garden of Eden: in other words, when God looked at the first humans and condemned them to futility and death, God also saw all of their descendants to follow, dispersed across time and space. Individual feelings about sin or salvation meant little within this ontological framework; as the *New England Primer* put it, "in Adam's fall we sinned all."[9]

From the time of Jonathan Edwards and the eighteenth-century revivals and through the early nineteenth century, Congregational theologians—the post-Edwards generation led by men like Samuel Hopkins, Nathanael Emmons, and Nathaniel William Taylor—struggled with this doctrine and its inherent unfairness. The metaphysics were daunting: though the old-style federal theology did not sit well with people learning to chart their own paths in a new democracy, the alternatives were every bit as difficult. If in some way human beings could actively choose to sin—even if in the first pristine moments after birth—then did that not diminish God's sovereignty, his governance over the world? Did every person enter the world a brand-new moral being, theoretically sinless? Not surprisingly, perhaps, "New England was one vast sea," as Harriet Beecher Stowe described it, "surging from depths to heights with thoughts and discussions on the most insoluble of mysteries."[10] In churches all across the region, as across American society more generally, Congregationalists were pondering the power of ancient and seemingly arbitrary decrees, whether the human race sat under the penalty of Adam's sin or there was room for self-improvement, if not transformation.[11]

This was the age of the spirit, after all, when revivalists promised freedom from the "hoary-headed error[s]" of the past and the possibility of "new-born truth," fresh from "the fountain of eternal purity and love."[12] Certainly, the converts who rushed forward to claim salvation believed themselves to be "born anew," suddenly and ecstatically loosed from the penalty of sin. This was also the hope of abolitionists and temperance reformers, who emphatically looked ahead rather than behind. Their opponents argued that the past was fixed, that African Americans were under the "curse of Ham" (the punishment for one of Noah's wayward sons) and women subject to the curse of painful childbirth and subjection to men imposed in Genesis 3:15 after the sin in the Garden of Eden. But as John Patterson Lundy, an Episcopal priest from Philadelphia, declared, "Christ came to do away with every curse entailed upon mankind by reason of sin, the curse in which slavery originated included." Christian salvation meant "freedom to every captive and bondman, both as to soul and body."[13]

The question of precedent also shaped the quiet but earnest discussions among Congregational churches about the binding importance of ancient documents like the Cambridge Platform or the writings of the original Puritans. The past certainly "mattered" to the sons of the Pilgrim fathers, just as Adam's sin somehow mattered to humanity—but how and why were far more complicated questions.

VERSUS UNITARIANS

For all its promise and energy, the early nineteenth century was one of the most difficult eras in the long history of New England's churches. It was a time of theological dispute, organizational loss and upheaval, and in the end permanent division between Unitarian and Trinitarian Congregationalists. The conflict, formalized with the establishment of the American Unitarian Association in 1825, ran deep, harking back to the mid-eighteenth century and a series of emotionally fervent religious awakenings that shook the transatlantic world. To some the explosion of religious feeling signaled the presence of the Holy Spirit and a brand-new spiritual dispensation; to others it was fanaticism run amok, threatening to bring down the entire Christian edifice.

A small but influential group within the larger world of New England Congregationalists, the first Unitarians were people who longed for a simpler, more rational faith, one appropriate for an "age of reason." This meant not only avoiding revivalistic excess but leaving behind the paradoxical doctrine of the Trinity—God as both one and existing in three persons, Father, Son, and Holy Spirit—and the unrelenting syllogisms of Calvinist theology. Rejecting an angry God who saved and damned according to an inscrutable will, Unitarianism emphasized God's availability to all, shifting the focus from Calvinist metaphysics to the development of Christian character. "We have no fears for Christianity provided it be presented fairly to the understandings of men, and in its original purity and simplicity," the *Christian Register* declared in 1827; "but we have great fears . . . if it is to make common cause much longer with prejudices and superstitions, which the world has outgrown, or is fast outgrowing."[14]

In the early nineteenth century, theological differences between Trinitarian and Unitarian Congregationalists escalated in a long series of disputes about money and property. The first signal came in 1806, after Harvard's chair of theology fell to Henry Ware, an avowed liberal. Shaking the dust of Cambridge from their shoes, orthodox Calvinists built a new school twenty miles to the north, in Andover, Massachusetts. In ensuing years, Andover Seminary's story of exile would be repeated in hundreds of local churches across eastern Massachusetts, as congregations splintered and the orthodox Trinitarians left to form new churches of their own. In 1854, historian Joseph Clark estimated that somewhere around a fifth of all the congregations formed in Massachusetts since 1620 had left the Trinitarian fold to become Unitarian. Even worse was the symbolic impact: of the thirty-nine churches whose pastors had helped frame the 1648 Cambridge Platform, a full third had been "expunged from the present list of evangelical churches." In Boston, all the city's oldest and most prestigious congregations had departed, with the Old South and Park Street congregations the lonely exceptions.[15]

The messy separation was the downside of old social privileges. As long as New England society was socially and theologically homogeneous— and as long as the people of the town accepted the local minister as their chaplain and first citizen—Congregationalism was the order of the day, a durable and flexible bond uniting the local community into a single parish. In return, the town paid the minister's salary and took oversight of building repairs, while the other "sects"—Baptists, Methodists, and Quakers primarily—carved out various exceptions and for the most part grudgingly accommodated New England's so-called Standing Order.

Not so, however, in the early nineteenth century. The Massachusetts state constitution, ratified in 1833, put an end to religious establishment and the taxation system, forcing the Congregational churches for the first time in their history to rely on their members for financial support. But by this time, the arrangement was far less controversial than it might seem. In fact, to many local churches, the official end of the parish system was a welcome change, especially in the wake of complicated and sometimes ruinous disagreements between Unitarian and Trinitarian Congregationalists over church buildings and the selection of ministers.[16]

The focal point was a dispute within the church in Dedham, Massachusetts. In 1817, the church members—those who could testify to an experience of faith and had been accepted by the rest of the congregation—clashed with the citizens of the town over the choice of a new minister. When the town parish appointed Alvin Lamson, a known liberal, the more orthodox church members immediately rejected him. Each side claimed the upper hand in making this decision, the church for spiritual reasons and the town as the taxpayers legally bound for paying Lamson's salary. The case ended up in the Massachusetts General Court and resulted in a ruling, the so-called Dedham Decision of 1820, which upheld the claims of the town rather than those of the church members: the assets of the Dedham church belonged to all the tax-paying citizens of the town, not the inner circle of certified believers. As a consequence of what one historian has called "bad law, bad history, and bad congregationalism," many local churches across eastern Massachusetts found themselves negotiating complicated spats over land, buildings, and valuables like the communion silver. In many cases, the orthodox ended up on the defensive, forced to build new structures from scratch and seeking retribution where they could. In Dedham, the Trinitarians erected their building right where their enemies could not miss it, directly across the street.[17]

In the meantime, the annual celebrations at Plymouth Rock had become regular occasions for ministers, Unitarian and Trinitarian both, to tweak the opposition. Liberal John Allyn unfurled the first charge in 1801, when he cited the famous line from John Robinson's farewell to his departing Pilgrim flock, calling for "more light and truth to break forth" from God's "holy word." It was clear the famous pastor of that original Pilgrim band was open-minded, Allyn declared, and he would have been in full sympathy with those seeking freedom from Calvinist determinism. Even though Unitarians might not hew to the exact form of Pilgrim belief, they had still inherited a full measure of the "noble spirit of liberty" the Plymouth settlers personified.[18]

The next year, Adoniram Judson Sr., the orthodox pastor of Plymouth's Third Church, turned the tables, beseeching the gathering to "tread in the footsteps of our pious fathers" and to "seek the good old way" of doctrinal orthodoxy and "primitive simplicity." There was no doubt that the Pilgrims believed in the divinity of Christ and the "total depravity of man," he said. Calvinists all, the Pilgrim fathers would never have abandoned the beliefs for which they endured exile and persecution. The right path for their descendants was backward, to the original purity of 1620.[19]

After the Dedham debacle, Trinitarians were not content with yearly sparring. Lyman Beecher, an open foe of all things Unitarian, arrived in Boston in 1826 and immediately launched a publication with the provocative title *The Spirit of the Pilgrims*. The opening number declared in no uncertain terms that "the orthodox feel themselves to be *the proper and legitimate representatives of the pilgrim fathers*," an "extraordinary race of men" whose aims were "great, noble, and comprehensive." The Unitarian "sect," said Beecher, was but a "small minority" of the churches of New England and had no legitimate claim on the Pilgrim legacy, past, present, or future.[20]

Not only that, Unitarians did not understand their own church polity. In 1830, Hartford pastor Joel Hawes published a *Tribute to the Pilgrims*, opening with the complaint that "there are but few among us, I fear, who clearly understand the *principles*" of Congregationalism. Hawes also dropped a broad hint about the source of the problem, those attacking the foundations of the faith "with no small share of acrimony and violence." He devoted one large section of his book to a narrative history of the New England churches, explaining the eighteenth-century Unitarian arguments against religious revivals as "the first open departure from the faith of the pilgrims—the first visible, decided step in the progress of that system of error which has spread its blighting influence over so many of the churches of New England."[21]

Unitarians rose to the challenge, though in the long run the orthodox would reap the spoils of battle, more by default than conquest. Unitarians certainly had their own fascination with the Pilgrims, a "liberal ambivalence with New England's religious past," as Joseph Conforti describes it. As historian Jan Dawson writes, "Puritanism was, paradoxically, both an affront and a stimulus to the romantic spirit," appallingly dogmatic but at the same time dedicated to "radical self-examination" and "absolute truth." Indeed, for every stark portrait of a Puritan moralist from the pen of Nathanael Hawthorne was a nostalgic novel by Lydia Maria Child or Catherine Sedgwick.[22] Fundamentally, however, it was difficult, if not downright irritating, to see the Trinitarians claiming the entire historic tradition as their own. Enough of the "great parade" of the "faith of our Pilgrim Forefathers," a reviewer in the Unitarian *Christian Examiner* declared. "We revere the ... Pilgrims too," he said, "but for what they did, not for what they believed." The true legacy of Plymouth was "resistance to spiritual tyranny," not "doctrinal speculations." In a public response to Hawes, the noted social reformer Samuel May praised the Pilgrims as "good old Puritan non-conformists" and returned the orthodox charge of narrow sectarianism. Their theology was simply out of step with the times, he said, "peculiarly offensive in this age of the world, and in our country."[23]

By the 1840s, however, Unitarianism itself was changing, increasingly defined by new radical voices like that of Theodore Parker, who championed intellectual freedom and discovery. Parker, in fact, explicitly warned his fellow Unitarians against fetishizing the past as the source of religious truth. "Anyone who traces the history of what is called Christianity," he declared in a famously controversial sermon on the "Transient and Permanent" in Christian faith, "will see that nothing changes more from age to age than the doctrines . . . insisted on as essential to Christianity and personal salvation." "The heresy of one age," said Parker, "is the orthodox belief and 'only infallible rule' of the next."[24] Echoing Parker's spirit, social reformer and popular lyceum speaker Henry Bellows defined Unitarians as simply "the only consistent Protestants," who "do not recognize the lines and boundaries" erected by sectarian zealots. And a contributor to the *Monthly Religious Magazine* closed the final chapter on Puritanism by declaring that "the progress of the world has made their theology obsolete." In the "blessed" nineteenth century, when "the word of God is better understood than ever before," he said, "shame be upon us all" if we insist on using our "gloomy ancestors" as the benchmark of piety.[25]

Compare this attitude with that of the Reverend Alvan Cobb, who urged his Plymouth congregation in 1831 to "resist any innovation" in defending "the correctness of the faith of our Fathers, and of their religious practice." For the orthodox, older was by definition better in every way, and the Unitarian departure only confirmed that conviction. As Rowley, Massachusetts, pastor Isaac Braman declared in a sermon on the church's founders, "Had any one at that day openly . . . denied the divinity of Christ . . . or indeed any of the doctrines of grace, he would have been considered a monster, more to be shunned than the pestilence that walketh in darkness."[26]

As Unitarians ceded rhetorical ground, the orthodox readily occupied it. By the 1830s and 1840s, the Puritan and Pilgrim past was for them not just a point of pride or an argument against Unitarianism. In the wake of the Dedham decision and religious disestablishment, it was becoming an important new argument for the superior virtue of the Congregational Way, providing the orthodox with an identity that would have been thoroughly improbable just a decade before. Suddenly they were martyrs of religious persecution, a beleaguered minority enduring oppression and exile for the sake of truth, just like their ancestors. We are "reproached for

[our] Congregational partialities and habits," one pastor complained, "as though all the evils in the world had their source in Congregationalism." It was bad enough to endure the taunts of "infidels and vain persons," from whom such treatment might be expected. Even worse was the mockery they received from "some others, from whom better things might be hoped." By this time, there was no need to say the word "Unitarian."[27]

VERSUS PRESBYTERIANS

Of course, the world beyond New England offered many, if not more, opportunities for martyrdom. In the increasingly competitive world of nineteenth-century American Protestantism, Congregationalists would have to face the "sleepless jealousy of minor sects" and their determination to undermine the Congregational Way. "The truth is," said leading spokesman George Punchard, that "while Congregationalists have been sleeping in their fancied security, other denominations have not been idle," pressing their "peculiar tenets" with confidence and zeal. Undeniably, "they who make the *most noise*, have the *best cause*."[28]

Punchard did not name names, but it is likely that he had his eye on the astonishing success of Baptists and, in particular, American Methodists. From a little known, mostly English, sect at the time of the Revolutionary War, within fifty years' time Methodism had overtaken all other American denominations, from just 2 percent of American churchgoers to 34 percent. Though a genuine popular religious movement, harnessing the zeal of laypeople across the backwoods South, urban Northeast, and Ohio Valley, Methodism was also a thoroughly top-down institution. Bishops assigned lesser clergy to local church posts and to evangelistic "circuits" made up of scattered and often impoverished congregations; laypeople met in local class meetings, larger quarterly meetings, and even larger annual meetings. "Everything about Methodist doctrine and practice demanded individual initiative and action," historian John Wigger has written. "But the Methodist system also demanded order and cooperation. The movement's extraordinary growth is largely an indication of how successful early Methodists were in balancing these two impulses."[29]

Congregationalists had none of these advantages. While Methodists were out changing the religious landscape, the New England churches were dealing with a decentralized system of church organization and a tradition of local independence already two centuries old. Though they sent out scores of evangelists in the late eighteenth and early nineteenth centuries—mostly men from the Connecticut Missionary Society to Vermont and New York—"unlike their Methodist counterparts," historian James Rohrer writes, Congregational evangelists "could not help but think of the church first and foremost as a covenanted community of regenerate saints. Although they longed for the salvation of individuals, they could not conceive of the lone, solitary Christian." The goal was to create stable, covenanted communities of faith that could sustain themselves over the long haul. As a result, many evangelists were reluctant to plant churches in thinly populated areas; Congregationalism was a faith best suited to towns and small cities.[30]

For a while at least, the solution seemed to lie in an alliance with Presbyterians, a partnership that promised practical efficiency but also threatened to unearth some old problems. Though Congregationalists and Presbyterians were sister denominations with the same historical and theological roots in the English Reformation, the two were never completely comfortable alongside each other. During the colonial era, few Presbyterian churches existed within New England, and few Congregationalists outside of it—this by mutual agreement. Today their differences might seem slight, but in an era specially attuned to questions of authority and freedom, they loomed large. Presbyterian churches were not independent and ruled by the consent of members but united under a system of presbyteries and synods, anathema to most New Englanders. By 1800, however, the two had drawn closer together, especially in Connecticut, where virtually from the beginning Congregational polity had been more centralized and more adaptable to Presbyterian style and practice.[31] Moreover, as the nation's religious culture began to shift, and Methodists and Baptists began to reap success, the two old Calvinist denominations began to realize that their futures required an end to their historic differences.

The result was the Plan of Union, an agreement formalized in 1801 to share in organizing churches in the newly opening western states, from New York westward to Illinois. Under the Plan, neither denomination could proselytize for its own system; instead, each individual new church would choose a Presbyterian or Congregational polity, or something in between, depending on the preferences of the members themselves. In practice, the vast majority of new churches, especially in more sparsely settled regions like Illinois, chose Presbyterianism. Tellingly, not a single Congregational church was organized there until 1833.[32] The disparity owed much to differences of polity. In the Presbyterian system, the local presbytery owned the deed to all property and alone had the authority to ordain candidates for the ministry. Above the presbytery, the regional synod and, above that, the General Assembly had authority to decide and enforce rulings on doctrine and practice. This meant that Presbyterianism promised isolated churches more support than Congregationalism could ever supply. It also meant that when a local church declared itself Presbyterian, it became part of an institutional structure, one that proved relatively easy to join and all but impossible to leave. Presbyteries rarely granted letters of dismissal to churches yearning for Congregationalism.

The Plan of Union also suffered under other pressures. As Presbyterians waded through their own protracted struggle over doctrinal standards—a split between New School and Old School factions that lasted from 1837 to 1852—Congregationalists became their common source of vexation. Both Old School and New School worried that the looseness of Congregational polity would open their churches to lax standards of doctrine, and specifically to the disruptive influence of Oberlin Seminary in Ohio. "Congregationalism, in New England, is admirable," one critic explained; "but in mixed communities, where there is no unity of sentiment, where all manner of wild opinions and movements abound," it was heresy waiting to happen.[33]

"Oberlinism," as its detractors called it, was a radical view of individual salvation with equally radical implications for society, identified with the theological seminary at Oberlin College and its outspoken leaders, Asa Mahan and Charles Finney. It promised that Christians could be free from sin, not just in an ontological sense but in a visible, practical one: one could conquer the will to sin by the power of the Holy Spirit—to become in a sense morally "perfect." Calvinists took a dim view of this teaching, as it tended to skip lightly over the power of original sin and bore an uncomfortable resemblance to a popular Methodist teaching on "Christian perfection" drawn from the writings of John Wesley. But that was not the only problem: Oberlin-style perfectionism had a broad and explosive impact on pre–Civil War American society for it not only promised individual moral perfection but encouraged the fervent expectation that social evils like slavery, alcoholism, and sexism could and should be eradicated as well. Oberlin itself modeled the new dispensation by admitting African American and female students, including future suffragist Lucy Stone and Antoinette Brown, who was ordained by a Congregational church in New York in 1853.[34] These teachings did not affect all Congregational churches west of the Hudson River, but they would find a more congenial home there than among Presbyterians. The perfectionist strain in western churches, often manifesting as a fervent commitment to abolitionism, created an uproar that would take many years to abate.

It was at this point, in the mid-1840s, as both parties were contemplating separation, that western Congregationalists began to unify around their Pilgrim heritage. A meeting with Presbyterians in Detroit, held in 1845, left many of them openly angry, complaining that their denominational partners had done nothing more than laud their own accomplishments and disparage Congregationalism as a "great mischief." The delegates decided it was time to take their own path or, as one of them phrased it, "to maintain and advance in the West, the polity of the Pilgrims."[35] The next year they met separately in Michigan City, Indiana. There the frustrated Congregational delegates underscored their allegiance to the New England past, resolving to "declare to the world our abiding adherence to the doctrines and principles of the gospel as held by the Puritan Fathers and our devotion to that form of Church polity which we have received at their hands, and which is our rightful inheritance."[36]

By the 1850s, the gloves were off. In Ohio, Congregational pastors and laymen took the formidable step of meeting together to form a more permanent organization. In early 1852, forty-four churches gathered in Mansfield, Ohio, and, in an amazing show of unanimity, drafted a statement of doctrine and a constitution, as well as a resolution against slavery. To one observer, the spirit of the meeting was almost surreal. "I can scarcely look upon what has transpired here as anything but a dream," he said. "It so transcends my expectations and differs so much from what I feared, that I say to myself as I walk from my lodgings to our [meetings]—How can these things be real?"[37] Other associations of Congregational churches began to spring up in other western states, always with great enthusiasm and few of the traditional fears among New Englanders that their constitutions and conventions would subvert the independence of local churches.

Western churches provided the impetus for the first denominational gathering since the Cambridge Synod of 1648, a meeting held in Albany, New York, in October 1852. In fact, without the leadership of Congregationalists beyond the Hudson River, it is doubtful whether their eastern siblings would have moved at all. Many New Englanders viewed the prospective meeting with open dismay. "I have seen no one yet who has a definite idea of what is to be done or attempted in the forthcoming Convention of Congregationalists at Albany," the editor of the *Congregationalist* complained. "Some of the brethren have said it would be undignified," Massachusetts clergymen agreed, to commit themselves "to a measure, of whose character and objects they know so little." In the end, New England clergy decided to attend, because, as one observed with a sigh, "we should have to share in the responsibility of what was done, whether good or bad."[38]

Called together by the New York Association, the delegates' first act was to formally terminate the Plan of Union, officially parting ways with their old allies. "They have milked our Congregational cows," was the memorable complaint, "and made nothing but Presbyterian butter and cheese."[39] Other important actions followed. The Albany Convention delegates—463 from churches in seventeen different states—voted to support the Maine Temperance Law (at the time the benchmark for prohibition legislation), excoriated slavery, and agreed to raise $50,000 for the construction of church buildings on the western frontier, a challenge met and exceeded the following year when local churches gave nearly $62,000 toward that effort. The Albany Convention also established the American Congregational Union, later the Church Building Society, to oversee the work previously done in union with the Presbyterians. Finally, the delegates voted to reissue the works of all the "Standard Congregational authors" from the seventeenth century, yet one more sign, as one western observer noted, of the "rising interest in the polity and institutions of the pilgrims."[40]

The Albany Convention was a curious mixture of modesty and bravado, setting the denominational tone for generations. Although they were putting an end to the Plan of Union, the delegates took great pains throughout to emphasize their "unsectarian" goals in emphatically ecumenical language. The Christian faith, they declared, "forbids us to attempt to promote the interests of our particular denomination by any measures that shall infringe on the rights, or obstruct the prosperity, of other portions of the great family of God." The virtual absence of any "external machinery" in Congregational polity made this fairly likely, of course. "Our polity is the worst possible for all sectarian uses," declared the conference preacher, Joel Hawes. "The only bond that binds us together is the unity of the spirit, kept in the pledge and culture of peace."[41]

But in fact, in the years after the Albany Convention, the Congregational churches began to rally far more purposefully around their unique heritage, specifically the celebration of Forefathers' Day. Preaching on 21 December 1857, Newton, Massachusetts, pastor J. W. Wellman applauded plans to "inaugurate a new and far more general commemoration of that grand event" among Congregationalists. It was time to celebrate the "incomparable worth of the church polity of the Pilgrim Fathers" and to give it "a position and power as it has never yet enjoyed."[42] By the 1850s, this meant wresting the Pilgrim heritage not from Unitarians or Presbyterians but from the more secular rituals growing up around Forefathers' Day. In the years before the Civil War, when President Lincoln would finally declare Thanksgiving a national holiday, Americans had begun to observe the December date as a time for family reunions, with games, get-togethers, and large sumptuous meals.[43]

Congregational leaders insisted, however, that Forefathers' Day was actually theirs, a special day they could set aside for denominational purposes. The power of those original Pilgrims was a "fire from heaven," the *Congregationalist* declared, a "Promethean spark," to be kept alive by their descendants, the "Vestal virgins" keeping watch for the good of the nation. In the 1850s, this meant that commemoration of the Pilgrims was a rallying symbol for fundraising on behalf of western churches. As the *Congregationalist* asked its readers in December of 1856, "Do you feel stronger confidence, as the years roll on, that the good old Puritan faith is the faith for our day? Then give generously to carry it over the breadth of our land."[44]

CODIFYING CONGREGATIONALISM

Behind the celebration, however, western church leaders quietly wondered how the New England legacy really applied to their situation. In the midst of all the rhetorical flurry and bother about the Pilgrim fathers, no one had paused to spell out any of the details—it was clear the heroes of Plymouth had a particular design for church order that was decidedly not Presbyterian, but beyond that the details were blurry. Western Congregationalists knew their circumstances were different, if not unique. They had no patience with "sectarian" religion or dogmatism—"there is scarcely a . . . single church in the West," an Iowa correspondent wrote in 1853, unwilling to admit new members "that doubt or deny some of its minor peculiarities of doctrine." But they were not averse to more top-down unity. "We are not . . . substantially *alone*, as are those churches in New England with which we sympathize," the ministers at the General Association of New York had explained in 1848, but they were surrounded by a diverse round of competitors. The truth was, "we are not acting upon Society as it was in our fathers' day . . . but as it is in this living and teeming Present."[45] "You have in the older states a quiet settled way of conducting ecclesiastical affairs," a western correspondent wrote to New Englanders in 1852, "which leaves you almost destitute of language and ideas in which to describe the conflict and turmoil which reigns" throughout the West.[46] Thus, instead of prizing local independence, westerners tended to value connection: the Congregational Way beyond the Hudson, a Chicago pastor declared, was one of "conciliation, charity, liberty, and fraternization."[47]

As western Congregational churches began to distance themselves from their former Presbyterian allies, they began to ask questions about denominational polity long since settled in New England. The question came up in Illinois in 1859, for example, about the possibility of electing elders to "take oversight of discipline" and thus free the pastor for more spiritual matters. The idea seemed eminently reasonable, except that "elder" was a term used by Presbyterians: each local church had a "teaching elder," or pastor, and "ruling elders" with authority to provide moral and spiritual watch over the congregation, with a set of deacons acting as trustees of property and finances. The Congregational system had deacons only, a practice that dated back to the early seventeenth century. In the discussion, ministers worried whether appointing elders "does not introduce an element of the Presbyterian system into our churches"; more pointed critics objected fervently to reviving a "cumbrous and useless appendage." Piecing together conflicting evidence from the New Testament, the Cambridge Platform, and Congregational practice over time proved so confusing that the delegates tabled the matter in frustration.[48]

The New England churches were of limited practical help. A Jamestown, New York, pastor reminisced in 1866 that, some forty years before, "the subject of the church polity was almost lost sight of in New England. The treatises on that subject by the early fathers, Mather, Cotton and others were out of print, and the leading seminaries ignored the whole matter."[49] Indeed, as a contributor to the *New Englander* admitted in 1843, "we have no established usages." They are "not printed in a book" or "enforced by authority."[50] Thoroughly in agreement, a committee of prominent Massachusetts clergymen declared in 1845 that the great principles of the Puritan fathers were "not at present sufficiently understood, nor generally observed," noting that "the churches in Massachusetts are, to a great extent, without any well defined and settled principles of ecclesiastical polity."[51]

In the meantime, many laypeople understood their polity as little more than local independence and, judging by the constant complaints from clergy, as a system free of any constraints. Enumerating the reasons "why I am a Congregationalist," one enthusiast focused almost entirely on the system's open-ended possibilities. "I love Congregationalism," he declared, "for its simplicity and its freedom from forms." Its only rule was the Bible, and its only "formulas" were meant "to ascertain whether its members believe in the Word or not." Whereas other churches ("Romanism, Episcopacy, Methodism and Presbyterianism") awakened "pride of power," Congregationalism was free of all the "machinery" other sects used to ferret out heresy. In fact, "its cases of discipline are comparatively few and rarely protracted"—not a surprising outcome for a system with few external demands.[52]

Yet before the 1830s, manuals, catechisms, or books of standard procedure were few and far between, an absence that reflects both the Puritans' antipathy to written liturgies and creeds and the lingering authority of the Cambridge Platform. The next attempt after 1648 to spell out Congregational "usage"—a term much preferable to words like "rule" or "procedure"—was Cotton Mather's *Ratio Disciplinae*, published in 1726. But even Mather's account was descriptive rather than proscriptive, laying out the "PRACTICES in which [the churches] generally manage and uphold their *Principles*." Ever sensitive to criticism, even Cotton Mather knew he was courting conflict by putting procedures down on paper, and therefore he opened his book with an "attestation" from his father, Increase Mather, who in turn buttressed his authority with a long list of references to other Puritan divines.[53]

After Mather's time, Congregational polity grew ever more chaotic. The religious revivals of the early eighteenth century and the nineteenth-century divide between Unitarians and Trinitarians raised a whole host of issues about procedures, especially in cases of church discipline. Records show that local churches constantly ran into problems with errant pastors and church members and standards for baptism and membership. The established form provided by the Cambridge Platform harked from a time when church comity was the order of the day. Disputes that could not be resolved within the local congregation could be referred to an ecclesiastical council composed of representatives from surrounding churches, who would presumably make an impartial decision. If that failed, the church could simply call another ex parte council—or another—until unity finally prevailed.

Two hundred years later, the system's basic flaw was all too apparent: the external councils had no power to enforce any of their decisions, and defendants found it distressingly easy to ignore their rulings and call other councils, this time filled with friends and allies, until they were vindicated. Local associations of ministers had little, if any, authority over local congregations either; in fact, in some cases no one seemed to know their proper role. In one southern New Hampshire church, for example, the congregation voted to remove its minister, but he simply refused to leave; when a council ruled against him, he produced a reversal from the Piscataqua Association of Ministers, a body no one in the church had ever heard of. Church members were equally difficult to discipline. In one church, a deacon unable to account for money given to foreign missions never came before the church; in another, a church member accused of immoral behavior turned up with his lawyer. In 1835, an extended argument in South Reading, Massachusetts, over the obligation of parents to have their children baptized, went on for months, grinding through one council after another. When asked for a ruling on the necessity of baptism, the church deacons appeared at a loss; their only rejoinder was that they "considered it a principle upon which the Church had always practiced."[54]

It took another century after Mather before anyone else dared to define Congregational practice, but by the 1830s manuals and catechisms were multiplying rapidly. Maine pastor Thomas Upham issued the first volume in 1829, and perhaps knowing his audience, he gave it the same title as Mather's, *Ratio Disciplinae*. But his effort would not be the last. Over the next twenty years, books on Congregational procedure by well-known authors appeared in a steady stream: New Haven pastor Leonard Bacon's *Manual for Young Church Members* (1833); a treatise *The Church* (1837) by Bangor Seminary president Enoch Pond; *A Guide to the Principles and Practices of the Congregational Churches of New England* (1838) by John Mitchell, pastor of Jonathan Edwards's former church in Northampton, Massachusetts; and *View of Congregationalism* (1840), written by George Punchard, pastor of a church in Plymouth, New Hampshire, and later secretary of the American Tract Society.[55] Groups of clergy, some official and others ad hoc, also attempted to impose clarity. In 1837, the General Association of Connecticut issued new publications of Congregationalism's founding documents, the Heads of Agreement and Articles of Discipline and the Cambridge and Saybrook Platforms. In 1846, a Massachusetts Committee on Congregationalism, composed of five leading pastors, tried to put an end to handbook writing with one of their own, a *Manual of Church Principles and Discipline*.[56]

The churches not only welcomed these efforts to restore order but saw the old Puritan way as a weapon for spiritual battle. Military metaphors abounded, in fact. Richard Salter Storrs, then a pastor in Braintree,

Massachusetts, rejoiced that "the spirit of the Puritanic times is reviving," harking back to those hallowed days when "the Mathers, and Cottons, and Wises, stood forth as its expounders and defenders." Still, he warned, "there remaineth much land yet to be possessed. Ignorance, fanaticism, and superstition are not yet driven from the field."[57] Writing in 1844, Z. R. Hawley, the author of the much-quoted *Tract on Congregationalism*, saw the providence of God "arousing the public mind to the great Principles of our Puritan fathers." Only this revival would help the churches recover the ground "lost through our supineness" and do battle for their faith. "Books are not adapted to accomplish all that his needed," he said; we must also have "*small arms* and *heavy artillery*."[58]

In that spirit, New Englanders determined that all the churches, especially those in the West, should have direct access to the actual words of the founding fathers themselves. In 1847, Bela Edwards, a professor at Andover Seminary, called for the establishment of a "Puritan Library and Museum" to preserve the treasures of the seventeenth century. In part, the model was the Congregational Library opened in London in 1831, but Edwards dreamed of much more. He envisioned a full collection of the works of the English Puritan divines, surrounded by a broad array of philosophical and historical writings and ancient manuscripts. Edwards also wanted the Puritan Library and Museum to collect "relics." By this he meant portraits of great men, from Elder Brewster down to "the patriarchs who have just finished their labors," men of true "moral and intellectual worth." Edwards also hoped to collect "miscellaneous memorials" or "cherished articles" of these same men, arguing that "we should feel a deeper interest in the doctrines preached by the fathers of New England, if we had visible and tangible memorials of their existence and labors." The Library and Museum would instill the kind of denominational pride the times required, demonstrating "the spirit and labors of what might be called the heroic and martyr-age of our history" and instilling "lessons of veneration and love." In the years that followed, the library achieved surprising success: from an initial gift of fifty-six books from friends and supporters, the collection had grown to 3,500 books and "some unknown thousands" of pamphlets in 1863.[59]

But what of Congregationalists not in the neighborhood of Boston? In response to the call at the Albany meeting for the republication and wider distribution of these works, Massachusetts pastors organized a Doctrinal Tract and Book Society and began sending to the churches in the West boxes upon boxes of seventeenth-century literature, *New England's*

Memorial and Bradford's *History of the Pilgrims*, as well as selections from the writings of John Robinson and his immediate followers on the original church polity. "We need to circulate more books: containing the Sacred Literature of the Pilgrim Fathers and their descendants—Mather, Cotton, Edwards, &c," an Illinois layman declared in 1853, "and also works containing their confession of faith and rules of church government. Many members of our denomination have been living in Illinois a dozen years," he noted, "and have not seen one during this time."[60] Not everyone was equally enthusiastic, however. The Michigan churches accepted the donation from the East with thanks but urged each church to adopt "some plan for adding to them . . . such works of Theological value as would be most desirable for the use of their Ministers." The Iowa churches asked the members of the Doctrinal Tract and Book Society to "enlarge their list" with smaller (and presumably more readable) publications, which they promised to distribute.[61]

These efforts, however slight, initiated complications that Congregationalists would deal with for the rest of their history. How could a system dedicated to the principle of freedom and openness to the moving of the Holy Spirit codify its rules? And, more than that, who had the authority to write down these rules on behalf of everyone? Did New Englanders have a special right to speak for everyone? The western churches, not those in New England, proved the most sensitive and the most articulate on these matters. Thomas Beecher, Lyman's son and pastor of a Congregational church in Elmira, New York, posed the problem directly in a sermon preached to the Chenango Association in 1865. Congregationalism, he said, was not some slavish imitation of "New England church order, or Old England order, or primitive church order, or even apostolic church order." It was "the simple theory . . . that where two or three are met in Christ's name, there he comes to"; it was the "abiding faith that the Spirit of God dwells with every true believer." New England Congregationalism "as an ism," said Beecher, ended up as "somebody's digest of Congregationalist usages and precedents," or the pronouncements of "Doctors A, B, C, and D, great men of New England, in virtue of the great churches that make them conspicuous." But in fact, he said, "he who tries to make a Congregational church only makes a fool of himself," for such churches "grow by the piety and spirit of the members" and "thrive by the Spirit of God and that only."[62] Beecher was not the last to make this argument about the essential formlessness of Congregationalism—in future years, his words would reverberate powerfully.

Embracing the Pilgrim and Puritan fathers allowed Congregationalists to move from an established position to a competitive one, providing a strong common identity as they ventured into the early nineteenth-century religious marketplace. Even more, however, it allowed them to imagine themselves as a denomination without running the risk of sectarianism, the assumption that they alone possessed the ultimate truth of Christianity, and to defend their system as best without falling into Biblicism, the claim that it was the only one authorized by scripture. In years ahead, as we will see, this particular self-awareness would propel Congregationalists into leadership of Protestant efforts in ecumenical cooperation and ease their encounter with liberal theology and historical criticism of the Bible. At the same time, however, those Pilgrim fathers would pose problems much more complicated than their seventeenth-century prose and densely reasoned theology.

Nineteenth-century sectarianism rested on a particular understanding of history, one fixed on the power of beginnings rather than the processes of time, on continuity rather than change. Historian Sidney Mead used the word "historylessness" to describe this attitude, so pervasive to American religion even today. At the core is the conviction that the first-century Christian church was the standard for everything to follow. All of the years between this mythic past and the present—in other words, the actual processes of human history—were "aberrations and corruptions," all "better ignored."[63]

Fascination with beginnings was the hallmark of the new "upstart sects," groups deeply critical of the established denominations. Alexander Campbell, leader of the Disciples of Christ, ran a regular column in his newspaper, the *Christian Baptist*, entitled "A Restoration of the Ancient Order of Things," which urged a complete rethinking of every church practice, including hymns, worship, and the role of the pastor.[64] In fact, the most ardent evangelicals refused any name whatsoever: the radicals who left the Presbyterian, Methodist, and Congregational churches in the first waves of the revivals simply called themselves "Christians," accepting no creed but the Bible, no church polity, and no theological system. Abner Jones, one of the leaders of the movement in New England, had become a Baptist during a revival meeting, but then, as he later reminisced, he decided to "believe and practice just what I found required in the bible and no more." "When I had searched the New Testament through, to my great astonishment," he said, "I could not find the denomination of baptist mentioned in the whole of it": neither Christ nor the apostles ever used the term, referring to each other only as fellow Christians. "After this examination I denied the name of baptist, and so I have continued to do until this day."[65]

The Congregational churches were in many respects worlds away from the Disciples of Christ and Christians, and as direct descendants of the Pilgrims and Puritans, they had no immediate need to tout their system as the most biblical. Thus, in his manual of Congregational usage, Northampton pastor John Mitchell was careful to deny that the New Testament prescribed one standard of church organization, though he did believe that Congregationalism produced the best "practical Christians." Enoch Pond was similarly equivocal, describing the Congregational system as "more nearly in accordance with apostolical usage" and "better adapted" toward church organization than other groups, but in his view the Bible account was far too slim to make a full-out argument.[66] Thomas Upham circled around the question by citing Enlightenment philosophers John Locke and René Descartes to argue that the Congregational Way reflected "the decisions of our natural understandings"; here was Christianity in its most pure and basic form. The Bible supported the primacy of Congregationalism, Upham wrote, but only indirectly, "so far as any information can be obtained from that source, in respect to ecclesiastical concerns."[67]

Congregationalism was perfect only in the sense that it was the most basic form of Christianity, the simplest and most open to all Christians everywhere. As Joel Hawes wrote in 1830, "if the millennium were to commence tomorrow," there would be no need to change anything. As the plainest, most fundamental form of Christianity, he argued, Congregationalism was positioned best to overcome the incivilities of the religious marketplace, to bring all Protestants back to their original unity. Indeed, said Hawes, "without relinquishing or altering any one principle of their organization, or polity, they might admit to their communion the whole world, converted to Christ, and extend the hand of fellowship to *all* Christians of whatever name or denomination." While other groups (Episcopalians, Baptists, and "papists") insisted on pushing their sectarian idiosyncrasies, Congregationalists had already achieved the millennial standard of peace and unity and would be fully prepared to "embrace in the arms of Christian fellowship, all who love the Lord Jesus Christ in sincerity and truth, however much they might differ in certain points of form and ceremony."[68]

But amid all these celebrations of Congregationalism was an open question about history: What kind of system did the tradition support?

How faithfully should they follow seventeenth-century standards like the Cambridge Platform? Every guidebook proscribing the correct way of holding a congregational meeting or debating the merits of pew rents versus Sunday collections was already well into speculative territory. The fathers themselves were famously reluctant to impose universal rules on local churches, and, perhaps not surprisingly, as Congregationalists were wresting their heritage away from their Unitarian cousins, they fell into a long-running dispute within their own ranks about the defining features and the organizational specifics of "true Congregationalism."

For the most part, nineteenth-century Congregationalists ignored this inconvenient reality, but they could do this only for a time. For all of the confidence and unity the Pilgrims bestowed, they also saddled Congregationalists with a self-understanding that would not wear well in years to come. The next chapter deals with a major national meeting held in Boston in 1865, when for a brief moment Congregationalists dreamed of an updated statement of faith and a single, standardized account of their characteristic polity. Here, speaker after speaker struggled to explain how Congregational belief and practice could be both faithful to the Pilgrim and Puritan standard but also adapted to the peculiar circumstances of the nineteenth century. In the end, the meeting generated more frustration than resolution: to some the seventeenth-century heritage provided the final word, while others worried that it was dangerously outmoded. What was missing in 1865 was middle ground, a language for change or an accounting for historical process. In all the long days of debate and dispute, they were unable to imagine a Congregational system adapted to the problems of the present day and still faithful to the original vision of the founders.

CHAPTER THREE

The Boston Council of 1865

For those who sat through it, the Boston Council was an exercise in patience amid adversity. For ten days, over 500 attendees, two-thirds of them ministers, crowded together in the Old South Meetinghouse, stifling in the oppressive humidity of a Boston summer. All that time, they withstood continual assaults by the noise of the surrounding streets—the meetinghouse was in the center of the city's business district—and sat through a relentless schedule of speeches and sightseeing. Most of the delegates had traveled long distances to Boston only to find themselves sweltering through dense, closely reasoned reports read aloud from the Platform and then followed by a flurry of nitpicking that monopolized what little discussion time was left.

In terms of time management, New Haven pastor Leonard Bacon was a prime culprit, reading aloud a report on Congregational polity that spanned two separate sessions on two succeeding days. Even the newspaper reporter assigned to the event appeared to have had trouble staying focused on the content. A brief article in the *Boston Evening Transcript* read somewhat cryptically that "Dr. Bacon of New Haven presented a long report on ecclesiastical polity, which he read, remarking that the document was a great thing. The assembly were of the same opinion before he had concluded the reading of the able production."[1]

Chicago pastor Will Patton's memory of the reports was painfully similar. "They were very long," he said, and "they covered much of the same ground several times over." Bacon's paper was so lengthy, Patton told his congregation, that by the time the distinguished pastor was through, the delegates had no opportunity for discussion. "With all respect for those who prepared these reports," Patton said, "I must express serious doubt whether they added, on the whole, to the value of the exercises."[2]

Despite the logistical difficulties of a large meeting held in the thick of an East Coast heat wave, the Boston Council was an important step forward. Standard historical accounts place the event as a precursor to the more consequential meeting that would be held in Oberlin in 1871, when Congregationalists finally united under a national denominational

Leonard Bacon
(Courtesy of
Congregational Library)

structure. The Boston Council has also served as a kind of benchmark for the demise of Calvinism in American culture and its defeat by the forces of liberal tolerance. The document produced by the 1865 council, the so-called Burial Hill Declaration, has long been seen as a major step toward Congregationalism's future status as a flagship liberal denomination.[3]

The reality was more complicated, however. Though the Boston Council may have taken care of some unfinished business with Calvinism, it was not a triumph of liberalism. Beneath all of the disagreements, discussions, and lengthy reports was a question about the authority of the past over the present, about the importance of continuity and the necessity of change.

The practical purpose of the Boston meeting was never in doubt, however. Whatever the disagreements between those who felt an emotional tug toward the founders and those who thought the whole thing an annoying eastern affectation, everyone understood the urgency of the moment: it was time to refit traditional Congregationalism for aggressive expansion into the South and West. With the Civil War winding to its conclusion, the way was clear for the program of church building first proposed at the Albany Convention of 1852. To do this, the churches needed first to put some important things in writing—at the very least a common declaration of faith and a description of their polity—so that they could press their case more effectively in the postwar South and the opening West.

This task forced Congregationalists through a field of nettles that they would have preferred to avoid. Arguing through detailed statements of polity and declarations of faith seemed, at the very least, a potential imposition on the independence of local churches, if not antithetical to the spirit of the original Pilgrim fathers. But beyond that, the delegates to the Boston meeting came with two different agendas, both based on their recent historical experience. The Congregational churches in the West had just separated from the Presbyterians and, though they recognized the importance of unity and structure, were deeply wary of anything resembling the narrow, rule-bound sectarianism they believed they had escaped. New Englanders, by contrast, prized the traditional autonomy of local churches—though in the wake of the Unitarian schism also saw the need for doctrinal clarity. Which approach was the more truly Congregational? And which was most true to the Pilgrim legacy—or did the principles and practices laid down in the seventeenth century matter at all?

As Congregationalists traveled to Boston in the early summer of 1865, they were not the only Americans facing questions about the past. The end of the Civil War brought bitter division over the path the Confederate states should take back into union. To many the past was still fresh and painful; the Radical Republicans in Congress argued that the South had heavy dues to pay for the sin of slavery and years of fiery treasonous rhetoric. In their view, only a long, humiliating penance would even the score. Others, including Lincoln himself, hoped to move forward quickly. Dwelling on past injuries would serve no one, they insisted; only some careful forgetting would bring about a better future. The path to reunion should be short and simple.

History weighed heavily in 1865, as it would for many years to come. Northern Republicans would continue to "wave the bloody shirt" every election year, urging their followers to "vote the way they shot." Southerners would romanticize the "Lost Cause" and the wanton destruction of agrarian simplicity by Northern aggression. In fact, the only forgetting that took place was about the freed slaves, most of whom ended up as sharecroppers, somewhere between past and present, bondsmen in everything but name. Within this larger context, it is not surprising that Congregationalists would become more and more preoccupied with history, throughout the course of the late nineteenth century. The debates at the Boston meeting of 1865 echoed a long and complicated argument about the past in American culture itself.

Hopes ran high for the Boston Council. Here finally was the long-delayed follow-up to the Albany Convention, when the western churches would finally have their say in a national meeting. Fittingly, the call for meeting came from the General Association of Illinois, at the request of a gathering of Congregational churches in the upper Midwest in April 1864. The Illinois resolution began by listing the advantageous circumstances of the times: shackles being "struck from millions of slaves" and "vast regions and populations" opening up to "free thought, speech and free missions."[4] Even after the meeting was over, Will Patton enthused about "the many Congregational churches that will soon dot the South, now that the gospel and the polity of freedom can have unrestricted access to those fertile regions, from which slavery has hitherto shut out Puritan influence." The South, in other words, was an open field just waiting for Congregational missionaries, if they could only get themselves organized. The times called for a "more general and thorough indoctrination" in Congregational principles and more "national concert and co-operation."[5]

Others had narrower hopes, that the Boston Council would put an end to confusion over Congregational belief and practice, unsolved by the flurry of manuals and guidebooks in the decades before the Civil War. A New Hampshire pastor bemoaned the "widespread departure, and in some quarters an actual apostasy, from the primitive faith and polity." "There is a prevailing indifference to Congregational principles," he said, manifested as "ignorance," "careless neglect," and even "sheer cowardice." Instead of a "sliding scale of faith," a Rowley, Massachusetts, pastor agreed, the council should reaffirm the standards set by the Westminster Confession and the Cambridge Platform. Nothing has "stood better the test of time than the formulas of the Puritan churches," he declared, "whose great principles have as little occasion for change of language" as the Bible itself.[6]

All across the country, the churches were ready. In short order, every state association, with the exception of New Hampshire, signed on to the proposal, agreeing to a preliminary planning meeting at the Broadway Tabernacle in New York City in November 1864. At this meeting, in keeping with the aggressive outreach urged by the Illinois Association, the delegates commissioned a series of reports on home and foreign evangelization, church building, ministerial education and support, as well as local and parochial evangelization. In keeping with the call for greater clarity on Congregational principles, they commissioned two more papers that were to describe the denomination's common beliefs and practices. One was a declaration of Christian faith and the other a statement on church polity, the latter to be prepared by men well known to the Congregational rank and file: Leonard Bacon, church statistician Alonzo Quint, and Ohio churchman Henry M. Storrs. Trying to keep things simple, the meeting planners asked the churches to appoint delegates during meetings of local conferences or associations. Knowing their audience, they emphasized that the proposed council would be "wholly destitute of any power or authority over individuals, churches, or other organizations."[7]

These optimistic plans, however, ran up against the ragged emotions of that fateful spring. The Boston Council met barely two months after Lincoln's assassination, and collective shock over the event was still fresh. Many council members were not ready to forget the crimes of the Southern states, and throughout the council's solemn and lengthy proceedings anger bubbled up at random intervals. Even mild and bespectacled Alonzo Quint, who had just returned from service as a Union army chaplain, burst out in protest during a discussion of the civil rights of rebels, declaring them "uncommonly stupid and ignorant" and "unfit to come back and be trusted with a vote."[8] Quint let fly again at the delegation from Great Britain, who were present at the council. Still deeply angry over British support for the Confederacy, and egged on by hisses from the other delegates, he denounced them as "always ready to follow the powerful, and always ready to crush the weak," "robbing in India [and] plundering in Ireland."[9]

Sometimes bitterness boiled over. A report on evangelization in the South prompted Samuel Pomeroy, who was both a Republican senator from Kansas and president of the Atchison, Topeka, and Santa Fe Railroad, to declare that it would suit him better "if we spoke out a little more plainly about hanging somebody." When the delegates responded with applause, Pomeroy pressed on: "I am very willing to mingle our justice with mercy to the common people of the South . . . but it does seem to me it is time somebody was hung." Pausing for yet another round of applause, he further advised that "some wholesome hanging, I think, would have settled this question in the minds of the American people long ago; and I do not believe that a convention, even of this character, composed largely of clergymen,—men who love forgiveness and mercy,—would be harmed if it adopted a little stiffer resolution on this question."[10]

The other source of tension was the structure of the meeting itself. The increasingly exhausted delegates met for ten successive days, from nine to five on weekdays, with many evenings given over to committee meetings or patriotic gatherings; on Sunday they were shuttled around to local churches. While the meetings proceeded on the lower floor of the Old South Meetinghouse (and then later the nearby Mount Vernon Church), a constant, disruptive stream of visitors milled around the upper galleries. The lack of decorum did not go unnoticed. "After all our Congregational friends have said about *order* and *quiet*," the editor of the Methodist *Zion's Herald* commented wryly, "they have at this council been more disorderly, noisy and demonstrative than Methodist Conferences usually are."[11]

Moreover, behind all the noise and commotion was consistent confusion about the basic procedures that had been set so carefully at the Broadway Tabernacle meeting. Three days into the proceedings, delegates were still offering resolutions to the platform, even though the rules required (or seemed to require) that all new motions had to be brought first to the business committee. Resolutions about a common order of worship, about ordaining revivalists, and about defending the Bible from error all ended up tabled. Enthusiasm for raising funds for evangelism burned high, as the delegates repeatedly upped the amount—without, apparently, providing a mechanism for churches to contribute. Moreover, efforts to streamline discussion with time limits failed repeatedly in a room full of professional clergy.

On one score, however, the meeting's agenda was crystal clear: the newest stage of Congregational history would unfold under the protective shadow of its storied past. In some respects, Boston was a strange choice for a conference whose spirit and inception came from the western states. Of the 500 or so in attendance, 200 of them came from twenty-seven states and territories in the West, and at first the planners had focused on Albany, Cleveland, or Springfield, Massachusetts, as venues. Boston ended up as host, Patton explained to his congregation, "for continued historical and practical reasons." Not only was it the site of the oldest churches and other preceding councils, but it was the "metropolis of New England" and the place where most of the denomination's benevolent societies were still located. And of course, said Patton, only Boston could host a real "family gathering, at the old Puritan homestead."[12] In his opening address, Andrew Stone, the local hospitality chair and pastor of Boston's Park Street Church, welcomed everyone to "this cradle of the Congregational order, and of Puritan principles." "We would have you feel that you have come *home*," he said, "and that all the doors and hearts of the old home are open to your return."[13]

The organizers also added a number of deliberate historical references. They appointed as moderator William Buckingham, the governor of

Connecticut and a direct descendant of the clergyman serving as assistant moderator during the adoption of the Saybrook Platform in 1708.

The last great event of the council would be a visit to the famed Burial Hill in Plymouth, but in the intervening days, visitors saw a great deal of Boston—taking a boat excursion hosted by the Collector of the Port and attending a strawberry festival at a mansion in Cambridge. Almost immediately after arriving in Boston, the council members accepted an invitation to assemble at the First Church in Charlestown, Massachusetts, "a spot around which cluster many patriotic and sacred associations," including both the church organized by Governor Winthrop and the Battle of Bunker Hill, then being honored for its ninetieth anniversary.[14] They met there on Sunday and listened to fond reminiscences of "that hallowed spot"—"the most sacred spot, I believe, on this continent," said James Miles, pastor of the Charlestown church. An awestruck New York delegate agreed. "Next to Plymouth Rock in political significance," he said, "this is most important." The assembly finished the day by forming a procession up Bunker Hill, to "look upon that shaft," and they heard an account of the battle and of the newly erected memorial by the president of the Monument Association.[15]

The Pilgrim fathers were regularly recalled throughout the ten days of meetings, sometimes as the allies of progress and more often as the defenders of an unchanging past. The report on evangelization in the West and South declared that only "the spirit, the principles, and the modes of organization" of "Puritanism" would truly reconstruct the Confederacy. "We can assign no reason why their ideas are not just as precious and just as potent in restoring society at the South as they were in constructing it in New England. Bible principles never grow old," the report concluded, "and their value and their adaptation undergo no change."[16] Similarly, the report on ministerial education called for men who are "the sons of the Pilgrim Fathers," "breathing the same spirit of devotion to the authority of the Scriptures, to earnest and progressive religious thought, and to a piety of deep experience." The "great ideas that cluster historically around old Plymouth Rock" ought to be the basis of all theological education, "thoroughly imbued with the spirit of the Pilgrims."[17]

The delegates did not just invoke the Pilgrims, they identified with them, having just "emerged from the stormy deeps of a civil war" to find themselves "standing on the verge of a vast and mysterious continent of the future." We do this day, they said, "lift the psalm of thanksgiving where our fathers lifted it, mingling, as did theirs, with the roar of the Atlantic surge, to Him that sitteth King and Lord for evermore."[18]

After a while, the New England filiopietism began to grate, especially on some of the western delegates. After listening to the report on evangelization, Edward Beecher, who had been the minister at Boston's Park Street Church before taking on a post in Galesburg, Illinois, voiced his frustration. From the very first day of the council, he said, "I have felt . . . afraid, that there would be a disposition to spend the time in talk, in remembrances of the Pilgrims" without accomplishing anything concrete.[19] Other westerners chimed in. Asa Turner, veteran of American Home Missionary Society work in Iowa, warned that harping on "what our forefathers believed two hundred years ago . . . will not satisfy the people of the West." Outside of New England, the churches "want to know what living men now believe, what living men now preach and teach."[20]

Julian Sturtevant, long a leading figure in the battle for Congregationalism in the West, addressed the problem head-on in an opening sermon. His text was from the prophet Jeremiah: "Thus saith the Lord, Stand ye in the ways, and see, and ask for the old paths, where is the good way, and walk therein, and ye shall find rest for your souls." As president of Illinois College, Sturtevant was a veteran of conflicts with Presbyterian-style "sectarianism," as he phrased it. Like many westerners, he wanted a clear mandate and plan of action but was deeply wary of any retreat into dogmatism. And so his opening sermon was masterfully diplomatic, praising the Pilgrims and Puritans without explicitly endorsing them.

Sturtevant was adamant in his reverence for the past: whatever superiority we claim for the present day, he said, "we owe to the principles which our fathers established, to the institutions which they founded, and the lessons which they taught." Moreover, as we assemble "around the old hearth-stone, and the cradle of our political and religious liberty," he declared, we should take care to "trace out those same paths, through all the intricacies and sorrowful confusions of the present."[21]

The ultimate goal, however, was to not to praise the past but to engage the present. Sturtevant warned against a "servile imitation of the fathers," insisting that the true Pilgrim legacy was a spirit of adventure and openness to the new. In this way, the ancients would bring Congregationalism—and American Protestantism more generally—into the future. In fact, only a renewed, confident, and "nonsectarian" Congregationalism would equip the Protestant churches for the challenges ahead. After all, he argued, the Congregational system was the one that all other churches were unconsciously striving to achieve, the least exclusive and isolated of all Protestant denominations. Some day, when the "ceaseless conflict of the sect system" finally burned itself out, Sturtevant predicted, the weary combatants would look around "for some platform on which the whole church of God can stand together," and they would find it "in the independency of local churches, built on the everlasting foundations of the simple truth as it is in Jesus."[22]

THE DECLARATION OF FAITH

The committee report on the declaration of faith, presented the next day, was not an auspicious beginning for the national gathering. The committee of three—Joseph Thompson of New York's Broadway Tabernacle, Edward Lawrence of Hartford Seminary, and George Park Fisher of Yale—had interpreted their task narrowly and produced a short statement based on the Cambridge Platform, buttressed by explicit reference to the tenets of Calvinism. Those "historical and venerable symbols," they said, pointed toward "the faith as it has been maintained among the churches from the beginning." The document was too brief to satisfy the council, however, and it immediately went back for revision. The council also added five more seminary professors to the committee: Samuel Harris (Bangor), Edwards Park (Andover), Noah Porter (Yale), James Fairchild (Oberlin), and Joseph Haven (Chicago).[23]

From there, the day went downhill. Leonard Bacon came forward to begin reading the first installment of his report on church polity, and then, hours later, Henry Martyn Dexter, editor of the *Congregationalist*, hustled onto the platform with a disturbing bit of news. He held in his hand a communication from the Massachusetts Convention of Congregational Ministers, a group familiar to most of the Bostonians in the room as a survival from the earliest days of the Massachusetts Bay Colony, by long custom still open to both Trinitarian Congregationalists and Unitarians. Mostly moribund, the organization did little except to administer funds for the Congregational Charitable Society, another ancient institution that predated the Unitarian–Trinitarian divide. But the letter Dexter read aloud warned the council that it might want to think twice before organizing any kind of separate Congregational denomination. Why should the group of Trinitarians gathered at the Old South Meetinghouse take the name for themselves? Given their common historic roots, weren't Unitarians every bit as Congregational as they?[24]

The flummoxed delegates groped for a response. Everyone knew that Unitarians and Congregationalists were two different denominations—or were they? After all, at the time the Boston City Directory was still list-ing the two groups as simply "Trinitarian Congregational" and "Unitarian Congregational." At that point, the council broke for Sunday observance, hoping the matter would resolve on its own. But on Monday morning, the delegates returned to discover that leading Boston liberals Ezra Stiles Gannett, Cyrus Bartol, and George E. Ellis had published an open letter in the local press, criticizing the Boston Council for usurping the name "Congregational." They also added a carefully veiled challenge. "If the name does not belong to us," the Unitarians declared, then what of all the money tied up in the Charitable Society, most of it in the form of ancient bequests given to churches before the denominational split?[25]

The clearly frustrated Trinitarians struggled to dismiss the Unitarian charges, declaring that only they could trace an "uninterrupted line" back to Plymouth Rock. "It is needless to quote authorities," they fumed in their official committee report, because Congregationalists have always assumed theirs was the only true claim to the "ancestral name," as their "heritage from the fathers." The answer should be obvious: their claim was "as clear as history can make any historical fact."[26]

But the Unitarians were not ready to back down. They were fresh from their own national meeting, chaired by the governor of Massachusetts, where the rhetoric had been every bit as optimistic and ambitious as the Trinitarian one. "The crust of ecclesiastical and theological usage . . . has been broken up," as one speaker had declared, and "there is a longing for light, a hospitality for truth, a willingness to hear, and do, and accept new things." Within this new era, said Boston pastor James Freeman Clark, "we, a feeble, forlorn hope of the army—a mere advanced post of the com-ing squadrons—have secured a little position, which we are holding until the rest of the great force shall arrive."[27]

The Unitarians then lapsed into the standard defense of their Pilgrim heritage. "We are children of Puritanism," the Unitarian *Christian Register* declared, "and inherit its glorious idea." If anything, the Trinitarians were the unfaithful ones, still clinging to "old errors" and refusing to follow their birthright to its logical conclusion. Though modern-day Unitarianism "has features which were not seen by our fathers," clearly "God leads his children into a higher truth." The Unitarian message ended with an aside that would be, in the long run, far more troubling than the future of the Charitable Society: if the so-called orthodox were honest with each other, they would admit that they had already traveled a long way from their original purity. Could they honestly say that the sentimental liberalism of Henry Ward Beecher, one of their most widely known preachers and pastor of the Plymouth Congregational Church in Brooklyn, was in any way related to the sturdy truths of a Cotton Mather or John Winthrop?[28]

The charges echoed as the delegates took up the report on the reworked declaration of faith, many of them more determined than ever to claim their Pilgrim heritage. The new version was not just longer, it also contained numerous references to the Westminster and Savoy Confessions and the absolute authority of the Bible. Sensing a rumble of displeasure, Broadway Temple pastor Joseph Thompson explained that the committee felt it necessary to include two "essential ideas," already laid on the table by delegates from New England and from the West. On the one hand, the statement of faith needed to embody the "historic unity of our body in that grand system of theology which has been the life of our churches here"; on the other, it had to be broadly ecumenical, avoiding "any offensive statement of peculiarities of doctrine." In fact, however, the document took a sharply defensive tone, railing against the "dangerous errors" of the invisible Unitarians in the room, those who rejected the "supernatural revelation of Jesus Christ" and "the fact of sin and the hope of resurrection."[29]

The phrase that burned most brightly was the declaration's unequivocal stand on "the system of truths which is commonly known among us as Calvinism."[30] Leonard Bacon took the lead in defending this tenet, taking aim at those who believed that Congregationalism "consists in believing nothing in particular." We would not invite Arminians to join us, he said, for "we would fall out by the way very speedily." Though Bacon did not spare all fellow Calvinists (he denounced "the entire Presbyterian system of imposing confessions of faith" as an "idol set up in the church of God"), he was not willing to jettison the entire Reformed tradition. All Congregationalists, he said, "hold in substance to that great, strong, iron-ribbed doctrine which was the common faith in the Reformation, passed down from Paul, Augustine, and Calvin, and, then through Jonathan Edwards" and his followers. Though no one proposed swallowing any theological systems "at a gulp," Bacon was adamant that roots mattered—the past had a direct and eternal claim on the present. Noah Porter, Yale president and another committee member, agreed. Calvinism was, and always had been, a defining feature of Congregationalism, he said, and the source of its intellectual rigor. The statement was simply designed to express "our faith as Calvinists, our faith as unsectarian, and our faith as reforming Puritans."[31]

The ensuing discussion was intense, beginning with a motion to strike the words "which is commonly known among us as Calvinism." New York delegate and veteran abolitionist Joshua Leavitt had no complaint with Calvinism itself—"I am so firmly a Calvinist that I have never been afraid that the system which is called Calvinism could not stand alone and take care of itself without being continually dinned into people's ears under the name of Calvinism"—but he did worry about the practicalities of identifying the denomination with a single system of faith, especially in the sparsely churched western states. "We have seen our congregations melting away from us under the use made of these ancient, worn-out, obsolete confessions," he warned. Many able preachers have refused to lead our churches, he said, in dread of the "scrutiny and screwing to which they might be subjected by an examining council to see whether they were Calvinists or not."[32] Julian Sturtevant reiterated the point of his opening sermon: the problem was not Calvinism or any doctrinal statement per se but the very idea of an ancient statement of belief as a modern-day authority. "I want a declaration of doctrine that goes the whole length of stating, in living original words of our own, in this year of grace 1865, what our view of that system is." Any Congregational declaration, Calvinist or not, should be written to address the needs of the present day.[33]

Andover seminary professor Edwards Park, who had spent much of that past week shuttered in the basement of the Mount Vernon church with his fellow committee members, was not happy with the response to the declaration. "We are Calvinists, mainly, essentially, in all the essentials of our faith," he declared. In his view, anyone who had pursued a three-year course of seminary instruction, studied the Bible in its original languages, and did not come out a Calvinist was "not a respectable man." Park was unequivocal: "This is an historical name; and I would not be cut off from our historical connection with the great fathers of our churches."[34]

This was the phrase ringing in the ears of the unhappy delegates as they prepared for a forty-mile trip down the Massachusetts coast to Plymouth harbor.

BURIAL HILL

Thursday, 22 June, was bright and sunny, as hundreds of Congregationalists set off for the great excursion to Plymouth. No doubt the open marshy countryside and smell of salt sea air were a welcome relief from the grit and noise of downtown Boston. But not everyone enjoyed the trip down. Will Patton recalled long earnest conversations about the council proceedings, with many delegates worrying that Congregationalists would

Burial Hill

never agree "in any exposition of our doctrinal views." Some saw nothing but days of "serious discord" ahead.[35]

But once they reached Plymouth, the gloom began to lift. The party's first stop was the famous Burial Hill, in Patton's words, "that most sacred of all spots in America." The "place and its memories were full of inspiration," Pilgrim descendant Amory Bradford recalled, as the delegates stood "among the graves of their Pilgrim ancestors, whose heroic achievements they celebrated."[36]

Imagination was a definite advantage, as very few Pilgrim ancestors actually rested in that spot. By the late nineteenth century, Burial Hill contained over 2,000 marked graves—and many more unmarked—with only six actually dating back to the seventeenth century. What remained of the first settlers was a series of unmarked graves some distance away on Coles Hill, signified only by a plaque.

Undeniably, however, the spot was still dramatic. Rising 165 feet above the town of Plymouth, which was nestled right below, it afforded a "splendid panorama of ocean and country." To the south were the hills of Manomet and, just beyond that, Cape Cod. To the north lay the old Pilgrim towns of Kingston and Duxbury, to the west a rolling stretch of unbroken forest, once the home of the Pilgrim's Native American ally Chief Massasoit. When the delegates looked east, they could see Clark's Island, where the settlers conducted their first Sunday worship, and imagine Provincetown far beyond, the first landing place of the Pilgrim fathers.[37] The delegates were clearly awestruck. "Standing on that summit, with their bones beneath our feet, and looking off to the harbor into which, God-led, they sailed, freighted with the world's liberties," Will Patton later told his congregation, "we first reverently engaged in prayer," thanking God for those "noble men" and for the principles they stood for.[38]

At this hushed moment, Alonzo Quint stepped forward, holding in his hand a new declaration of faith, which he had written on the train down to Plymouth, using his top hat as a table. "It was an audacious proceeding," Connecticut pastor John Gulliver later told the *Independent*, "which no one but a soldier, a Democrat, and an old-school man—all in one—could possibly have attained to."[39] But Quint had, in fact, consulted privately with the business committee before the trip to Plymouth and received permission to prepare a new declaration on his own, a clear departure from the platform rules already in place.

In any event, this was not a moment for procedural niceties. Introduced by the assistant moderator, Quint stood and said simply, "I have been directed by the Business Committee to read a paper which is in their hands. The idea was entertained that it might possibly meet the views of all present." The so-called Burial Hill Declaration did not differ substantially from the existing committee version, except that it made no specific mention of Calvinism. It was broadly ecumenical and, as church historian Williston Walker later described it, had "the merit of reasonable brevity."[40] In his own postmortem analysis, published in the *Congregational Quarterly* in 1866, Alonzo Quint insisted that it was "merely a declaration," simply stating "what was the permanent and united faith of the churches."[41]

Despite the absence of Calvinism, however, the Burial Hill Declaration was not a liberal document. On the whole, it looked backward rather than forward, explicitly tying Congregationalists to the legacy of the original Pilgrim fathers. "Standing by the rock where the Pilgrims set foot upon these shores," Quint's document opened, "upon the spot where they worshipped God, and among the graves of the early generations," we do now declare our allegiance "to the faith and order of the apostolic and primitive churches held by our fathers." The two and a half centuries that had elapsed since Pilgrim days had "only deepened our confidence in [their] faith and polity."[42]

The effect on the audience was "instantaneous, and favourable," said Amory Bradford, though more for the document's delivery than for its content. "The sentiments of the first report were all there, but they were expressed in a vigorous and resonant rhetoric," which "caught the ear and enchained the attention at once."[43] The declaration came as surprise to most of the council, as Will Patton explained, but with just a few modifications, it was "solemnly adopted with streaming eyes."[44] Ever the Calvinist, Leonard Bacon declared it "God's providence" that no vote had been taken on the declaration of faith the night before. As we stand on "the holiest spot of all the earth" and "become, all of us, more deeply and fervently conscious of our relation to the past," he said, we are embracing our responsibilities toward "the boundless continent, and to the boundless future."[45]

No one wanted to ruin the moment. Even those who felt slightly ambushed by Quint echoed his rhetoric in their objections. "In the name of our forefathers," said George Allen of Worcester, "I protest, from this consecrated hill, against that Declaration. It is sectarian." But Yale's Noah Porter weighed in to settle the matter, declaring the statement firmly "in keeping with the traditions . . . which we have received from our fathers."[46] The delegates immediately united in the Lord's Prayer and then, said Patton, passed "reverently around the ancient graves," wending their way down to the village of Plymouth. Reassembling on the "celebrated Rock of Landing," they again "joined in praise" and assembled for a group photograph amid the docks and fishing shacks in Plymouth Harbor. At their visit to Pilgrim Hall, they "deposited many interesting relics of the Fathers" and finally found their way to a nearby orchard for some outdoor refreshments.[47]

Even while picnicking, the delegates continued to rhapsodize. Local host Andrew Stone declared it fitting that the council meeting reached its climax at Plymouth, where all Congregationalists could enjoy "closer communion with the fathers and their ever-living principles. It is well," said Stone, "that we follow the stream back to its fountain, that we may drink again at the ancient spring fresh and pure." With the solid bulk of Plymouth Rock beneath their feet, he said, "we are at one with the fathers of that common and blessed experience."[48]

Will Patton told his Chicago parishioners that, all told, "We preserved our historical continuity . . . to the general system of doctrine as our Puritan fathers."[49] But that unity rested more on the emotional experience of Burial Hill—a deeply ingrained, long-standing sense of connection with their Puritan ancestors—than on theological syllogisms argued in the assembly hall. In 1865 this connection proved a way of avoiding dogmatism, of staking Congregational identity on Calvinism or a set of doctrines; it did not, however, solve another ultimately more intractable problem, defining the Congregational Way itself.

Back in Boston, the delegates faced one very large final hurdle, Leonard Bacon's report on church polity. Because the document was so lengthy and so little time was left for discussion afterward, many of them left Boston unsure about the extent of its authority over local church matters. In truth, the report was such a formidable object that it defied any attempts at clarification from the floor. Consequently, formal objection did not arise until the second-to-last day of the meeting, in the form of a "minority report" from Joshua Leavitt. Leavitt took issue first of all with the way the statement on polity had been presented; it was much too detailed and complex to be swallowed whole in one meeting. On that everyone could agree. But Leavitt went further, objecting to Bacon's liberal use of the Cambridge Platform to back up his points, complaining about its "antiquated phraseology" and "uncouth and lumbering logic." Taking up a familiar refrain, he argued that the Platform had been written for another time and place, "the circumstances in which our Pilgrim Fathers then found themselves, only twenty-eight years after the first settlement in Plymouth." Any document that old, Leavitt contended, could hardly speak to "our present situation, duties, and responsibilities."[50]

Leavitt's remarks set off a storm of other responses from weary and frustrated delegates. The committee never intended to create a single code of practice, Alonzo Quint retorted, much less try to enforce it. The goal was only to "put on paper, in the clearest way, the principles, and . . . present usages of the denomination." Quint took special umbrage at Leavitt's irreverent description of the Cambridge Platform as "uncouth." "I don't think that a little spice of antiquity will hurt us," he rejoined, "any more than I think that the gray hairs, which are quite plenty in this congregation, now injure the appearance of this body."[51]

Bacon, who had been advocating for the relevance of the Cambridge Platform in Connecticut for the past two decades, was prepared to answer Leavitt. For many years now, he said, he had become "profoundly and increasingly interested in the Congregational church order, particularly its "natural growth and development from its roots, which are its first principles." Yes, he allowed, the Cambridge Platform was an old document subject to many years of reinterpretation; but rather than discard it, Congregationalists should be reading it more carefully and critically than ever. What they needed was a deeper understanding of the principles the Platform had codified so long ago—they needed to take their own history seriously. To prove his point, Bacon returned the next day with one of those very documents, a record of the Massachusetts colonial government authorizing the Cambridge Synod. As was his wont, he read several pages aloud and commented at length.[52]

More than just a visual aid, the document was a symbol of historical continuity, not as literal or dogmatic as Edwards Park's argument for Calvinism, but nonetheless representing a providential framework bequeathed by Jonathan Edwards and the Puritan forefathers. The story of the church, as Bacon had explained to a Yale audience in 1848, "is like the grain of mustard seed sown in the earth . . . yearning and working toward the light, building itself up by materials . . . assimilated from the soil and from the air, and so growing into a tree."[53] This was a metaphor first used by Jonathan Edwards to explain the logic of original sin and now applied to an argument about the millennial unfolding of Christian history toward a future perfect time. A fully grown oak tree "preserves its identity of substance, and sameness of eternal principle" with its original acorn, theologian William G. T. Shedd explained in 1856. "It does not, and cannot, turn into something different." Additions and subtractions were a "departure from the archetype," he said. Just as "the tree would be another than the oak," the individual "would not be a true specimen of humanity."[54]

Nineteenth-century Protestants also understood change and continuity within the deductive principles of commonsense rationalism, a system of thought dominating Protestant seminaries throughout most of the nineteenth century. Commonsense rationalism held that truth could be found in a careful analysis of biblical texts, as if they were propositional statements with a limited set of implications, self-evident to anyone thinking clearly. In the same way, nineteenth-century Protestants assumed that history—specifically the history of the Christian church—unfolded as a series of logical deductions from a first premise. The Christian story was "a continuous line of connections," Shedd explained. "The Historian follows the line backwards up toward the point of beginning . . . until he reaches the beginning of human history, where the basis for the whole process was laid by a fiat, supernatural and creative." The divine ideal might evolve over time, but it would never change its basic direction. The true historian, said Shedd, would not be unduly impressed by "improvements," because the "progress of the present and the future must be homogeneous . . . with the progress of the past."[55]

This was not the same as mere "development." Well into the late nineteenth century American church historians were careful to distinguish their fairly mechanical understanding of historical change from the more open-ended theoretical model identified with George Wilhelm Friedrich Hegel and being taught in German universities. Though American scholars particularly admired the scholarly sophistication of church historians Johann August Wilhelm Neander and Lawrence Mosheim, they worried about their tendencies toward "speculation" and "doubtful theory." Enoch Pond, for example, praised Neander's "childlike simplicity" and "humble piety" but deplored the "development-theory" of history as *pantheistic, atheistic,* [and] *fatalistic.*" It is "false in fact, heretical in its tendencies, and positively injurious in its bearing upon the cause of historical literature and truth," he warned, and declared that "the sooner we renounce it and return to the simple natural methods of the Bible and of our fathers, the better it will be for all concerned."[56]

Though the ultimate work of divine providence, change was not a mysterious, invisible process. Alert and pious historians, said Shedd, would instantly recognize "deviations" from the authentic path of history. Heresies, sins, and mistakes "cannot be regarded as . . . necessary parts of the great historic process, any more than the diseases of the human body can be regarded . . . as the normal development of the organism." In effect, he argued, "man is the same in all ages, and history is the repetition of the same lessons."[57] An Ohio pastor, preaching at a church dedication in Sandusky in 1848, said much the same thing to his congregation. Christians studied history in order to understand God's original principles, bringing out truths "undiscovered in a former age" but clearer under the light of "intellect and improved methods of reasoning." What could be simpler? "Truth moral and religious, like mathematical," he said, "is immutable as the throne of God."[58] "Whatever goes to make up the spiritual history and embodiment of God's universe," a contributor to the *Congregationalist* agreed in 1857, "is as indestructible as are the particles of matter which constitute God's physical creation."[59]

In the same way, then, as Bacon explained to the delegates at the Boston Council, true Congregationalism was simply the natural outgrowth of its own first principles, planted long ago by the English Separatist Robert Browne and codified in the Cambridge Platform. Far from being old and irrelevant, that old document was an "inevitable necessity," not simply to be taken at face value but containing all the truths that nineteenth-century Congregationalists required.[60]

Western delegates were unimpressed. Visibly impatient with the glacial pace of the council proceedings, Edward Beecher agreed that a "calm historical analysis" of the Cambridge Platform was a wonderful idea and that the Platform was, no doubt, worth studying to understand the "causes that were operating at the time of its development." But even this, he warned, would never free Congregationalism from "local influences, and, if I may say so, from New Englandism." Beecher then announced his intention to vote against Bacon's report.[61]

Congregationalists did not settle the polity question in 1865—the delegates gave general assent to Bacon's report but referred it to a committee of twenty-seven men, composed of clergy, seminary professors, lawyers, and judges, where it languished for seven years before its final publication.[62] Yet in many ways the council was a solid practical achievement. Even Unitarian critics pronounced it "less narrow than we had anticipated." It mitigated bad feelings between western and eastern factions, challenging New England provincialism as well as the more extreme antisectarian feeling in territories involved in the Plan of Union. Delegates left Boston believing that the world lay before them waiting to be evangelized. Will Patton went home to his Chicago congregation and rhapsodized over the "grand impetus that has been given to the work of evangelizing our whole land, on each sea board, in the central mountains, valleys and plains, and along the shores of the Lakes and Gulf."[63]

Others were less satisfied. The young Theodore Munger, a future leading liberal theologian, found the Boston Council and the Burial Hill Declaration genuinely depressing. There could be no "advanced, liberal, orthodox Christian thought," he said to a friend, until they "cut loose from the moorings of Plymouth Rock," or at least had "as much respect for the nineteenth century as for the fifteenth or the second. I hope I live to see it."[64]

But by then the Pilgrim ship had already sailed. In the Civil War's aftermath, New England's founders would enjoy greater and greater prominence. The war itself, historian Joseph Conforti writes, "encouraged the moral rearmament of New England's heroic past—the forefathers' crusading spirit now consonant with the righteousness of the Union cause."[65] The Puritan thanksgiving feast was on its way to becoming a beloved American institution, and the town of Plymouth gearing up to attract the tourist trade. Plymouth Rock would soon become the signal attraction, sitting under a Greek cupola with an array of goddesses representing Faith (a female figure with her foot on Plymouth Rock and her arms cradling a Bible), Morality, Education, Law, and Liberty.[66]

In 1870, the 250th anniversary of the Pilgrims' landing would be another pivotal moment for Congregationalists. The unparalleled opportunity to

enjoy the national spotlight and step into the center of American patriotism and pride meant that any reservations about New England filiopietism would quickly subside. This wave of celebration also proved the final
answer to the tensions around doctrinal declarations and statements of
polity. In 1871, on the heels of the Pilgrim celebration, Congregationalists
organized their first National Council and took their first major step
toward denominational unity.

CHAPTER FOUR

The Pilgrim Jubilee and What Came of It

Congregationalists marked the Pilgrim jubilee, the 250th anniversary of the famous landing at Plymouth, by minting a silver coin. Designed especially for church members, it was hailed as an object of beauty and superior craftsmanship, ranking "with the very best specimens of the medalurgy [*sic*] of the country." On one side was an open Bible with the words "Whose Faith Follow"; on the other, a depiction of the Pilgrims' arrival in New England. The tableau featured twelve figures—a carefully selected biblical number—with six kneeling and the rest standing around the figure of William Bradford, his hands clasped in prayer. "The application of a powerful magnifier," the *Congregationalist* enthused, will show that "every one of these faces and figures carries its own characteristic expression." Surely this was a memento that belonged in the hands of every Sunday school student, as a "quickener of faith and virtue."[1]

The coin's more practical purpose, however, was to help with fundraising. The Albany Convention and the Boston Council had set high financial goals for the churches to meet, and the $50,000 pledged for church building at Albany in 1852 proved only a third of the actual costs tabulated in 1865. But even then the council delegates seemed almost giddy with optimism and voted to have the churches raise $200,000 for church building and $750,000 for evangelizing the South and West. Still not satisfied, in 1870 denominational leaders announced a new goal of $3 million to be raised during the jubilee year. All of it would go toward building many more churches and schools, a grand denominational infrastructure stretching from Boston to the Deep South, the Great Plains, and on to California. Hopes for the jubilee coin ran high: "There is no reason why, if wisely and energetically managed," the *Congregationalist* enthused, it should not raise "at least as much as the vastly inferior medals of our Methodist brethren netted to them during their recent Centenary year."[2]

The coin did not sell well, unfortunately. Months into the campaign, only one in every twenty Congregational churches had purchased the anniversary souvenir, prompting the *Congregationalist* to warn, in a string of economic metaphors, that "the credit of the denomination is at

The Pilgrim Jubilee Medal (Courtesy of Congregational Library)

stake." While other Protestants were raising millions for their own causes, "the sons of the Pilgrims of Plymouth" had managed only a "meager and shameful pittance"—"a lamentable disgrace to all concerned."[3]

Given the ambiguities of money and wealth in 1870—Americans were only beginning to understand the depth of graft and greed in Washington and the imperial ambitions of the Gilded Age's "robber barons"—the Pilgrim jubilee coin is a curious artifact. Here was a product, a representation of secular currency, minted and mass-produced in order to raise money for church projects. Without making too much of this one episode, as the coin was apparently not all that popular among church people, it is still a useful metaphor for economic and cultural changes taking place among Congregationalists and in American society in the Gilded Age. Like so many aspects of life during this time, the past was being monetized. Old chairs and tables in New England barns and attics were becoming antiques, worth far more than their brand-new counterparts, "consecrated" as historian Joseph Conforti writes, "by the values understocked by Gilded Age America: character, craftsmanship, simplicity, good taste." This was the time when history—especially New England history—was becoming a tourist attraction, with popular destinations like the House of Seven Gables in Salem, Massachusetts, and the replica of a colonial town in York, Maine. The past, in other words, was becoming something to purchase and own.[4]

Like many Americans in the late nineteenth century, Congregationalists began to memorialize their past, uniting around symbolic objects like the Pilgrim jubilee coin and joining in corporate rituals honoring Forefathers' Day. The post–Civil War decades were a time of general yearning for public ceremonies of memory, especially in the wake of epic personal loss on both sides of the conflict. Southerners instituted the rites and symbols of the Lost Cause, holding days of remembrance for heroes of the Confederacy. In the North, the first celebration of Memorial Day came in 1868, setting in motion a string of parades and public ceremonies conducted by veterans' organizations in small towns and cities across the country. It was during this time, writes historian Michael Kammen, that "American memory began to take form as a self-conscious phenomenon."[5]

Commemorations did not necessarily mean Americans were interested the past itself, however. The Columbian Exhibition in 1893, marking the 400th anniversary of Columbus's arrival in the New World, made little mention of the man himself, nor did the Louisiana Purchase Exposition, organized to honor the centennial of the Lewis and Clark expedition, feature much information about the trip. In fact, the public anniversary rituals of the late nineteenth and early twentieth centuries focused on the glories of the future rather than those of the past. The main attraction at the national centennial celebration, held in Philadelphia in 1876, was a grand hall chock-full of enormous exhibitions demonstrating American achievements in industry, agriculture, and technology. Visitors could marvel at the amazing dynamo, the future power source of American industry, reaching to the pavilion's glass ceiling, or they could stand in awe at silver cups and trophies of every description, their elaborate carvings depicting American success in agriculture, warfare, mining, and seafaring. Within this great mass of machinery, the exposition included only a few historical exhibits, which were framed in ways to uplift the superior virtues of the present. The cradle of Peregrine White, an infant born on the journey to Plymouth, was on display, for example, but mostly as a "mute witness of the wonderful story of American progress with which all tongues are busy now."[6]

Memorializing turned Congregationalists toward the future as well. The year after the Pilgrim jubilee, in 1871, they met together in Oberlin, Ohio, to form the National Council of Congregational Churches, officially beginning their existence as a denominational institution. The move toward a common organizational structure had been under way for twenty years or more, at least since the Albany meeting in 1852, but the formation of the National Council was jarring, as it marked an open departure from two and a half centuries of local independence. In the 1870s, however, arguments were relatively rare: it was enough to celebrate the past in special denominational gatherings, in Congregational Clubs and Forefathers' Day celebrations, and to leave the specifics to another generation.

THE PILGRIM JUBILEE

As the commemoration of the Pilgrim landing approached, Congregationalists seemed almost taken by surprise. In fact, the event attracted no notice at all until the last week in December 1869, when Henry Martyn Dexter issued a national call for celebration. Denominational pride was at stake, he warned, pointing out recent developments among Universalists, Presbyterians, and Methodists, and in particular the way these occasions had "awaken[ed] Christian gratitude." Methodists alone had raised some $4 million at their jubilee in 1866. It was high time, said Dexter, for all the "earnest sons of the Pilgrims, East and West, North and South," to come together and raise "our denominational labors of benevolence to the highest possible standards of efficiency." He proposed a "grand Congregational Thanksgiving" at the next Forefathers' Day in December. Deploring the "infelicity" that "nobody seems to have remembered the special historical significance of 1870," Dexter began floating a number of possibilities for celebrations to cover the entire year: a convention in Chicago on 21 July, the day that the Pilgrims left Leyden to begin their trip to New England; or 18 September, the Sunday nearest the date on which the Mayflower left Plymouth, England.[7]

But as Dexter likely knew, the problem was not so much public indifference as it was Congregational polity. John Todd, pastor in Pittsfield, Massachusetts, was dubious toward Dexter's suggestion, warning of "the great difficulty in creating any enthusiasm for Congregationalism" in local churches.[8] John W. Harding, a pastor from Longmeadow, Massachusetts, complained that simply "garnishing the sepulchers of the Pilgrims, and clapping hands over brave memories of our past" was pointless. "The best memorial, by far, that we can build to the memory of the Pilgrims," he said, would be for each local church to get to work and accomplish something on its own.[9] In that spirit, Leonard Bacon complained about making Chicago the "federal head" for any national meeting and warned that it would be an occasion for "unauthorized and irresponsible individuals" to "majestically speak for, and dictate to" the churches all around the country. "Let the talk be much more about the Pilgrims," Bacon urged, "their principles, their self-sacrifice, their unconscious greatness and the grandeur of their work, than about 'our common Congregationalism.'" Besides, he added, 21 July was the date of Yale's commencement.[10]

But Dexter also received many personal letters from leading Congregationalists, most of them college presidents and pastors of very large churches, who immediately recognized the practical benefits of a united public celebration. Amherst College president W. A. Stearns urged him to "by *all means, move* in favor of the '250th' for Congregationalist America and mankind. The opportunity must not be lost." "There is so little in our denominational polity . . . to attract public attention," wrote J. W. Andrews of Marietta College, or to inspire larger loyalties. "I was thankful that . . . some one would notice the time and propose the proper commemoration," wrote Iowa College's George Magoun. "Let us do something worthy while we can! And do it in the line of furthering and giving practical impulse to the principles for which the *Fathers* lived, and labored, and suffered." "Your main idea is excellent," Joseph Thompson agreed. "The year itself must be made memorable." But as the pulpit spellbinder of one of the denomination's largest churches, New York's Broadway Tabernacle, Thompson was not one to waste an opportunity. He encouraged Dexter to keep the priorities clear: "December 21 must be the day for raising money."[11]

Every step toward celebration, however, was a journey across a tightrope. At all costs, the celebration was not to compromise the independence of local churches. In February, the Church of the Pilgrimage in Plymouth issued a cautiously worded call for a meeting to plan the year's commemorations, urging all "who revere the Fathers and who love their faith" to "enter with earnest and affectionate zeal upon its commemorative endeavors." The church was also explicitly vague about the source of the idea—"someone to whose judgment we defer"—and was careful to disclaim any "thought of dictation, or desire to claim pre-eminence" over other Congregationalists.[12]

Momentum grew quickly, with a "National Pilgrim Memorial Celebration" set for April in Chicago. The planning committee, which included some familiar figures from the Boston Council as well as a few rising stars—Alonzo Quint, Will Patton, and now Dexter—also issued a recommendation that during the month of May, every Congregational pastor preach on "our obligations to the Pilgrim Fathers, the influence of their faith and polity upon the character of the nation; and the duty we owe to the memory and principles of the Fathers, to maintain, enlarge and transmit the inheritance we have received at their hands."[13] Further, the group announced the goal of raising $3 million for denominational purposes: funding education, helping churches in debt, and building a grand Congregational House and Congregational Library in Boston.[14]

And so, in late April, Leonard Bacon got at least part of his wish: he was the main platform speaker at the Chicago convention. The meeting proved to be a great and "unexpected" success, with over 600 delegates present, most from outside New England. Bacon's lengthy historical overview, which, the *Congregationalist* reported, held his audience's attention "for we know not how long," embodied the fervent spirit of the meeting.[15] The statement issued by the convention was equally emphatic, sprinkled liberally with verbs like "honor," "reverence," "wonder," and "venerate."[16]

Perhaps a bit overfed on seventeenth-century history, the leaders of the Chicago meeting appointed a committee to provide a condensed statement of the Pilgrims' beliefs and their "self-denying devotion." Led by Henry Martyn Dexter—like Bacon, not known for his ability to summarize—the end product was far from concise. Though the authors apologized that the jubilee handbook was hastily prepared and "exceedingly fragmentary and inadequate," it nonetheless featured a day-by-day chronology for the years 1620 through 1621, supplemented by pages of dense and flowery prose from the works of British and American historians.

There was no mistaking the handbook's central theme: throughout, it glorified the Pilgrims for their bravery, tolerance, and independence. "From the rise of the Papacy to the Reformation," it declared, "the theory of the Church was that of an all-embracing centralized organism," imposing "submission and unquestioning obedience from the people." The Pilgrims, under the leadership of the radical English Separatist Robert Browne, brought a new spirit of liberty and freedom. More than any other factor in American history, Congregationalism was the "mother of our civil liberties."[17]

The next event was the December anniversary. The secular gathering in Plymouth did little to impress Congregationalists this time around, despite the involvement of luminaries like John Greenleaf Whittier and President Ulysses Grant. Not only did the event feature a ball, which the editor of the *Pacific*, the denomination's journal of record on the West Coast, excoriated as an example of "low, shuffling taste," but the Pilgrim Society held its celebration in a Unitarian church where, the *Congregationalist* noted disapprovingly, the service was "accompanied by suitable music, but no prayer." The editor also found it "a little singular" that the main speaker at the Plymouth gathering was Robert Winthrop, a descendant of the first governor of Massachusetts Bay but also an Episcopalian. Even worse, the New York festivities featured transcendentalist poet and philosopher Ralph Waldo Emerson, "who is not much of a church man of any kind."[18]

At their own event in Boston, Congregationalists explicitly and emphatically tied the Pilgrim legacy to the rise and the preservation of American democracy. The point, as one speaker declared, was "not to idolize, but to idealize the fathers."[19] Once again Leonard Bacon gave an oration on the Pilgrims, "displaying a great familiarity with the topic," as the *Congregationalist* reported, "and making it evident to all his hearers that it has been with him the subject of patient, laborious, and profound study, and investigation." A host of other speakers, some more successfully than others, labored through more tributes to the Pilgrim fathers, all verging toward the same theme: Congregationalism was essential to American freedom. With new threats emerging everywhere—the last speaker on the program, evangelist Edward Norris Kirk, raised the specter of "Romanism"—Congregationalists needed to rally around their historic legacy. "To prevent the fight," Kirk declared, "we must understand ourselves."[20]

In that spirit, other commemorations multiplied. In local churches across the country, the jubilee year meant Pilgrim memorial meetings, church suppers, and creative displays of historical nostalgia. A festival in the Ipswich, Massachusetts, church featured hymn singing accompanied by "instruments of the olden time, [which] rendered a number of old tunes with fine effect." Celebrations on the West Coast, where Congregationalist churches were sparse, were equally, if not more, uplifting. The San Francisco–area churches held their own memorial festival in the city's public pavilion, enjoying a lengthy oration on the Pilgrim fathers and a "simple and frugal" reception where they lifted nonalcoholic toasts to California, San Francisco, Plymouth Rock, John Robinson, and the matrons of early New England.[21]

A Pilgrim jubilee in Providence, Rhode Island, organized by the local churches, was a similarly impressive affair, with speeches by Dartmouth president Mark Hopkins, Andover professor Edwards Park, and Henry Martyn Dexter. Apparently choosing to overlook the fact that they were meeting in Roger Williams Hall, dedicated to the memory of a man the Puritans had once banished, the celebrants took every possible opportunity to praise the courage and long suffering of Williams's old nemeses. The grace over dinner included a reminder that those ancients ate not in mid-Victorian splendor but "with their loins girt about, their shoes on their feet, and their staffs in their hands."[22]

After a while, all of the Congregational celebrating became too much for even sympathetic outsiders. The Baptist *Watchman and Reflector* ran an article on the "heroic fortitude" of Roger Williams, reminding their Congregationalist friends that those very same Puritans who fled the state church in England "immediately established a State-church in America, and almost at once entered on a career of similar persecutions." Two hundred years ago, the *Watchman and Reflector* observed on Thanksgiving Day 1870, "this very month and at this very hour, one member of the Baptist church in Boston was lying in prison," while another was avoiding an arrest warrant by hiding in the marshes of East Boston. They should all be thankful this day, said the Baptist newspaper, that "our Congregational brethren" have finally been delivered "from the chains that bound their fathers."[23] The Methodist editor of *Zion's Herald* was simply irritated. "The dear old [Pilgrim] fathers and mothers" have been "taken out of their graves and made to sit afresh for their portraits," he said, while "their children and principles go on multiplying, ad infinitum." Indeed, "it is a little strange," the editor continued, that "among all the references to [the Pilgrims], no one ever remembers . . . an original Mayflower man, who was executed for murder not many years after the arrival."[24]

WHAT CAME OF THE JUBILEE

If other Protestants were sometimes skeptical toward the Pilgrim fathers, Congregationalists grew more determined than ever to appropriate their legacy. The late nineteenth and early twentieth centuries, the American heyday for organizations of every kind, saw the rise of Congregational clubs all across the country and a growing variety of different ways to commemorate the Pilgrim fathers. These were mostly social groups, providing regular occasions for men—and, once a year in June, their wives—to hear a talk on a relevant subject and enjoy a good dinner together. A safe alternative to the lodge and secret society, both enormous distractions to church men during this time, and a denominational version of the popular New England clubs springing up among homesick exiles, Congregational clubs offered gentlemen of substance an opportunity to meet with their peers from other churches.

These clubs grew steadily throughout the late nineteenth century and eventually spread across the country. Boston's was the first to form, in 1869, but others soon followed, in Cleveland, Ohio, in 1875 and Minnesota in 1878. Of the twenty-seven clubs formed nationwide by 1888, ranging from Syracuse, New York, to San Francisco, just about half (fourteen) were located east of the Hudson River. By 1902, when enthusiasm for the clubs was at its peak, national membership had grown to over 6,200, a figure that included some fifty-three local groups. Boston remained the epicenter, with its two clubs alone numbering some 600 members.[25]

The Boston club organized a major observance of Forefathers' Day in 1875. Up until then, the major denominational event was a somewhat drab and churchy "Congregational Festival," held in late May and, as one critic put it, laboring "under the disadvantage of commemorating nothing in particular."[26] In contrast, the Boston banquet put on public display everything that was admirable about Congregationalism. The evening's festivities included poetry, prayer, hymn singing, and not one but four orations on the courage of the Puritan ancestors.[27]

The 250th anniversary also set in motion a more serious purpose, creating a single institutional structure to unite all the Congregational churches. Just as with the jubilee, at every step of the way, organizers negotiated a tension between the principle of local independence—now being uplifted as the central tenet of the tradition—and a gathering momentum toward greater union. In 1870, the Rhode Island churches called for "the holding of stated general councils once in two or three years, for the purpose of securing greater unity of feeling and action in the churches," though, of course, "in full accordance with the Congregational theory."[28] Likewise, the success of the Chicago Memorial Convention prompted a call to state conferences and associations "to unite in measures for instituting on the principle of fellowship, excluding ecclesiastical authority," a permanent national body.[29] Though Congregational polity did not theoretically allow for any form of authority beyond the local church, the *Congregationalist* saw little danger of "ecclesiastical tyranny." If anything, the spirit of the times was far too individualistic already, with too many actions being taken by "self-constituted organs of the denomination, and in club rooms, and by so-called leaders in the church," with "driblets of opinion flow[ing] from local associations and conferences." If they were lucky, however, the *Congregationalist* predicted, "within one or two years, a National Council of Congregational Churches in the United States, holding stated meetings at suitable intervals, may become an accomplished fact of Congregationalism."[30]

Nowhere was the prospect of coordinated action more welcome than in the isolated churches of the West. True, few were able to participate in the celebrations in Chicago and New England, but the uplifting of the Pilgrims at least temporarily boosted the spirits of "the dispersed," as they called themselves.[31] The more important development, however, was the talk of serious fundraising—though many western observers were skeptical of success. The Chicago celebration was a wonderful event and the speeches were glorious, the editor of the *Pacific* noted that May. "But we do not notice that any pledges in money were placed upon the table."[32] For their part, western Congregationalists chose to emphasize the biblical meaning of "jubilee" as a time in a fifty-year cycle for forgiving financial debts. For some institutions along the West Coast, this seemed the only way. The *Pacific* itself was just barely scraping by despite constant economizing, the editor confessed, adding that "we need a hundred thousand dollars for the Pacific Theological Seminary and as much more to carry on other auxiliary institutions of the churches here." Appealing to all those "who value the independence of the churches" and prize the tradition of "ecclesiastical liberty," the *Pacific* declared it time to work together and "let the strong help to bear the burdens of the weak."[33]

They would get their wish the next year, when the first National Council met in Oberlin, Ohio. This meeting would be the first of many more to come, a time for invoking the Pilgrim tradition of local church independence in the service of national unity—setting in motion a central contradiction that would define Congregational church politics for the next century.

OBERLIN

Planning a national meeting was no easy task for people long accustomed to acting independently of each other. In the months leading up to Oberlin, anxious Congregationalists could not even decide on the right noun for the gathering. "Council" was a familiar denominational word, but in 1870 it brought to mind the Roman Catholic meetings going on in the Vatican, where the talk was of papal infallibility.[34] As November approached, organizers were still undecided, having considered "association," "union," and even "syndicate," without coming to agreement. In fact, at the actual event in Oberlin, draft versions of the proceedings simply left a blank space for the title while the arguments continued. After hours of debate and a "state of uproar," they finally settled on "council," but far from unanimously.[35]

The other issue was the place for the gathering. The idea had originated in Boston, and the call for the meeting had been issued by the General Association of Massachusetts.[36] But New England had just hosted the Boston Council in 1865, and western churches felt they deserved their due.

Not only the most financially needy, they were also the fastest growing segment of the denomination. In fact, by that time, the First Church in Oberlin was the third largest in the denomination, with nearly a thousand members, far behind Henry Ward Beecher's Plymouth Church (close to 2,000) but certainly level with the Park Street Church in Boston (975).[37]

The choice of Oberlin was also as symbolic in 1871 as Boston had been five years before. The council meeting announced the end of hostilities between orthodox Calvinists and the radical perfectionist theology long identified with Oberlin Seminary. The shift began at the Albany Convention in 1852 when Oberlin was, according to one observer, finally "received into the fellowship of the denomination as a national body." But even in 1871, a bit of sarcasm was difficult to resist. One retired Oberlin professor told the gathering that after being "under the ban so long, we appreciate the privilege of associating with the very chivalry of orthodoxy," exulting that "we now have the stamp of respectability!"[38] But in the end the tone was collegial. After a stirring address by Oberlin's aging president, Charles Finney, the moderator of the National Council declared that "we stand to-day on the grave of buried prejudices." Oberlin "was finally and fully initiated into the fellowship of all the wise and good."[39]

Still, New Englanders fresh from their Pilgrim jubilee struggled to adapt to the world beyond the Hudson River. Even Oberlin's inclement weather made them think of Plymouth Rock. "The skies were leaden and unpromising, the air was keen and frosty," the *Congregationalist*'s correspondent reported—"quite in keeping with the associations of the past" for the "sons of the Pilgrims."[40] (For very different reasons, delegates from the far western states also declared Oberlin remarkable for its spiritual tone and overall morality. "Think of being in a place a whole week," the correspondent from the *Pacific* told his readers, "without having your ears saluted with oaths," or "seeing a drunkard reeling through the streets."[41]) Perhaps a bit wary after a long year of jubilee celebrations, the *Congregationalist* urged the New England delegates to stay humble and keep their orations short. Though we are "attached to our usages," the Boston paper urged, with a tip of the hat to Oberlin, "we do not pretend to have already attained perfection."[42]

Without doubt the council was an important achievement. Its self-described purpose was to "express and foster the substantial unity of our churches in doctrine, polity, and work" with "as simple an organization, with as few officers, and with as limited duties" as possible. As a representative body created by the local churches, the council had no legislative or judicial authority of its own.[43] Nor did it allow for any permanent officers except a bookkeeper; even the constitution was barely a page long. The list of restrictions was so lengthy, in fact, that some of the delegates thought that the two-year cycle of meetings was going to be a pointless exercise—if the council had no authority to do anything, then why meet? But most delegates were relieved that the meetings would be an occasion for talking rather than legislating and certainly preferred not to wade into the icy waters of Congregational polity.[44]

Between regular protests about its lack of authority, the council did initiate some important actions. It called for broad support for denominational projects—the Publishing Society, benevolent and missionary societies, the building of a Congregational House in Boston—and recommended a new creed to replace the Burial Hill Declaration, which by then had outlived its usefulness. Even more, the council proposed the raising of $100,000 to aid church growth in the West.

Despite these achievements, Congregationalists worried that they would be accused of denominational bigotry. The Oberlin Council therefore issued a ringing "Declaration on the Unity of the Church," almost twice as long as its constitution, promising to cooperate "with all the churches of our Lord Jesus Christ." "As little did our fathers in their days, do we in ours," Congregationalists declared, "make a pretension to be the only churches of Christ." The Oberlin gathering vowed to begin a "new epoch of our history" in a spirit of unity and friendship.[45]

"NEW-FANGLED" CONGREGATIONALISM

Over the next two decades, progress was uneven: Congregationalists were neither as united nor as skilled at running meetings as the success at Oberlin had led them to believe. Delegates to the next council meeting, held in 1874 in New Haven, were preoccupied with questions about their role and the extent of their authority, egged on by worried conservatives who threatened to block any kind of change in the existing order. At times the debate was simply painful. "It was not so much what was said," observer E. Lyman Hood recalled, "as it was the manner of the saying," arousing an "antagonism seldom if ever equaled in any discussion in the Council." The *Independent* pronounced the New Haven meeting mediocre at best. "If the Congregationalists are to perpetuate their system of councils," the editor chided, "they must learn to suppress bores."[46]

The new denomination did not have the luxury of starting slowly. The national councils of the late nineteenth century faced a host of knotty issues with little power to untangle them. How would Congregationalists respond to the needs of the freed slaves, the rise of Mormonism, or the government's treatment of Native Americans? "There is no lack of brains in the Congregational denomination," one critic moaned; "but the brains are too little brought to the front." Though the institutional structure of "new-fangled Congregationalism" promised much, he complained, it was being railroaded by "statisticians, certain editors of newspapers, and a few agents who have access naturally to a large number of people." As a consequence, their Protestant competitors continued to sweep on by: "If we do not look out," he warned, "we shall become, as a denomination, what the Methodists were a generation ago, and lose that character of dignity and intelligence which has been our distinction in the past."[47]

Congregationalists also had more personal issues to deal with, as the scandals surrounding Brooklyn pastor Henry Ward Beecher escalated during these early years. In 1870 the enormously popular Beecher, known for his florid pulpit style and rumored dalliances with female church members, was accused of adultery with Elizabeth Tilton, the wife of Beecher's friend and influential publisher Theodore Tilton. A lurid controversy ground on for years in court trials and newspaper exposés—Beecher's congregation exonerated him not once but twice during this time—and ended with a hung jury in 1875. Though in private correspondence church leaders debated his guilt or innocence, they had no doubt of the potential damage Beecher's sexual misdoings might cause. "Congregationalism, my dear brother," Dartmouth president A. D. Smith wrote to Henry Martyn Dexter in 1875, "has a little too much to bear, just now, and we must be careful that the burden not be increased." The "infatuated, mesmerized, [and] spellbound" members of Plymouth Church were not helping the denomination's larger cause either. "*Beecher may be the rock on which Congregationalism is to split,*" Smith worried, urging Dexter, as editor of the *Congregationalist* to "have an eye to these things, my dear Sir, and head them off, as best you can."[48]

These rumbling insecurities prompted a new spurt of handbooks and manuals dealing with Congregational polity. The National Council commissioned Michigan pastor A. Hastings Ross to write one of the first in 1883. Ross's *Pocket Manual of Congregationalism* settled a few old questions about ordination and membership, but more important, it laid out a more contemporary model of local church governance, with well-defined roles for church trustees and committees and a complete set of parliamentary rules for guiding church meetings. During this time, the newer state conferences, those outside of New England, also began issuing manuals of their own.[49] The National Council called for another iteration of Ross's manual in 1892, with a sample set of bylaws and more explicit procedures for organizing churches and admitting new members. This did not, however, slow another round of handbook publishing: George Boynton's *The Congregational Way* (1905) and Will Barton's *Pocket Manual* (1910) and *Law of Congregational Usage* (1916). Historian Williston Walker issued his study *The Creeds and Platforms of Congregationalism* in 1893, to provide access to the original texts of statements on polity dating back to the English Separatists.[50]

The National Council was slightly more successful in putting together statements of faith. In 1880, at the request of the Ohio delegation, the council commissioned work on a new creed, to finish the work begun at Burial Hill. The goal was to create a new document, written "in our living tongue" and explaining "the doctrines which we hold to-day." While testifying to "belief in the old doctrines," it would "define these doctrines in modern phraseology that the world should know exactly what we believe."[51]

The Creed of 1883 was the work of twenty-five men, only three of whom did not sign the final document. It would prove a strong but flexible standard for ordaining missionaries and ministerial candidates—Williston Walker declared it "simple, clear, and modern."[52] But in an age of growing polarities between religion and science and belief and nonbelief, it did not please everyone. Critics found it far too short and general, especially around contemporary debates over evolution and the infallibility of the Bible. Massachusetts pastor William DeLoss Love complained that almost anyone could sign the Creed of 1883, even a "professed Christian man who believes that we are descended from monkeys." Boston social reformer Joseph Cook denounced it as a "fast and loose compromise" and a "tissue of latitudinarian loopholes."[53]

In a broad sense, Cook was right, at least about the denomination's liberal leanings. Congregationalists could already boast leading innovators in theology, from Horace Bushnell to Theodore Munger, and were widely known for the pulpit eloquence of men like Henry Ward Beecher and George Gordon, who presided over Boston's Old South Church for more than forty years. Moreover, over the course of the late nineteenth century, meetings of the National Council became occasions for Congregationalists to publicly align themselves with progressive causes. The St. Louis Council in 1880, for example, seated the first woman delegate, Amanda Bell of Denver, enrolling her "without question." The Minneapolis Council of 1892 appointed Reverend George C. Rowe, "an honored member of the

African race," as an assistant moderator, beginning a long-standing practice of including an African American official on the platform. Council meetings also provided, for the first time, a denomination-wide forum for issues of national significance and brought to the national spotlight local churchmen like Washington Gladden, an Ohio pastor and leading figure in the Social Gospel movement. By the turn of the century, in fact, he was a genuinely beloved figure among Congregationalists and a regular speaker at council meetings. Gladden's speeches and popular books also introduced the churches to ideas that most would not have encountered on their own, from the radical labor movement for Christian Socialism to the Pentecostal power of the Holy Spirit.[54]

In retrospect, then, the Pilgrim jubilee marked the beginning of a gradual and deeply consequential series of changes. During the late nineteenth century, the certainties of men like Edwards Park, who could not imagine Congregationalism without Calvinist doctrine, were giving way to a "new-fangled" version of denominational life, symbolically tied to the Pilgrim legacy but in reality defined by a progressive social agenda and the modern methods of parliamentary procedure. More than that, by the turn of the century, the old Puritan churches, the heirs of Cotton Mather, Jonathan Edwards, and Lyman Beecher, had become one of the most liberal denominations in the country.

In many ways, that very New England legacy made the transformation possible. Congregationalists themselves would have credited the democratic and civic values of their Pilgrim ancestors for their progressive cultural role, assuming that they were merely living out those seventeenth-century principles in their nineteenth-century world. But more important than what that historic identity gave to Congregationalists is what it helped them to avoid. In the years before the Civil War, it shielded them from the competition to be the most "biblical" Protestant group—claiming and maintaining their status as "sons of the Pilgrim fathers" was legitimacy enough. In 1865, Congregationalists side-stepped the demands of Calvinist orthodoxy while gathered at the top of Plymouth's Burial Hill. And in 1870, memorializing Pilgrim history with coins and clubs and celebrations helped them overcome remaining obstacles to creating a denominational organization.

Historical memory worked in other ways as well. The more powerful the investment in their Pilgrim roots, the more Congregationalists would find themselves encountering a new set of assumptions about the relationship between the past and present—ideas so challenging and significant that they would divide the Protestant world into angry factions and forever alter Western society and thought. These are enormous ideas with enormous consequences, but best explored on a smaller scale, in the very different careers of two leading scholars of Congregationalism, Henry Martyn Dexter and Williston Walker.

CHAPTER FIVE

Scribes and Scholars

The Careers of Henry Martyn Dexter and Williston Walker

Congregationalists sat through their first and only major heresy trial in 1886, feeling angry and humiliated. The stakes were high: leading faculty at Andover Seminary had been accused of teaching unorthodox theology, in particular the theory of future probation—that souls condemned to hell would have a second opportunity to repent and be saved. Speculation about the ultimate fate of unbelievers was nothing new in Christian thought; in fact, this latest Protestant reworking of Roman Catholic purgatory came with a respectable pedigree from a German university. It also offered a compassionate answer to the increasingly thorny problem of the damnation of the heathen—no longer a theoretical question during a great age of missionary expansion.[1]

But the central issue in the Andover controversy was not theology— it was history. Five faculty members stood accused of holding doctrines antagonistic to the school's written constitution and "the true intention of its Founders as expressed in those statutes." The Andover professors had transgressed not just the law of God but the will of the men who had first organized the seminary in 1807.

Actually, the story was even more complicated than that. Andover had been founded as an orthodox alternative to liberal Harvard, as a bastion of scholarly rigor and Trinitarian doctrine, but its foundation was riddled with fault lines. For a variety of reasons, most reflecting intricate points of difference among early nineteenth-century Calvinists, Andover had two sets of founders with two slightly different understandings of what Protestant orthodoxy actually entailed.[2] Standing together against a common Unitarian enemy, they smoothed over these disagreements with an airtight faculty creed, to be required of all new professors, recited in public, and renewed every five years. The so-called Andover Creed was an exercise in specificity, spelling out condemnations of "Atheists and Infidels" as well as "Jews, Mahommetans, Arians, Pelagians, Antinomians, Arminians, Socinians, Unitarians, and Universalists." Just in case anyone had been left out, the Andover professors also declared their enmity to "all other heresies and errors, ancient or modern, which may be opposed to the Gospel of Christ, or hazardous to the souls of men." The seminary's founding documents also committed the faculty to the standards of the Westminster Confession of 1643 and a lengthy Associate Creed that spelled out specific guidelines for curriculum, course content, and personal piety.[3]

For all the orthodox intentions of Andover's founders, the network of creeds was a recipe for confusion: not only did Westminster and the Associate Creed contradict each other on some basic points, but no one knew precisely which professors were to be held responsible to what statement of belief. Some drew salary off an endowment established by one set of Calvinist founders and were presumably responsible to their set of doctrinal standards. But at the same time all faculty were to be responsible to the Westminster Confession, even though the two standards were logically inconsistent. This was the historically confusing standard the Andover professors had violated when they published a set of essays entitled *Progressive Orthodoxy*, an important and challenging statement of the liberal "new theology" of the late nineteenth century, the last chapter of which made reference to future probation.[4]

The accusations came from the Board of Visitors, yet another unwelcome visitation from Andover's past. This board was also a creation of the seminary's nervous founders, a three-man body appointed to monitor application of the creeds. Until the Andover case, they had rarely made an appearance, a fortunate thing in one sense, but it also meant that no one really knew the extent of their authority, especially in relation to the school's other governing body, its Board of Trustees.

To make matters worse, the Andover case went public, and soon Congregationalists found themselves an object of mockery. Since the uneasy days under the Plan of Union, Congregationalists had taken secret pleasure watching their Presbyterian competitors labor through one heresy dispute after the other, from the Old School–New School rift during the Plan of Union days to the trials of liberals David Swing, Henry Preserved Smith, and Charles Briggs in the late nineteenth century. (It was no small compliment that Briggs eventually fled the Presbyterian Church and became a Congregationalist.) The Andover case, involving the denomination's premier educational institution and its leading intellectuals, was a deep embarrassment to a tradition nationally known for its liberal thought and long proud of its freedom from dogmatism. It did not help matters that the Unitarian *Christian Register* was one of the first to

Henry Martyn
Dexter (Courtesy of
Congregational Library)

parody the antiquarian creed in print, setting its ponderous imprecations against Arians, Pelagians, Antinomians, Arminians, and Socinians to a grim Gregorian chant.[5] As the Andover case ground on, eventually moving into the Massachusetts court system, the seminary's vaunted reputation and the prestige of Congregationalism itself teetered dangerously.

At the center of the case was Henry Martyn Dexter, editor of the *Congregationalist*. The very picture of a scholarly Victorian gentleman, with a high brow and carefully groomed graying beard, he was one of four men who had first urged the Board of Visitors to pursue heresy charges. Dexter was by far the most outspoken, declaring in the pages of the *Boston Evening Transcript* that the Visitors should have pressed criminal charges rather than theological ones. In his view, the Andover professors were guilty of a "stupendous *breach of trust*." During the course of the trial, which lasted from late December 1886 to early January 1887, Dexter served as an expert historical witness, introducing "a vast amount of documentary evidence from the creeds of the churches, and from sermons," to explain the founders' intention and the many ways in which current faculty members had departed from it.[6]

In the end, Dexter and the Visitors lost their case—the Supreme Judicial Court ruled that they needed to provide specific evidence of heresies being taught in the classroom, and they were not likely to find many allies among Andover's student body. The prosecution obtained only one conviction, which was later overturned on jurisdictional grounds, and four of the professors faced no penalty whatsoever. But Andover itself would never be the same: the long trial brought heavy legal costs, bad publicity, and a steady decline of students. By 1890, the seminary's graduating class was down to thirteen. "I feel as if a cyclone had swept over one part of our country," Andover professor Edwards Park wrote to a colleague in 1891, "and prostrated the strongest castle in it."[7]

Andover's restless ghosts had had their revenge, it seems. The school's lengthy debacle proved that the past was not always the willing ally of progress: sometimes those angry old specters rattling chains in the attic demanded their due from the living.

Over the next several decades, Congregationalists did their best to avoid another direct confrontation. It was clear they needed a better way of making good on their debt to the past, one that would leave the original legacy intact but provide a clear rationale for change. And, in fact, the intellectual tools were already at hand by the 1880s, in a new understanding of history that would ultimately replace faith in divine providence with secular explanations of change and development.

Chapter 6 will take up the experiences of laypeople as they sifted through Sunday school lessons about the book of Genesis and sermons on the so-called new theology; this chapter deals with the writing of Congregational history itself, and the passage from one set of narrators to another, from the world of denominational scribes to professionally trained historians seeking a more objective rendering of the past. It is a story best told through the lives of Henry Martyn Dexter and Williston Walker, who was by the turn of the century the leading scholar of Puritan and Congregational history. The passage from Dexter's influence to Walker's ascendency was decisive and, for Dexter, personally painful. By the end of his career, Congregationalism's most eminent historian would see the popular tide turning decisively against the historical certainties he had worked so hard to establish.

THE RISE AND FALL OF HENRY MARTYN DEXTER

Henry Martyn Dexter's first major book was as ponderous as its title, *Congregationalism: What It Is; Whence It Is; How It Works; and Why It is Better than Any Other Form of Church Government.* It began as a sermon, but by the time Dexter finished it in 1860, the text had grown considerably, from a few sermon notes to an article in the *Congregational Quarterly*, to the "moderately sized volume" requested by the publisher and then to a work of some 400 pages. Written in segments and delayed by the onset of the Civil War, *Congregationalism* finally appeared in 1865, just in time for the Boston Council, where it was enthusiastically received.[8]

Until his death in 1890, Dexter was Congregationalism's leading historian. A graduate of Yale University and Andover Seminary, he spent most of his career as a church pastor, beginning with his first charge in Manchester, Massachusetts, in 1844. No detached academic, Dexter brought energy and passion to every post he filled. In 1849, he became pastor of the conflicted Pine Street Church in Boston and through patient effort guided its transformation into one of the city's liveliest Congregational churches, with the largest Sunday school in New England. Dexter was also an enthusiastic observer of Boston's burgeoning urban culture during this time; his favorite thinking place, he said, was the crowded city streets, as he walked back and forth from his post at Pine Street to the offices of the *Congregationalist*, where he had begun work as an editor. His first book, *Street Thoughts*, testified to his early idealism. Dexter clearly had no love for the affected dandies and the uncaring rich who crossed his path—and even less for the inebriated. His sympathies lay with the Irish and African American laborers he encountered on his way through Boston.[9]

Around this time, Dexter began his true service to his denomination as a writer and editor. In 1858, he helped found the *Congregational Quarterly*, a monumental effort combining learned articles and denominational news as well as a census of local churches—as complete as was possible at the time. His larger claim to fame was as editor of the *Congregationalist*, the journal founded in 1849 as an alternative to the stodgy and unloved *Boston Recorder*. Under his leadership, the *Congregationalist*, based in Boston and deeply concerned with people and events there, but always with a primary focus on national politics and culture, became one of the most important voices for the emerging denomination.

Dexter's abiding love was New England history. He was born near Plymouth, Massachusetts, came from a long line of eminent Puritans and Pilgrims, and developed a lifelong fascination with the first colonists. In fact, Dexter pursued Pilgrim lore throughout his lifetime, and in nine transatlantic voyages scoured the British Museum and Bodleian Library, as well as smaller repositories in the Netherlands and New England, to create a catalog of 7,250 titles. Dexter's "Collection towards a Bibliography of Congregationalism" was an astonishing achievement, containing rare and unique items, a number of which he included in his own collection (donated to Yale University upon his death). "I will venture to say," George Ellis, a Unitarian and fellow member of the Massachusetts Historical Society, noted at Dexter's death in 1890, "that no human eye has ever seen, and no human brain has ever wrought upon, so many of these dynamites of divinity as the eye and brain of Dr. Dexter."[10]

Dexter's other fascination was the church polity of those original Puritan churches, which he saw as the template for modern Congregationalism. When his first church in Manchester became mired in a quarrel over property, each side bringing in top-notch legal talent, Dexter served as an expert witness on Congregational procedure. His testimony ended up as the decisive factor in the case, and in the welter of confusion over church polity at the time, Dexter became a much sought-after authority. His second major work after the history published in 1865 was a *Handbook of Congregationalism*, which appeared in 1880. By this time, Dexter's particular understanding of the Pilgrim churches was becoming broadly influential and increasingly difficult to refute.

This was, after all, the system "which Christ and the Apostles established in the earliest days of the Christian Church, and which emerged from the hierarchical eclipse of fourteen hundred years" through the "pious studies, labors, and sufferings of our Pilgrim fathers."[11] By virtue of those seventeenth-century ancestors, Dexter maintained, Congregationalism had the truest claim to historic biblical standards and the least contamination by the intervening millennium of Roman Catholicism. His first book, *Congregationalism: Whence It Is*, laid out a rationale and procedures for a wide range of practices, including the formation of new churches, taking in new members, and dismissing pastors, all supported by a dense network of footnotes citing biblical texts and English and American Puritan divines.

Dexter did not approve of deviations from the original Congregational Way for the sake of convenience. In a lengthy footnote to a discussion of the proper ordination of clergy (he was arguing against the practice of ordaining roaming "evangelists"), he rejected any modification to the wisdom of the fathers. A friend had suggested that it was time for "improvement upon the rigid practice of the past" by the "more excellent way" of the present. But how, said Dexter, "can an illogical inference from the fundamental principles of a system be safely engrafted upon that system?" An ill-considered "improvement" would only "undermine and uproot" those very principles. In Dexter's view, if a nineteenth-century critic wished to change Congregational polity to make it more simple and convenient, he had to show how it fit into a "logical" unfolding of the original practice. Congregationalism was, Dexter argued, a set of practices drawn directly from biblical texts "interpreted by common sense." The small household churches described in the New Testament were the true model, and the modern Congregational system grew "naturally and inevitably" into its present form, "necessarily" entrenching itself "in the hearts of those who look to the Bible simply for their faith."[12]

DENOMINATIONAL HISTORIES

Not everyone agreed with Dexter's argument. The years before the Civil War witnessed a growing fascination, on both sides of the Atlantic, with what was known as "ecclesiastical history," and by the mid-nineteenth century all the major Protestant denominations had established their own historical societies and their own argument for primacy over the rest. The Presbyterians were the first to begin, in 1791, when the General Assembly appointed two Princeton professors, John Witherspoon and Alexander McWhorter, to gather old church records and write an authoritative account. At the point of reunion between the Old and New School in 1852, the General Assembly approved a motion to form a Presbyterian Historical Society and build a special library for housing old records. Baptists organized their historical society at about the same time, in 1853, to "encourage and promote a knowledge and appreciation of Baptist history," and a Western Methodist Historical Society formed in Cincinnati in 1839, to "procure, collect, and preserve all the necessary and suitable materials for a complete and authentic history of the Methodist Episcopal Church, west of the Alleghany range of mountains."[13]

The spirit behind these efforts was sharply defensive. "If the reminiscences of the past be not collected by us," the founders of the Methodist society warned, "our adversaries will write what they call history respecting us." Baptists hoped to set the record straight about the first New England colonists. "Trace back the record of church history to the early centuries," they declared, "and it will be invariably found that every time of quickening and reformation has produced Baptists." And though Princeton professor Samuel Miller described his foray into Presbyterian history as a "humble attempt," his stated purpose was to prove beyond a doubt that the Presbyterian system was "more truly primitive and apostolical" than "any other Church, now on earth."[14]

The goal of denominational history writing was to demonstrate con-tinuity with the first-century Christian churches, which by virtue of their proximity to the Bible were the standard of truth against which the entire history of the Christian church would be measured.[15] Thus, as a Baptist author claimed, his own tradition had maintained "the nearest resem-blance to primitive Christianity." A Methodist editor asserted that "in point of doctrine, experience, discipline, and economy, we come nearer to the apostolic standard than any other evangelical denomination," including "those who boast a higher antiquity, and a more direct succession from the Founder of the Christian Church."[16]

Dexter was no less competitive. In the preface to *Congregationalism*, he freely admitted his intention to "unfold and defend" a system of church with a "special Divine aptitude" to bless the entire nation. "If a fellow Christian is an Episcopalian, or a Presbyterian, or a Methodist," he declared, "I want him to be such with all his heart and soul and mind and strength; and equally I desire an earnest Congregationalism in all who accept the democratic, as, at once, the primitive and the peerless polity."[17]

But history, he believed, was clearly on the side of his own denomination. In 1876, when the Massachusetts Supreme Court was considering a petition to revoke the 1635 banishment of Baptist dissenter Roger Williams, Dexter took the occasion to issue a lengthy defense of the Puri-tans. A few "excellent—if not erudite—people," he said, were demanding "historical justice" for a man now seen as an advocate of "perfect religious liberty." Dexter aimed to set the record straight with a heavily footnoted display of his own arduous research, and he challenged his opponents to do better. "Any historian who shall go on to reproduce the former slan-ders" against the Puritans with all of the evidence before him, said Dex-ter, was simply "paying better fealty to indolence, or prejudice, than to the truth." Though the Baptists of the present day might be "quiet and well-behaved persons," the "simple, inexorable fact of history remains," that their seventeenth-century ancestors were "coarse, blustering, con-ceited, disagreeable, impudent fanatic[s]" who would be unwelcome in any nineteenth-century church. Who could blame the Puritan authorities for banishing them? "They never dreamed that they were settling the Bay in order to afford harbor for all sorts of persons who could not live comforta-bly elsewhere," said Dexter. They should not be condemned by the court of modern opinion for failing to rise above the standards of their day.[18]

When the Congregational press republished Dexter's "Monograph" in 1880, the *Christian Leader*, a Universalist paper, immediately took him to task, attacking both his scholarship and his moral reputation. "Years ago," the editor I. M. Atwood wrote, "we found him translating Calvin's Latin in a way that defied the grammar and menaced history," and since then "we have had a careful eye on his philological and historical exploits." The Roger Williams book only confirmed what Atwood had long suspected. In his defense of "his godly Puritan ancestors," Dexter had added "to the original sin of perversion the actual sin of prevarication."[19]

Clearly angry but ever the gentleman, Dexter attempted to mollify his "brother editor" in a personal letter of response. But Atwood refused to back down, even in private. The "Monograph" is "of great value for its researches," he wrote back to Dexter a few months later, and a "fine specimen of literary art." "But it seems to me to be the work of a strong partisan, with 'pre-suppositions' on the very subjects of inquiry," and flawed by a "fatal gift of perversion." "Whatever the literal accuracy of its facts," Atwood scolded Dexter, "a work written in that temper is not authentic history. It puts the author's bias before the candor of historical inquiry, and makes the facts yield, not what is in them, but what is in his mind." Atwood's obvious personal dislike went beyond a simple scholarly disagreement. "Why, I am no saint to be sure," he wrote, "but if I had been guilty of the crookedness which appears to me to mark your course in that matter, I should expect all the world to laugh at me if ever I took on lofty airs of impartiality again." Dexter refused to be drawn into the fray, however, and in his own response, several more months later, he assured Atwood of his own "good conscience" and standing within the historical profession, referencing "scores of notes of warm approval, written unsolicited to me by many of the most eminent historical scholars of America and England."[20]

If he had been witness to his own eulogies, however, Dexter might not have been as confident. Upon hearing of Dexter's death, Unitarian George Ellis eulogized him before the Massachusetts Historical Society, where they both were members, in kind but measured words. He remembered Dexter to the society as "the most thoroughly erudite and scholarly, able and accomplished, if not, indeed, the very last man among us, of the original Pilgrim stock." Ellis lauded Dexter's "full attainment in deep and accurate historical lore" on behalf of "the unreduced, unmixed faith, principles, and religious polity of the Fathers of Massachusetts." This was double-edged praise, for Ellis went on to describe Dexter as "a faithful historian" but with "the tone and the spirit" of an "advocate and champion." "He could not recognize those who were parties to what he regarded as a 'doctrinal defection' as the rightful inheritors of the Congregational order," said Ellis, referring to the old Unitarian and Trinitarian conflict over their Pilgrim origins. Whereas Dexter had insisted that the earliest Congregationalists were thorough Calvinists, and that their descendants should be also, Ellis found "no organic necessity that they should have been such, or that their lineal successors in polity should retain their creed."[21]

Somewhat guardedly, Cambridge pastor Alexander MacKenzie rose to describe Dexter as an "advocate" who admittedly made no pretense to absolute objectivity "on the side of the great questions." At heart he was a churchman and an editor, not a scholar, MacKenzie said, and "his opinions were strongly held, and to them he persistently adhered." Similarly, John Sanford, who presented a full obituary to the society in November 1891, emphasized Dexter's career as a pastor and journalist, ending with slightly dubious praise for him as an "indefatigable and thorough student of history, his work being conspicuous for painstaking accuracy."[22]

When one of Dexter's unfinished works, *The England and Holland of the Pilgrims*, was completed by his son Morton and published in 1905, even his fellow Congregationalists were becoming wary of his reputation. Just fifteen years after his death, Dexter was already somewhat of an antique. In a review of the book, Chicago Theological Seminary president Ozora Davis cited Dexter's "painstaking fidelity to detailed accuracy" and "microscopic research" but quickly acknowledged that his loyalty to the Pilgrim fathers "betrayed him into special pleading." "On the other hand," Davis wrote, "we miss that glow and passion of occasional defense and pleading which is characteristic of Dr. Henry Martyn Dexter's work."[23]

THE EVOLUTION OF WILLISTON WALKER

Speaking to a gathering of Congregationalists in 1920, at the 300th anniversary of the Pilgrim landing, historian Williston Walker began by lauding that "well-known tale." He then laid out in plain historical language the story of the political and ecclesiastical events in England and in the Netherlands that led up to the Pilgrims' famous departure. Yet, "picturesque as was the Pilgrim immigration, and dramatic as were the circumstances of the long voyage," said Walker, they were "plain men and women of the English country-side"—real figures, not plaster saints. He warned against the "frequent mistake" that these Pilgrims came in simple pursuit of religious liberty. "This is to ascribe to them a distinction which they did not possess," he said, "and to which few in their age could lay claim." The only real freedom they sought was for themselves, and anything more was an "unintended consequence."

Williston Walker
(Courtesy of
Congregational Library)

In a few paragraphs, Walker attempted to teach his listeners something about historical change and causation. The American tradition of religious toleration, he said, evolved out of a variety of historical conditions and was the work of many different communities of faith. The Pilgrims were important, of course, but as one group among many and with no particular claim on the course of history after their time. The modern ideal of religious freedom "was no part of the Pilgrim ideal," Walker argued, "and to claim them as thus in advance of their age is to assert too much on their behalf." The Pilgrims might be exemplary in many respects, but they were hardly the seed from which an important American principle had grown; in fact, in some areas, said Walker, they were genuinely "backward." "It would be unjust," he warned, to attribute to them "an enlightenment which almost none of their age possessed," when the credit really belonged to those "far in the future."[24]

Walker gave this address at the end of an illustrious career. Educated at Hartford Seminary and the University of Leipzig, he taught first at Hartford Seminary and finished his career at Yale, serving as professor of history from 1901 to 1922. He became president of the American Society of Church History in 1907 and sat on the editorial board of the *American Historical Review* during his tenure at Yale. A slender dignified man with deep-set eyes and a large, drooping Victorian moustache, he was well known for two classic texts on Congregational history: *The Creeds and Platforms of Congregationalism* (1893) and *History of the Congregational Churches in the United States*, issued as the third volume of the prestigious American Church History Series in 1894.

Walker's denominational credentials were as distinguished as his academic achievements. He was the son of George Leon Walker, the pastor of Hartford's Center Church, the so-called Canterbury of Connecticut, established by Thomas Hooker and John Davenport and more recently led by Joel Hawes. The elder Walker was also a member of Andover Seminary's Board of Visitors and served with Henry Martyn Dexter on a committee to establish a memorial plaque for John Robinson in Amsterdam—this was Dexter's last dying wish. No less than Leonard Bacon himself preached George Walker's installation sermon in 1879.[25]

Without a doubt, Williston Walker represented the new trend toward rigorous research taught at Leipzig and slowly spreading into American graduate schools. When the American Historical Association was founded in 1884, history was still a gentleman's hobby, a marginal part of most college programs, usually fulfilled in an hour of recitation after lunch on Saturdays. Professorships in history were rare: in 1884, there were only fifteen full and five assistant professors in the entire country. Princeton had only one historian on faculty, and Dartmouth had none.[26]

But all this was changing. The new philosophy of history being taught in German universities, and then sifting into American scholarship in the late nineteenth century, reflected an entirely different set of assumptions about the relationship between past and present. The language of development in the works of Georg Wilhelm Friedrich Hegel, the most influential philosopher of history in the nineteenth century, may have sounded similar to that of Neander and Mosheim, but the meaning and implication were fundamentally different. To Hegel, history was not simply the unfolding of some organic inner necessity but a dynamic process of conflict, temporary resolution, and then another round of struggle. Hegelianism did not automatically eliminate divine providence, especially for those determined to maintain it, but it introduced disturbing new possibilities. In practical terms, as historian Elizabeth Clark writes, Hegelians were interested less in origins and more in change over time. In their eyes, it made no methodological sense to quarantine the New Testament from historical study, as previous scholars had done. The generation of biblical scholars led by David Freydrich Strauss, Ernst Renan, and Ferdinand Christian Baur "dispensed with the boundary that had silently cordoned off the unique era of Jesus and the Apostles from that which followed." The search for the "historical Jesus," a man no longer divine but raised in a specific time and a specific place, was on.[27]

As historical scholarship developed over the course of the nineteenth century, it became less and less the friend of orthodoxy. From more radical thinkers like August Comte and Karl Marx came an even deeper ethic of historical relativism, the idea that the actual structures of human thought are products of human time and development. Marx radicalized this notion further, writes Grant Wacker, by arguing that religious ideals "are not only historically constituted, but historically interested. What appears to be truth is, for the most part, not truth but ideology." "Precisely as the past was being rehabilitated," as Sheila Davaney writes, "its authority was being undermined."[28] It was one thing to study the Bible in its proper chronological context, analyzing ancient texts to provide a firmer grounding for modern faith and demonstrating through reason that the old stories were true and trustworthy. It was another to subject those same texts to scholarly standards of historical proof. Inevitably perhaps, biblical scholarship and Christian orthodoxy parted ways, for more often than not, the old stories did not meet this standard—it was not possible to prove that Moses had parted the Red Sea, much less that he had written the entire Pentateuch by himself, including the passages that narrated his death at the top of Mount Nebo.

American thinkers were far more reluctant than their European counterparts to adopt this stance, but they did absorb the basic lesson of historicism, that beliefs and values were not imparted from above but were part of an ongoing historical process. This did not mean abandoning all forms of certainty. In the United States, historicism meshed with a confidence that scientific thinking would open the way to unassailable truth. In his presidential address to the American Historical Association, Albert Bushnell Hart called for a "genuinely scientific school of history which shall remorselessly examine the sources and separate the wheat from the chaff." Like a scientist in a laboratory, historians were to "critically balance evidence" and "dispassionately and moderately set forth results."[29] If historicism provided the rationale for studying the past purely on its own terms, science was the means toward precise and exhaustive answers.

By the end of the nineteenth century, then, most American thinkers had adopted some understanding of historical perspective. They understood that beliefs and values were created and continuously re-created within the processes of history, and that the connection between past and present became clear only through diligent and painstaking research. For a time, most philosophers, social scientists, and historians also shared a broad set of assumptions about where this process was headed. Few would have allowed for out-and-out providentialism, but most were not willing to accept a purely random set of changes. This would change, however, and by the 1920s, leading thinkers were much more willing to believe that "the only logic history bears is what people commit to it, moment by moment."[30]

HISTORY AS DEVELOPMENT

Williston Walker's work on Congregationalism fits into this broad late nineteenth-century context. His major work, the *Creeds and Platforms of Congregationalism*, is "still unsurpassed," historian David Hall writes, for its careful editing and commentary on the historic documents it contained. The book itself was an argument for both the continuities and the development of the Congregational Way, an "unfolding of the Protestant Reformation with Congregationalism in a starring role," centered in the story of the Pilgrim Separatists who followed John Robinson to Leyden and then settled in Plymouth in 1620.[31]

Above all, Walker emphasized the natural adaptations of Congregational polity in response to the demands of the secular world. Speaking to a gathering of Connecticut churches sometime around 1905, he described the history of the denomination over the past several decades as a continual striving for efficiency and centralization in the face of growing confusion and chaos. At issue were efforts to allow local associations (or advisory councils) the authority to ordain and discipline pastors, a power that had long rested with local churches. "It may be objected by some," he said, "that these attempts to modify Congregational polity . . . are really a Presbyterianizing of Congregationalism," threatening the loss of local independence. But, in fact, the changes were the necessary adaptation to the challenge of the times, a course change in response to conditions the original Puritans could never have foreseen. With nearly 6,000 independent local churches and scores of ministerial candidates seeking positions, the possibilities for fraud, or at the very least mismatch, were obvious. While previous generations had established the principle of freedom as the denomination's fundamental hallmark, the great need of turn-of-the-century Congregational churches was greater standardization and institutional cooperation.[32]

Walker insisted, however, that these changes still reflected basic denominational "traits." Despite an enlarging external bureaucracy, local churches still aimed at the ideal set forth by the Puritans, that all of the members should be "regenerate." Though, for example, the founders themselves had abandoned the pure ideal with the Half-Way Covenant in 1662, allowing non–church members to have their children baptized, the basic principle still held that "personal followers of the Lord Jesus are the only proper active members of a church." Though the circumstances had changed, the deeper truth was still intact.[33]

The use of a Darwinian term like "traits" was not accidental: Walker saw the modern-day Congregational within an evolutionary framework, as the sum of changes demanded by unforeseen and unforeseeable circumstances. Rather than an acorn becoming an oak tree under the direct supervision of divine providence, present-day Congregationalism was more or less an accident of history. Instead of legitimizing change by looking backward to the example of the founders or, even worse, claiming some kind of divine imprimatur on the Congregational Way, Walker urged denominational leaders to take a firmly unsentimental understanding of their polity and press on to the future. "Modern Congregationalism has few representatives who would claim that its system is of exclusive divine authority," Walker wrote. Perhaps referring to Dexter, he acknowledged that "there have been prominent expounders of its polity in recent years who have held a *jure divino* conception of its claims." But few "modern Congregationalists" still looked to the New Testament for a "minute outline" or an "inflexible pattern to which it must in all particulars conform," Walker declared. The Bible provided "broad principles," and this was sufficient. Whatever "novelty" modern times had introduced, he said, present-day Congregationalism was "never more true to the main principles of faith and practice which it has inherited than at present."[34]

If Walker's work discomfited denominational leaders, their criticisms were muted: he was, after all, a trained professional. As the *Congregationalist* assured its readers in 1896, Walker's understanding of Puritan church government "is due not merely to inherited preferences, but is the outcome of historical research and independent thinking."[35] As such he was a potent advocate for change in Congregational polity. In 1909, George Gordon, the liberal pastor of Boston's Old South Church, congratulated him on an address that, Gordon said, won Walker widespread support. "I do not know how to explain it," said Gordon, "but all the conservatives have great confidence in you," though he added, "it is a misplaced confidence." "When a voice like yours, from the centers of unsuspected, hereditary, orthodox Congregationalism [by which Gordon meant Hartford, Connecticut], comes here speaking with prophetic clearness," he declared wryly, "we regard it as a voice from above."[36]

Unlike Dexter, Walker's admirers included outsiders and critics of the Congregational Way. After the publication of the *History* in 1894, he began correspondence with Charles Francis Adams, former railroad magnate, amateur historian, and grandson of John Quincy Adams. The irascible Charles had just published his own book, *Massachusetts: Its Historians and Its History*, which included a lengthy critique of what he called "filio-pietistic" reconstructions of the past, taking direct aim at Henry Martyn Dexter and his work on Roger Williams.[37] Walker's half of this correspondence does not survive, but it is clear that the acerbic Adams recognized in him a kindred spirit. "It seems to me," Adams wrote, "if you will permit an expression of opinion from one who is a comparative beginner in the study of New England history, that you have criticized, with justness, the thick-and-thin defence of the New England fathers . . . and that your contention that they have missed historic impartiality through a 'filio-pietistic' way of viewing events is amply proved." "I never could see much value, for instance, in the contention of the late Dr. Dexter that Massachusetts was a kind of private club, free to send out or admit members on terms inapplicable to a state." "It seems to me too," Adams continued, "that you have done a good work in pointing out the essentially persecuting character of much that the Puritans did. They certainly did not cross the Atlantic to establish religious liberty, and very few of them had any conception of religious toleration as other than an evil. To make them pioneers in tolerance is an absurdity."[38]

It was during this time that Congregationalists began to feel, for the first time, the pinch of cultural criticism. "Puritan," New York pastor Charles Jefferson complained in 1908, has become "a term of derision and contempt," that was "soaked in vitriol, hurled by slanderous tongues for the purpose of making blisters and inflicting wounds."[39] Adams's work was part of a larger reappraisal of the Puritan heritage within late nineteenth-century American culture, what historian Michael Kammen has called a "critical turning point" in American attitudes toward historical traditions. For many late nineteenth-century Americans, Puritanism represented something simple and natural, a forthrightness rapidly disappearing from their rapidly changing society. This would change by the early twentieth century with the advent of "scientific" history, itself a reaction to the genteel "filiopietism" of earlier generations. By the 1920s, "Puritan" had become a synonym for intolerance and religious bigotry. All in all, however, the historicizing of the Puritans spurred more interest rather than less. The turn of the century was a time of great fascination with old things, reflected in a growing mania for antiques, medieval architecture, and, as we will see in following chapters, historic pilgrimages and plays.

The historical importance of the Puritans and Pilgrims rose with new academic interest in denominational history. In the 1890s, the American Society of Church History commissioned a scholarly series, under the leadership of Philip Schaff, Henry C. Potter, and Samuel M. Jackson. (The volume on Congregationalism was the first to appear, written by Leonard Woolsey Bacon.) But laypeople followed quickly after. During this time, many Congregationalists, especially those outside of New England, began to form their own local church history societies dedicated to serious scholarly pursuits. The Illinois Society of Church History began meeting in 1891, its goal to collect materials "for the future historian" and to awaken interest in the story of Congregationalism in that state. A church history professor, the Reverend H. M. Scott of the Chicago Theological Seminary, was the founder, but the first members were largely clergymen and interested laypeople. Before long they were not content with merely gathering materials for a library and set out to do their own original research. The first annual report, issued in 1892, contained a list of serious topics for study, all with titles that would have interested Williston Walker much more than Henry Martyn Dexter. "We might inquire into the origin of Congregationalism in Illinois, how closely connected it was with New England, and how far its followers came from other States," one member suggested, and another proposed that "the story of Congregationalism and Presbyterianism in this State until they went their separate ways might be treated as a paper." "Chicago Theological Seminary must soon have a fuller, more complete history prepared," insisted another.[40]

Frank Hugh Foster, church historian at Oberlin Seminary, organized the first meeting of the Ohio Church History Society in 1889. "History is no mere record of events," he told the opening gathering. "It is a science which traces events to their causes." Indeed, even the history of a local church "must be studied as a piece of scientific history" and as such might "add to the sum of human knowledge." Foster was quick to add that, in the end, history served a doxological purpose: after the scientific work was done, the past would reveal the "excellencies of men of other ages," the superiority of truth to "the attacks of unbelieving men," and "the providence of God in the guiding of the church." History "magnifies the permanent, the divine, over against the transient and the human," Foster insisted, "and it encourages the minister to lean upon God, and to walk in the atmosphere of faith, and the consciousness of the presence of the Unseen."[41]

ANDOVER, PART TWO

Even so, Congregational history had come a long way between 1865 and 1900, from Henry Martyn Dexter's Pilgrim saints to Williston Walker's evolving Puritans. The deepest change was not in the content or even the purpose of their work—both wrote more or less with Congregational laypeople in mind—but in the ways both men applied Pilgrim and Puritan history to the present day. To Dexter, the men of early New England were literally family, spiritual ancestors with a special link to eternal truth. To Walker, the past was a different place with its own rules and language, "a strange country across the sea, from which explorers bring reports of customs and of interests which strike us as quaint or amusing," as he told an Andover Seminary audience in 1898. It was a "land in which men move as in a haze, unreal, nebulous, not flesh and blood as men and women whom our morning newspaper brings to our acquaintance."[42]

By then Andover Seminary (to return to our story) had good reasons for wishing its ancestors into abstraction—and was about to have a few more. In 1908 the Board of Trustees announced a decision to move the seminary back to Cambridge, and onto the Harvard campus no less. In pragmatic terms, the proposal made sense: Andover had been struggling to retain students and faculty since the infamous heresy trials, and its geographic isolation on the grounds of a secular prep school some twenty-five miles from Boston did not help. The new arrangement promised efficiency of scale, urban opportunities for students, and collegiality for beleaguered professors. When the Philips Andover school received its original land grant in 1780, the documents stipulated no removal from the South Parish in the town of Andover unless "the good of mankind shall manifestly require it." With the school's survival at stake, the trustees had no problem concluding that this time had come.[43]

The decision to move coincided with Andover's one hundredth anniversary, providing supporters an occasion for considerable fanfare. But behind the optimistic predictions was a deeper current of dismay from those who saw any contact with Unitarian Harvard as a fundamental betrayal. The Chicago-based *Advance* led the charge, objecting to the idea of "monkey[ing] around a Unitarian school" and pulling the seminary "over the hills just for the theological fun of it." "Congregationalists ought to know that what is good enough to build with long, hard labor is good enough to keep a long time."[44] It all came down to "denominational loyalty and fidelity to trusts and honor," another critic pointed out. Now Andover would be forming an alliance with a faith "it was founded and endowed and built up to oppose."[45] Some grieving alumni went further, proclaiming the death of Andover. "We are now only waiting for the funeral at the centennial," one wrote in April 1908. "Then the old hill will be deserted, with all its voices of memory and tradition." Others spoke of "perfidy" and "drift" and "betrayal." "Fogies and fossils we may be," a Missouri layman wrote, "but we do believe something," namely, the "gospel which the fathers believed and taught."[46]

At the bottom of these complaints was a nagging concern that the affiliation with Harvard was "against the logic" of the school's history. It did not "harmonize" with Andover's original orthodox design, as anyone with plain common sense could see—an understanding of historical progression that Henry Martyn Dexter and his generation would have strongly supported. The editor of the *Advance* went so far as to quote from *Congregationalist* editor Albert Dunning's recently written history of the denomination: Dunning had described the Unitarian schism of a century ago as the triumph of Trinitarians and "the ancient polity of Congregationalism" over its liberal despisers. "Why the historian himself should now whip around and think that even better results are to be achieved by doing just the opposite," he charged, "is difficult to understand." At least Dunning could attempt to be logically consistent with his own accounting of the past.[47]

Despite such protests, the move went as planned, and Andover celebrated its centennial year by decamping to Cambridge. The relationship between the two schools proceeded smoothly, so much so that by 1922 the leaders of both were drawing up plans for full affiliation and the creation of a new School of Religion in the building Andover had erected on Harvard's campus. The *Congregationalist* proclaimed a new era in the history of American religion, an "undoing of the past," with its schisms and splits, and the opening of a "new day of opportunity and accomplishment worthy of all that is best in her past."[48]

The signing date was just a month away when Andover's old nemesis, the obstructionist Board of Visitors, reared its head once again. For the past fourteen years, the Visitors had quietly acquiesced to decisions they deplored—and now the cup of wrath was full. The Board of Visitors took the trustees to court, charging that the plan to affiliate with Harvard was a legal breach of the school's original statutes. They demanded that the Massachusetts Supreme Judicial Court step in and stop the trustees from going forward. On the heels of this action they issued another charge, that ever since the move to Cambridge, Andover had been in violation of its founding promise to "maintain and inculcate the Christian faith as expressed in the creed" and to reject the errors of the long list of Mahometan, Arian, Arminian, and Socinian heretics.[49]

The court unequivocally upheld the Visitors' complaint, though not exactly on their terms. Chief Justice Arthur Prentice Rugg declared that "the joining of the seminary with another institution to form a non-denominational theological school is contrary to the avowed end and aim of the founders." But the real issue was money. Andover's endowment, now nearing $1 million, had been given, Rugg said, with the clear expectation that it be used to educate "orthodox, pious and Zealous Ministers of the New Testament." No outside conditions could mitigate the terms of this bequest. Indeed, in the end, the Visitors' attorney commented, the case was about not history or theology but "the sacredness of trust funds."[50] Andover's professors now faced the very real prospect of standing up in public—at Harvard no less—to declare allegiance to an outmoded and embarrassing creed. Within short order, most of the faculty resigned, and in 1925 the school closed its doors, seemingly forever.

In the end, Andover escaped its burden of history mostly outside the public eye, in a partnership with solidly orthodox Baptists, formalized in 1930. As the union of two seminaries, the Andover Newton Theological School was in no way a continuation of the past, but "something new under the sun, a unique undertaking," as one enthusiast put it, destined to transform American Protestantism for the better. In surprisingly short order, a century marked by doctrinal squabbles and denominational competition would be left behind, all but forgotten.[51]

The same was true all over the United States and the Western world, as people were learning to embrace the new and free themselves from the past. The modern society taking shape at the turn of the century was future oriented, confident of progress, and enamored of efficiency and improvement. It was also shaped by a new culture of consumption, an economy based on spending for pleasure as well as need, of grand department stores and ever more sophisticated advertising. It was a world by definition "hostile to tradition" and to anything old and well-worn.[52]

This was the context for a new kind of historical understanding, shaped and articulated by laypeople rather than professional scholars. In the late nineteenth and early twentieth centuries, the Pilgrims and Puritans would enjoy a new popularity in Congregational churches, but under far different terms than before. No longer saints or role models or authorities on seventeenth-century church polity, they were becoming figures of a vivid, modern, twentieth-century imagination.

CHAPTER SIX

Coming to Terms with the Pilgrim Fathers

We know a fair amount about the way that literary and educated men weathered the spiritual crises of the late nineteenth and early twentieth centuries, especially as they encountered historical criticism of the Bible. Many of them were leading Congregationalists, in fact: Newman Smyth at Andover and Yale, pastor theologians Theodore Munger and Lyman Abbott, and well-known preachers like George Gordon and Henry Ward Beecher. We also know quite a bit about the opposition, the fundamentalists who protested against these changes and took an uncompromising stand for biblical inerrancy. Despite their differences, however, they shared one important similarity: all of them had the time, the inclination, and the passion to work through their religious dilemmas on paper.[1]

But what of someone like Mrs. J. M. Templeton, a laywoman from Medina, Ohio, who described the "stir in our church circles, when we first learned that a real Job probably never existed"? Instead, they found out, she said, that "the story of Jonah and the whale is an allegory; the world was not created in seven days of twenty-four hours each, and that David did not write all the Psalms credited to him." While some people in the congregation preferred to believe the stories "told them at their mother's knee," Mrs. Templeton clearly did not. The bemused tone of her remarks suggests that to her the great spiritual crisis of the age was really about people who refused to grow up and accept reality. "This is a progressive age," she said, and "we are indeed a progressive people."[2]

This Congregational laywoman's offhand remark opens a world of meaning. It demonstrates, for one thing, surprising equanimity toward historical criticism among laypeople, even in small-town churches—in fact, we might wonder whether the "spiritual crisis of the Gilded Age" penetrated all that far beyond the ivied walls of leading universities. But even more than that, Mrs. Templeton's words suggest that something fundamental was changing within traditional Protestant piety. This presumably ordinary churchwoman took pride in being tolerant and accepting of new ideas, however uncomfortable, and she spoke about matters of doubt and faith with dry good humor.

Was this due to some larger devaluing of religion in modern culture? Perhaps Mrs. Templeton simply chose not to take her faith seriously. But stopping here, explaining this example of casual toleration as proof of religious decline would be, at the very least, a missed opportunity. As this chapter suggests, the rise of historical thinking, even about the Bible, was not necessarily an occasion for moral panic or radical doubt. Nor did it always result in apathy and disaffection from traditional faith. What we find instead are people learning to understand and accept ambiguity, the possibility that more than one thing might be true at the same time. In the words of one astute observer, writing in 1903, "There is not only a New Theology, of which much has been said, but also a new religious experience, of which very little has been said." Though this new theology was "less emotional," it was also "more ethical," "less intensified but more diffused." Though it "may seem less evidently divine," he said, "it is more evidently human."[3]

Nineteenth-century evangelical piety rested on certainties, that the Bible was true and Christianity the only way to salvation. Indeed, for all the emotion associated with camp meetings and revivals, the fundamental core of evangelical belief was rationalistic: God made logical sense to those with an obedient and humble mind. Mirroring Henry Martyn Dexter's confidence in the past, evangelicals had no doubt that the Bible was self-evidently true—no need for mystical revelations—and that its historical accounts took place exactly as written.[4]

In the late nineteenth century, challenges to certainty from science and biblical scholarship forced everyone to renegotiate the meaning of belief. On one side, fundamentalists intensified the standards of orthodoxy: instead of simply maintaining the old strongholds, they staked out aggressively new ground, even more difficult to defend. Thus, the Bible was not just infallible in its teachings, but it was inerrant, without any error of scientific, geographic, or historical fact; Christ would return, as Protestants had always held, but in a literal Second Coming, predicted with pinpoint accuracy by the words of scripture. Fundamentalism's certainties, therefore, were more solid and unassailable than anything evangelicals had needed or wanted before.[5]

On the other side were rationalists devoted to scientific standards of truth. Where nineteenth-century theology was vague and ethereal, the "tough-minded" found a "superior exactness," a far more direct and reliable grasp of reality. In the late nineteenth and early twentieth centuries, a new pantheon of secular saints and martyrs emerged: Copernicus and Francis

Bacon, Isaac Newton and Charles Darwin were lonely and mistreated heroes of a new order based on certainty rather than superstition. Science was "worthy of all reverence," said philosopher Herbert Spencer, to all but "the most perverted intellect."[6]

But what of everyone else? Leaving church was not always possible or desirable, especially when the pull of family and tradition was strong. Thus, some people learned to compromise, to accept ambiguity and paradox: the Bible could be at once a book of "Hebrew myths" and a spiritual guide to modern-day people, Christianity could be the one true religion, but that did not necessarily mean that Hindus, Buddhists, and Jews were all headed for perdition.[7] In other words, turn-of-the-century liberal piety refused to make forced choices between fixed positions, one right and the other wrong. "We are ready to let the other fellow have his belief," as one Congregationalist wrote in 1925, but we "refuse to give up the faith of our fathers." Perhaps, he sighed, we are just "Mavericks without a name or brand wandering over the no man's land between the hostile forces of Liberals and Fundamentalists."[8]

Many Congregational laypeople found themselves in this liminal space as the nineteenth century drew to a close and the twentieth century began to unfold. They understood that the past, with all its traditions, was important, but they knew at the same time that it was not absolute. They were relativists but also believers, skeptical of old pieties but unable or unwilling to leave them behind.

FUNDAMENTALIST HISTORY

Certainly many people in the broader religious world understood what was at stake. In his inaugural speech as assistant professor of New Testament literature and exegesis at Princeton Theological Seminary in 1915, conservative scholar J. Gresham Machen declared that "the centre and core of all the Bible is history." It is "a record of something that has happened, something that puts a new face upon life." Without this core, religion was just a set of ideals detached from truth or certainty. The "modern Church is impatient of history," said Machen, as merely the external form in which ideas are expressed. It makes no difference, then, if "history is real or fictitious," if Abraham was a historical person or a myth, or even if Jesus really lived and died and rose again. Religion had become independent of "the uncertainties of historical research," and all that was left were "lofty pieties."[9]

Turn-of-the-century fundamentalism made no bones about history. The Bible was true, one of its defenders argued in 1894, because it was "a true history of what took place at the time and in the place stated. The time given is the chronology of the history, and the place given is the geography of the history; and both these must be accurate, or it is not true history."[10] Believers were not to worry about the so-called new theology, for the Bible was more than able to stand up to criticism. "It is a striking and comforting fact," declared the editor of a fundamentalist journal, appropriately named *Truth*, "that every new discovery of the scientists who are examining ancient monuments and tombs and tablets, confirms the literal truthfulness of the Bible narratives." The Pentateuch (the first five books of the Old Testament) was not a "confused and contradictory jumble of myth and legend, as alleged by infidel Higher Criticism, but the most authentic history in the world, precisely accurate in every detail of its statements."[11] This was a high standard but a necessary one: the alternative to a historically accurate Bible was no Bible at all. Once a believer had accepted the possibility of historical or scientific mistakes, fundamentalists warned, "the brakes are gone." "He has discovered, he thinks, an error, a mistake, a slip of memory, a lie in this and that passage, and his head swims as he reflects that the next passage may be as bad, and he rushes on to an undone eternity."[12]

Leading secularists did not necessarily disagree. "Once the historical method is applied to Biblical science and church history," Ernst Troeltsch declared, "it is a leaven that alters everything." Indeed, historicism was "the most devastating of all modes of nineteenth century skepticism," eroding all forms of certainty. Writing in 1886, philosopher Henry Sedgwick observed that historians stood little chance of becoming true believers. In the end, the study of the past brought all "cherished convictions" down from their pedestals, "to take their places in the endless line that is marching past." To the historian, "the whole defiling train of beliefs tends to become something from which he sits apart." For the sake of peace, "he accepts the beliefs that are pressed on him by public opinion in his own age and country; but in his heart he believes nothing but history."[13]

CONTINUITIES

Somewhere in between these two poles—absolute faith or absolute doubt—Protestant laypeople continued to attend church, listen to sermons, and teach their children the tenets of Christianity. Even

Congregationalists, generally more liberal than most, still enjoyed many of the traditional evangelical pieties they had inherited from their parents and grandparents. One fairly typical rundown of "spiritual work" in the back pages of the *Advance* for April 1903 included numerous accounts of revival meetings in churches throughout the Midwest, Pennsylvania, and New York. In Sedalia, Missouri, for example, the church invited Reverend "Bob" Layfield to lead a seventeen-day revival, which resulted in eighty professions of faith from people of all ages, seventeen of whom became new members. The church in Washington, Pennsylvania, increased its numbers through "faithful, persistent house-to-house visitation, with hand-to-hand endeavor, and heart-to-heart talks." The excited pastor reported that "a great awakening seems apparent."[14]

Like many other Protestant pastors of their day, Congregational clergy tried to interest their members in broad topical subjects. In that spirit, a Cleveland, Ohio, minister organized "evening discourses on The Religion of Great Americans," and the church in Amboy, Illinois, hosted a series on "Great Forces That Determine Character." Somewhat more aggressively, the church in Fairmount, Indiana, advertised four lectures on "Reasons why every Sensible Man should be a Christian." Only one pastor advertised a series that might have troubled the orthodox. E. L. Graff in Champagne, Illinois, offered lectures on the early chapters of Genesis, including "Literary Forms in the Bible," "The Dawn of the Ethical Sense," and "The Hebrew Consciousness."[15] Unfortunately, we have no record of the reaction to Reverend Graff's lecture series. Did laypeople resist his views or applaud them? Or, for that matter, ignore them?

There is no doubt that laypeople were intensely aware of seismic changes in the religious world by the early 1900s. In the late 1880s, for example, Congregational Sunday school lesson plans still taught the traditional view, that the world was created in 4004 B.C. (following the calculations of Irish archbishop Ussher, who worked backward from the genealogies of Jesus Christ provided in the Gospel accounts). Thus, according to Bishop Ussher and the *Pilgrim Quarterly for Senior Classes*, Adam and Eve ate the forbidden fruit that same year, and Cain was born the year after; Abel was murdered sometime during the year 3875 B.C.[16] In 1901, the editors announced a change, declaring that the chronology of Bible events in previous issues of the *Pilgrim Quarterly* was "absolutely worthless." "The fossils in the rocks, the arrangement of the strata of soil, the signs of channels worn by rivers, all show the great age of the world."[17] By 1907, a graphic of the "Old Hebrew Idea of the Universe" replaced the chronological table, complete with layers of firmament, earth, and Hades, ready for comparison with the "Early Babylonian Idea of the World" on the next page. "If any one is in search of accurate information regarding the age of this earth, or its relation to the sun, moon, and stars, or regarding the order in which plants and animals have appeared upon it," the teachers' guide advised, "he must be referred to recent text-books in astronomy, geology, and paleontology. No one for a moment dreams of referring serious students of these subjects to the Bible as a source of information."[18]

Not surprisingly, Congregational laypeople did a good bit of wondering and sorting out of their beliefs in the early twentieth century. Writing in 1902, Theodore Munger described the current state of affairs as one of "mingled ignorance and bewilderment."[19] At the same time, though, the editors of the *Congregationalist* reported receiving questions about faith and modern scholarship "with increasing frequency." Thirty years ago, they noted, biblical truth was not an issue. "Tradition was accepted as authority, and when of great antiquity as final authority." But the last few decades had changed everything.[20]

This much is clear in the letters sent in to the *Congregationalist*'s popular advice columnist, Oberlin College president Henry Churchill King. Many of King's readers were demanding certainties, wanting to know the answer to the question posed by one layman, "Where Shall We Stop?" Doesn't the higher criticism "throw in doubt the incarnation, regeneration, miracles and the supernatural?" he wanted to know. "Will you give us light on this whole matter?" Others wrote to King in utter frustration. "I am troubled by the lack of demonstrable proof of the existence of God," another North Dakota layman confessed. "*Make it plain*," an "Octogenarian" pleaded, tired of feeling "in the dark" about faith.[21]

While King fielded some standard queries about Jonah and the whale and the sun standing still at the Old Testament Battle of Gibeon, many of the letters he received dealt with problems of historicity. If Jesus could see "the end from the beginning," an Ohio reader wondered, why would he change water into wine? Did he not see the evil of furnishing intoxicating drinks to wedding guests? If Jesus was limited by the knowledge of his day, another reader asked, and "mistaken in his eschatology and demonology," how could he be the "supreme authority in the spiritual realm" today? If Jesus believed in a hostile spirit world, must modern people do the same?[22]

King's usual response was calm and judicious. Taken in the proper doses, he advised one reader, a "gradual introduction to the facts which the historical and literary study of the Bible has brought out" could actually strengthen one's faith. His answers also reflected a growing consensus that the higher criticism was not only a reality to be accepted but a genuine help for those struggling with faith.[23]

Evidence from local churches mirrors this conclusion. In 1895, Amory Bradford, then pastor in Montclair, New Jersey, reminded his congregation that biblical criticism "is simply and solely an effort to get at facts." In the end, the "wave of critical inquiry" would "carry away many superstitions and traditions, while it will leave the headlands of truth clearer and grander before those who are reaching for realities. Criticism," said Bradford, "is the friend of all who love truth; the enemy only of those who are content with lies."[24] "The claim is often made," said George Warren Stearns at the bicentennial celebration of his Middleboro, Massachusetts, church, "that there has been a sweeping and fundamental change in preaching, and that the old doctrines are no longer believed." But, he declared, the Bible was not being discarded or the Gospel shunted aside. "It would be more truthful to say that the alert church seeks in every epoch to choose out of the wealth of her treasure of Christian truth such ideas . . . as are best suited to the varying conditions of the particular age, and therefore most likely to be effective."[25]

Many clergy made a distinction between actual historical realities and the spiritual truth they conveyed. A "church is like an individual whose body is constantly changing, but whose spirit abides the same," the Reverend Edward MacArthur Noyes told his Boston-area congregation at its 250th anniversary in 1915. "I suppose," he went on, "there is nobody in this audience who would subscribe to the five points of Calvinism as John Calvin stated them." Much of the old theology "seems to us mechanical," perhaps even "absurd and childish, mingled with much that is weighty and worthy." Nevertheless, gratitude was still in order. "They who dwell in fertile valleys, enriched by ever-flowing streams, may well recall with gratitude the rugged, snow-covered heights, where those perennial fountains have their source."[26]

BUSHNELL'S CHILDREN

Williston Walker credited the relative peace of the late 1890s to "mutual forbearance and good-will" between liberals and conservatives. "Not the least notable feature," he said, "has been the kindly sympathy and co-operation" of "conservative laymen, trained in the theological conceptions of a half-century ago" in receiving the ideas of a newer generation. "It is certainly a cause for gratitude," the *Congregationalist* agreed, that theological change in Congregational churches "has been unaccompanied by bitterness and is being made with mutual tolerance . . . [and] a growing respect by all parties for leadership who differ from one another."[27]

Without a doubt, theologian Horace Bushnell deserved major credit for this culture of forbearance. By the late nineteenth century, as Williston Walker observed, Bushnell's theology was "widely characteristic of Congregationalism," helping its people negotiate "recent theologic modifications" and accept the "mutual toleration of divergent interpretations."[28] Though controversial in his early career, by the end of the nineteenth century the Hartford pastor was a leading voice of Protestant liberalism, guiding the turn from the transcendent sovereign God of John Calvin, to a gentler divinity living in and through human society. Bushnell's theology replaced the metaphysical syllogisms of the New England theology, as it was called, with a faith in intuition and feeling. True religion, he said, consisted in following Christ's powerful ethical example, not endless logic chopping.[29]

For many Congregationalists, Bushnell's greatest influence was his book, *Christian Nurture*, first published in 1847. Bushnell's model of Christian child rearing drew directly from his conviction that God was, as he said in one of his most popular sermons, "present in small things." Godly parenting was a constant gentle push toward salvation, not a shove into a violent conversion experience. Christian nurture was about continuities, a home that in its daily routines and even in its physical design allowed a child to grow up a Christian, as Bushnell put it, "and never know himself to be otherwise."[30]

Spiritual biographies from Congregationalists coming of age in the late nineteenth century routinely testify to Bushnell's influence, describing a nondogmatic and warmly pious upbringing where continuity was the key. "My home was warmly, definitely Christian with a tendency toward liberality and freedom in religious thought," California pastor Albert Palmer wrote in 1925. Churchgoing was simply a part of life, said Charles Jefferson, of New York's Broadway Tabernacle. "It was nothing added to life, it was a part of life itself." A Topeka, Kansas, pastor recalled that "from the earliest days of my self-consciousness I found in me an 'unfeigned faith.'" "My home was Christian and my playmates also came from Christian homes," he said. "In the home of my boyhood the Christian ethic was the law of the household, the Bible was the most familiar book, and Jesus Christ the ever-present ideal." "The happy, hopeful, useful consistent Christian lives of my father and mother . . . has always been an irrefutable argument to me for the claims of the Christian religion," said one Iowa native. His own faith was simple and sincere. "My father taught me that I should pray only for what I thought was for my own or another's good, and that God would answer every prayer with a 'yes' or a 'no,' whichever answer was for the best."[31]

Perhaps not surprisingly, as one of the editors of the *Congregationalist* declared in 1905, "we shrink from the rules of ecclesiastics. We don't want to be caught in the wheels of too much machinery."[32] The 1896 "heresy trial" of W. T. Brown, a young graduate of Yale Divinity School, is a case in point. Complaining that his sermons had "seriously disturbed the faith of some of his parishioners," a small group of members in Brown's church in Madison, Connecticut, charged him with teaching heretical doctrines. According to Congregational practice, the matter was taken up by a council composed of representatives from area churches. Rather than take sides with Brown or his critics, however, the council affirmed the "right of the minority" to bring the matter to consideration and then urged the majority to "pay kindly respect to the tender scruples of those who may have differed from them in words of doctrine." The ethic for all was "mutual trust, forbearance, and helpfulness for all its members."[33] "One cannot be otherwise than soothed by the irenic tone of the document which was adopted, it is said, unanimously," the editor of the *Pacific* enthused about the case. This was the first time, the *Congregationalist* agreed, that a council had taken up "the orthodoxy of what has come to be called the newer religious thinking." In this case, the question was "not whether the new should supplant the old, but whether the old should exclude the new." The final message of this Congregational "heresy trial" was that "there is room in the Congregational denomination for both the older thinking and the newer." Congregationalism had never required blind obedience: "It asks only that they shall loyally seek the truth and use all the light God has given them."[34]

In an increasingly polarized religious age, the ethic of tolerance applied even to fundamentalists. Certainly to some, this new brand of religious conservatism was "dangerous propaganda," as Seattle pastor Chauncey Hawkins warned in 1922. "The day for 'playing safe' in the pulpit has passed," he warned, urging churches to meet "the challenge of the reactionaries."[35] But others took the opposite view. "Some one wrote me the other day from New York asking me to subscribe to a fund to finance the defence of Mr. Scopes," said Irving Maurer, president of Beloit College, referring to the infamous "monkey trial" taking place in Dayton, Tennessee, in the summer of 1925. "I shall not subscribe one dollar," he said. The fundamentalists were "absolutely right" in standing up for their convictions, he thought; in fact, modernists could take a lesson from their public courage.[36] This was not just liberal posturing. The pastor of the Congregational church in Chattanooga, Tennessee, refused to join in the denunciations of fundamentalists by Unitarians, Universalists, and Episcopalians. "I have tried, in my pulpit and in published sermons and statements," he said, "to let it be known that the Congregational Churches have room for both Fundamentalist and Modernist, if only each will keep his temper and give to the other the toleration he asks for himself."[37] Indeed, in 1923, the National Council of Congregational Churches issued a statement recognizing differences of opinion between liberals and fundamentalists and assuring both parties that "we love and know them all," and that "our fellowship is broad enough to include them all."[38]

Respect and tolerance for other views was a highly practical virtue for a denomination committed to ecumenical cooperation. From the late nineteenth century onward, Congregationalists were a leading voice calling for the end of denominational competition and division and one of the very first to support the establishment of the Federal Council of Protestant Churches in the United States and Canada in 1900.[39] Although the task of ecumenism often clashed with the competing ideal of denominational identity, dislike of sectarianism ran much deeper, dating back at least to the unhappy Plan of Union. Congregationalists consistently chose cooperation rather than individualism, pursuing unions with Methodists, Presbyterians, and even Episcopalians with concerted zeal. In the years before World War II, Congregationalists also took a leading role among mainline Protestant churches in establishing a middle ground between blind patriotism and blind pacifism.[40]

Yet tolerance was not just an ecclesiastical virtue or a political one—it was also an ethic for dealing with other classic irritants to the faithful, like Sunday bicycle riding. "I am not a bicycle rider, but a middle-aged, Puritan, Yankee woman," one reader of the Congregationalist wrote in 1896. "Often, recently, I have heard those of my own age and older speak bitterly, unkindly, in a very un-Christian spirit, of the bicycle riders spoiling our Sunday—of bicycles being the great enemy of the Sabbath. Every time, in my heart, I find myself defending the bicycle rider. I have taken pains to be observant and see in what way they spoiled our Sabbath. They pass my door on Sunday morning, singly or in company, and sincerely I say, God bless them! By how many voices will he speak to them today and draw near to their hearts and open their lives."[41]

The Reverse Pilgrims, from *The Book of the Pilgrimage: A Record of the Congregationalists' Pilgrimage to England and Holland* (Boston: Office of the Congregationalist, 1896)

Holding one's convictions loosely did not just apply to spiritual pieties—it could apply to historical ones as well. As Congregationalists adjusted to the new world of biblical criticism and multilayered truth—one in which the Bible could be false in one respect and true in others—they were also learning to appropriate their Pilgrim and Puritan heritage in a new way. The turn-of-the-century years, before the epic tercentennial of the Pilgrims' landing in 1920, saw a remarkable shift in the tone and the types of ways that Congregational laypeople remembered and enjoyed their past.

REVERSE PILGRIMS

Twenty-four Congregationalists set out across the Atlantic in the summer of 1896, on a "reverse pilgrimage" to England. The year itself had no particular historical significance, nor did the trip commemorate any notable event. It simply marked the eightieth anniversary of the *Congregationalist*, a denominational journal in a constant search for more subscribers. The pilgrimage was an opportunity to do some public promotion and provide an opportunity for a small group of people to have a wonderful time.

The travelers had little interest in reliving the challenges faced by their hardy forebears. Like many Americans of their time with a bit of discretionary income and a yen for European culture, these innocents abroad rode in comfort on an ocean liner and stayed at plush hotels. When they arrived in England, they were feted by lord mayors and bishops and hustled from one reception to another. Then just as quickly, the group crossed over to Holland for a whirlwind tour of Rotterdam, Leyden, and Amsterdam. At that point, they parted ways with Pilgrim history and traveled across Germany and Switzerland, maintaining a breakneck pace through Cologne, the spas of Baden Baden, the Black Forest, and Lucerne. The final leg of the journey landed them in Paris, where they spent the better part of a week before returning to London and then, no doubt reluctantly, retracing the route of the original pilgrims back to the New World.

The group was a lively one, composed of a few standard-issue clergymen but mostly comfortably wealthy laypeople—a lawyer, several businessmen, a military general, a doctor, and Albert Dunning, soon to replace Henry Martyn Dexter as editor of the *Congregationalist*. Three of those men came with their wives, but another nine were single, as were most of the twelve women in the party. The female contingent included a group of society women from Hartford, Connecticut, and two young professionals: Frances Dyer was editor of the Home Department of the *Congregationalist* and wrote weekly updates for publication, and Anna Burnham oversaw the children's curriculum produced by the Congregational Sunday School and Publishing Society. "Most, if not all, of the pilgrims have pronounced Puritan and Congregational sympathies," the paper reported proudly, also assuring readers that "the party has been made up carefully . . . of persons who would be congenial and would value especially the unusual privileges to be offered them."[42]

Even without a specifically historical errand, however, the trip spoke volumes about the people who made it a noteworthy event. The reverse pilgrimage of 1896 was a telling moment for turn-of-the-century Congregationalists—and for the many Americans who shared their cultural vantage point—not so much for the act of commemoration itself but for the way they understood and used their past.

This was, after all, an age growing used to "conspicuous consumption," in economist Thorstein Veblen's famous phrase, and an economy depending more and more on discretionary spending—a culture of desire, as it has been called—by ever more sophisticated advertising techniques. There is no doubt that the 1896 voyage was an exercise of wealth and privilege, and of the deeply ingrained Anglophilia among educated Americans of the time and Congregationalists in particular. Most of the English hosts recognized the material benefits of entertaining a sentimental group of wealthy Americans. Austerfield, one of the more enterprising towns on the pilgrims' itinerary, stole the march on others by sending an "Appeal to the American People" before the ship had left the docks of New York, advertising itself as "The Cradle of the Pilgrim Fathers" and the birthplace of William Bradford. Just to make sure their message was not lost, the town fathers also included in their brochure a description of the church, "wherein WILLIAM BRADFORD was baptized," and printed out the budget for much-needed renovation, so that "*its ancient character shall be preserved.*"[43]

The Americans were equally interested in marketing their experience. Just months after the pilgrims returned, the *Congregationalist* produced a beautiful souvenir volume, *The Book of the Pilgrimage*, chronicling the journey of "new world Pilgrims" to "old world shrines." Luxuriously illustrated, with gilt and beveled pages and filled with newsy accounts by Frances Dyer, it was declared a "must-have" for loyal church members— and all for a mere $3.00 (roughly $75 in present-day value). Laypeople responded eagerly, recognizing a product that combined educational opportunity with the beauty of a potential family heirloom. "I received the lovely volume in good notice," a churchwoman wrote to the editor, promising to make it a gift to her children. Just the act of receiving the commemorative book would, she said, "make good Congregationalists of all of them."[44]

Of course, by then Puritans and Pilgrims were regularly appropriated for use in the modern marketplace, usually as symbols of old-fashioned virtue. In the 1890s, for example, the *Congregationalist* began carrying regular advertisements for "Puritana soap," also known as "Nature's Cure." Puritana was the brainchild of Dr. Dixi Crosby, former head of the Dartmouth Medical College, whose "disease-conquering discovery" was composed of New England roots and herbs from an "original family recipe" and "compounded in the laboratory of Common Sense." Promising to cure everything from "weak lungs" to "starved nerves" and a "fagged brain," Puritana was just the thing to make "weak and weary men and women strong and healthy." The advertisement featured a simple line drawing of a Puritan maiden in cap and apron.[45]

It was clear that much had changed, even in the years between the 1870 jubilee and the reverse pilgrimage of 1896. From a simple silver coin,

An advertisement for "Puritana," from the *Congregationalist*, 2 April 1896, 534

the cultural apparatus around the Pilgrim and Puritan fathers had grown considerably, now tapping into energies that were transforming the lives of the urban middle class in particular. In a sense, historical figures were becoming less real, less tied to particular events and people, reflecting what historians have identified as a shift in the nature of personhood itself. The late nineteenth and early twentieth centuries were what religion scholar Ann Taves has called "the golden age of the subconscious," of growing awareness of a "secondary self" normally hidden from view. Behind each person's public persona, constructed on its own "chains of memory" and experience, lurked another with an entirely different set of memories—hidden knowledge of pain or fear or abuse. The old idea, that human character is a direct manifestation of the soul—that we are what we believe—was giving way to a view of human motivations that was indirect, complicated, and downright mysterious. Personal memories were no longer reliable explanations of the self.[46]

In a less complicated way, however, the reverse pilgrimage demonstrated a budding sense of humor toward the pieties that had drawn Congregationalists together as a denomination just a few decades earlier. This much is evident in a letter written by Morton Dexter, the irreverent son of Henry Martyn Dexter, to the rest of the group while he stayed behind in England. "I am as lonely . . . as an anti-tobacco lecturer in Germany," he complained. Once the excitement of the visit had died down, all the bishops, deans, and canons were "paying no more heed to me than if I were one of their own thirty-nine articles." "In spite of the ennobling influence which, as you must bear ready witness, I have sought to exert over you," he continued with a wink, "I have too much reason for believing that, only a few hours after you left me, you all . . . were 'half seas over,' and that it was Dutch courage' with which you sought next morning to inspirit yourselves." "And this, too," Dexter noted, "so soon after partaking of the cheering, but not inebriating hospitalities of Lady Henry Somerset," one of Britain's foremost temperance reformers. "I beseech you to pause ere it becomes too late," he declared. "Beware the flowing bowl—especially aboard ship!"[47]

Many of those back home were in on the joke as well. The Unitarian *Christian Register* noted approvingly "how comfortably and happily and sensibly" the New World pilgrims traveled to their ancestral home. "We heartily commend the enterprise of our orthodox contemporaries in trying to see so much of this world before they see the other." The *Interior*, a Methodist journal based in Chicago, described the trip as a "summer excursion" designed to "appeal to the sense of humor." "They pretend that they are pilgrims of the stock and times of Scrooby and Plymouth Rock," the editor noted, carrying a wooden crusaders' staff tied with apple blossoms, ribbons, and a lady's fan: a pretense "accepted with solemn gravity" and an "irrepressible twinkle" by their English hosts."[48]

Many laypeople were also taking up the cue, a fact demonstrated in the proceedings of the Congregational clubs and Forefathers' Day observances initiated in the years after the Pilgrim jubilee. By the 1890s, these celebrations had less and less to do with denominational fund-raising, much less the actual religious principles that brought the Pilgrims and Puritans to New England in the first place.[49]

Dry humor was a potent way of simultaneously embracing the Pilgrim heritage and keeping it a safe distance. The Congregational Club of Chicago held a formal banquet for the Tri-Church Council meeting in 1907 and laid out the entire program in antique script and what approximated seventeenth-century prose. Welcoming "ye Chicago menne of ye Pilgrim faith," the banquet organizers provided beneath each menu course "Wife Words of Antient Puritans and menne of yr time to illustrate ye things Eaten and Said," adding also a few from Methodists, "albeit not fo manie." The club members dined on Puritan Oysters, Massasoit Sherbet, Winslow Salad, and Ices from Plimouth Harbor, as well as Sweet Potatoes ("Ye like of which Pocahontas cooked") and Beef Tenderloin ("Roasted like unto ye method of Mrs. Brewster").[50]

We might think of these stories as a democratizing counterweight to the steady reduction of the Pilgrim myth by academic professionals. Laypeople once again had access to the romance and mystery of the past, unencumbered by the mundane realities so beloved by historians. These changing attitudes suggest a particular kind of remembering at work, one increasingly discontinuous with the real events and people of the past. Alison Landsberg's description of "prosthetic memory" is a helpful way of understanding this change, especially as it relates to turn-of-the-century American culture. Certainly, people of every age and time have created imagined connections with the past—in the early nineteenth century, Congregationalists built an entire denominational identity around their legacy as spiritual "sons" of the Pilgrim fathers. Modern memory is different, Landsberg argues, because it no longer serves as an exclusive link between a contemporary group and its direct ancestral tradition. "Through the technologies of mass culture," she writes, previously exclusive pasts are available to anyone, "regardless of skin color, ethnic background, or biology." Prosthetic memory allows one individual to assume the "archive" of another, to "suture himself or herself into a larger history." Direct correspondence between the reality of the past and the facts of the present is not strictly necessary. The past is, in a sense, a transferable commodity.[51]

Thus, in the years after World War I, Protestants of many different types learned to enjoy dressing up as people from long ago. The Knights of King Arthur, a group begun by a Rhode Island Congregational minister in 1893, boasted 130,000 members by 1918, each enlisted in a local "castle." Every boy adopted the name of a chivalric hero and created his own regalia, complete with shields and banners. When the young squire joined his local church, he was also knighted, in a "solemn and beautiful" representation of the medieval ceremony.[52]

This is the cultural context for the rising popularity of Pilgrim costumes and reenactments of historic events at the turn of the century. In 1896, the Plymouth festival of "Old Days and Ways" no longer featured speeches and "historical discourses" but had shifted to a program of dances and *tableaux vivants*, in which individuals recreated historic scenes by posing in seventeenth-century dress.[53] By the time of the Pilgrim tercentenary in 1920, the trend was reaching an apotheosis of sorts, as Americans everywhere became participants in the historic landing at Plymouth. In Omaha, the state of Nebraska launched a full parade of floats with citizens depicting the "Persecution of the Pilgrim Fathers," the "Landing on Cape Cod," and, slightly out of context, the Boston Tea Party and the Goddess

Pilgrim Tableau (Courtesy of Congregational Library)

of Liberty.[54] In the late summer of 1920, the Massachusetts town of Truro launched a full costume pageant, with a cast of more than 100 characters, including Indians, Mayflower voyagers, and several barefoot girls dressed in white, gray, rose, and yellow, who periodically danced across the stage to convey the idea "that the Pilgrims felt the unseen." As a follow-up to the stage performance, troops of Pilgrims with breechloaders and buckled hats trudged earnestly across the hills of Cape Cod, staging the discovery of a stash of buried corn in North Truro and recoiling in dismay as Samoset took John Winslow as a hostage.[55]

Congregationalists participated, too, in somewhat more staid fashion but with equal enthusiasm. This was the context for the Pilgrim tercentenary in 1920. The Congregational Commission on Missions seized on the anniversary celebration eagerly, recognizing the financial opportunities before them, and called for a "fresh dedication of life and treasure to the work of the Kingdom of Christ."[56] The tercentenary program also incorporated a range of social reforms. "The Pilgrim movement was more than a mere revolt against personal tyranny," the Social Service Commission explained. "If we are to be worthy followers of the Pilgrims and exemplify the best in their lives in the midst of the complex and perplexing problems of today, the church must have a program of social action and a method by which this program may be made effective." The Commission urged local churches to celebrate the tercentenary by conducting community surveys and campaigning for laws guaranteeing a six-day work week. The Pilgrim legacy also encompassed the goal of a "saloonless nation in 1920," as well as efforts toward peace and international cooperation, "recognizing our nation as part of the world's family of nations."[57] The denomination also launched a broad educational effort, a tercentenary correspondence course for local congregations, "Pilgrim Deeds and Duties." This was a fairly routine series of questions and answers to memorize—hardly as popular as the many works of fiction spilling from the Congregational press. It is likely that many more Congregationalists read Annie Russell Marble's tale *The Women Who Came in the Mayflower*, about the "Pilgrim mothers," the "noble women" whose "faith, fortitude and calm judgment were a constant source of strength to the men."[58]

The denomination also commissioned a public play, *Pageant of the Pilgrims*, written by Esther Willard Gates, the reigning expert in this popular turn-of-the-century art form. This play came complete with stage and lighting directions and a full script—and a warning to all readers that permission was required from the denominational publishing house in Boston, and $10 paid in advance. The play itself was relatively simple in terms of staging and costuming, a series of episodes in the life of the Pilgrim Colony introduced by a Questioner and an Interpreter. The last episode pointed toward the future, with a group of Adventurous Spirits "dressed in the colors of the sunset and dancing to alluring music" and a procession of "goldseekers, pioneers, Puritan clergymen, woodmen, trappers, and Jesuits" following them westward across the stage.[59]

HAVING FUN WITH THE BIBLE

Historical imagination not only brought the Pilgrims alive—it could also apply to the Bible. Certainly Congregationalists embraced the fervent, often sentimental, "Jesus piety" of their time, taking pious liberties with the Gospel texts. In 1903, a Nebraska pastor offered a series, "Twenty-Five Nights with Jesus," with talks on "His Superb Intellect," "His Beautiful Face," "His Honeyed Lips," "His Starry Eyes," and "His Loving Hands." It is perhaps not surprising that Congregationalists produced two of the most important imaginative religious best sellers of the early twentieth century: Charles Sheldon's *In His Steps*, an inspirational novel about ordinary people considering the question "What would Jesus do?"; and Bruce Barton's *The Man Nobody Knows*, depicting Jesus as a hard-driving modern businessman. Sheldon was a Congregational pastor and Barton the son of Will Barton, the author of a widely read history of Congregational creeds and a leading authority on church polity. In fact, the elder Barton was beloved in the denomination for his weekly column entitled the "Parables of Safed the Sage," short folksy stories written in King James English and providing "some wholesome lessons" about the spiritual side of "common things."[60]

During the World War I era, Congregationalists, along with many other Americans, also began to embrace the growing popularity of religious drama, writing short plays about their local churches or organizing larger costume epics of biblical and church history. They did not invent the trend; it reflected a general penchant for the visual and sensational—this was, after all, the age of Billy Sunday and Aimee Semple McPherson, of movies and vaudeville. It was also the result of a concerted push by many different denominations, including the Federal Council of Churches, to encourage quality productions in local churches.[61]

Biblical dramas proved enormously popular: not only did these present familiar stories in a new light to veteran churchgoers, they also captured the attention of outsiders. In 1921, Reverend Arthur Metcalf of San Francisco enjoyed great success by turning the story of Onesimus, the slave at the center of Saint Paul's letter to Philemon, the young man's owner, into a "scriptural play." "While the play was deeply religious," the editor of the *Pacific* enthused, this did "not spoil it with the general public not given overmuch to things of the Spirit." "The theater was once a church affair, and religious plays were commonly employed to teach religious truths," he continued. "Why not take the drama out of the hands of the commercialists and rededicate it to the service of religion—just as many churches are now doing with motion pictures."[62]

Pious intent covered a multitude of sins. Metcalf's other productions more than hinted at sensationalism: *Athaliah* starred the viciously depraved queen of Israel; *The Beasts of Ephesus* depicted the dramatic confrontation between Christians and the pagan priests of the goddess Diana.[63] In 1926, twenty-five of his Logan Heights Players staged *Potiphar's Wife*, the story of young Joseph's temptation by Pharaoh's lusty spouse. The *Congregationalist* heartily approved the play's educational intent, especially the way it portrayed the attempted seduction, "vividly and chastely." The audience also learned of "strange and informing" Egyptian burial and marriage customs through Joseph's wedding to Asenath, the beautiful daughter of the Priest of On, "loyal to the throne and zealous for a spiritual faith." Best of all, *Potiphar's Wife* clearly made a "profound religious impression worthy of the cost of time and effort." "The Bible and Christian history," the *Congregationalist* announced, offer "unlimited material for pen and voice."[64]

Productions like these were a curious mixture of biblical criticism and Hollywood sensationalism. The "Biblical data" behind *Potiphar's Wife* was taken from Genesis 37–47, the scriptural account coinciding with the reign of Amenhotep IV and "interfused with what can be known of this strong monarch." Though the playwright claimed that "all action of the characters harmonizes with what is known to be fact," the play had relatively little to do with the Old Testament story. He freely invented a pious love interest for Joseph as well as a nemesis, the evil priest Manetho, who is planning an insurrection against the throne. Act IV includes a retelling "in modernized form" of Joseph's reunion with his brothers and an opportunity for Asenath to meet her future in-laws. Reverend Metcalf also freely updated the narrative of the biblical story, claiming that "Pharaoh, stirred by the spiritual vision of the Hebrew, proclaim[ed] the Allness of the One God, and call[ed] the nation to worship in a pure monotheism."[65]

Biblical dramas also allowed Congregational laypeople to contemporize sacred texts, a privilege once the sole property of scholars and seminary professors. This proved the salvation of one local pastor, mired in the toils of a Sunday evening Lenten series, "Some Big Questions for Young People." Launching into a lesson on Abraham, he quickly discovered to his dismay that only a handful of them could even identify the biblical patriarch. But the quick-witted pastor remembered the fun earlier that evening as the group sat around the fireplace eating apples and playing a game of charades. When he suggested that the group act out their favorite Bible stories, they responded enthusiastically. The students produced four impromptu dramas, "in their own words and with their own acting" and with "the finest kind of reverence." The stories of Joseph, King David, the prodigal son, and Abraham included more swordplay and slang words than the original text, and some were "crude and ineffective." But they were true to the pastor's explanation that "The Bible is the laboratory experiment book of the successes and failures of men as they have attempted to do the things God wanted them to do."[66]

THE IRONY OF ANTIMODERNISM

Throughout all of the change in historical thinking, local Congregational churches continued to celebrate anniversaries and milestones. By the turn of the century, they had become far more elaborate than their early nineteenth-century predecessors, with more and longer bouts of oratory, varieties of choirs, and offerings of food. The core of the event remained the same, however, a Sunday morning meditation on the importance of history.

For the most part, the parade of local saints who had graced church celebrations in decades past was gone. Of course, some congregations, like First Congregational in Marietta, Ohio, still lauded their predecessors as "men of clear and high beliefs" and longed to "get back to the source" of the "moral and spiritual forces which still exercise such a far reaching influence." Similarly, in Pittsfield, Massachusetts, in 1900 the congregation heard a reading of a list of every Sunday school superintendent from 1850 onward and lengthy perorations on departed saints and the "moral tone" of the Pilgrim fathers.[67]

But by the turn of the century, those kinds of celebrations had an old-fashioned, conservative feel. For most Congregational laypeople and pastors, the past had become a different place, interesting in all its variety but clearly removed from the issues of the present day. This meant that more and more of the historical address was dedicated to explaining the past rather than praising it, often through lengthy descriptions of the political and religious context surrounding the church's founding and early days. For some congregations, this presented a challenge, as it did in Middleboro, Massachusetts, where the bicentennial sermon began with Christopher Columbus and meandered on through Shakespeare, Cervantes, and even the adoption of Gibraltar as an English protectorate. Other orations cast their nets less broadly but offered the same conclusion: a reminder of how swiftly and irrevocably times had changed.[68]

Certainly, the goal was not to uplift the superior piety of the ancestors. "Evidently a good deal of the carnal and a good deal of the temperamental existed in those ancient days," members of a Massachusetts church heard in 1926, just "as they exist in these more modern times." Indeed, though a New Jersey pastor congratulated his church that the "ministrations of the pulpit" had included "nothing unique and no attempt at novelty," he assured them that there was no need to dwell on older days. Although the past had "lessons," he said, "the revelations of the future" would be far greater still. In St. Louis in 1916, the pastor gave an address entitled "Religious Progress" and described that fifty-year-old church as a man just emerging from adolescence into "manhood." "The past lies behind," he said, and "the present and future are the main interest." The call to the present-day congregation, facing the rising horrors of World War I, was therefore to "put away childish things," those early obsessions which are "in themselves transient and trivial." Doubtless, the pastor said, the occupations of a generation past "have done something more or less for us, but we can well afford to forget them." In the face of unprecedented human suffering, the best response was to gather "what of wisdom or of strength we have acquired" and "turn ourselves without reserve to the work that is now at hand."[69]

Congregational church people demonstrated their freedom from the past in a variety of ways, some of them downright surprising given their historical tradition. A survey of worship practices in 1889 found a substantial number of churches including the singing of the Gloria Patri, the Apostles' Creed, choir anthems, and chanted psalms—all practices that would have been anathema to their Puritan ancestors.[70] Others constructed new buildings that bore little resemblance to the plain meetinghouse style of generations past—in fact, they painstakingly restored all of the features that their Puritan ancestors had so thoroughly rejected. In 1926, the Second Church of Newton, Massachusetts, dedicated a sanctuary with a chancel and stone altar, boasting that it was the first Congregational church to do so. The typical Sunday service began with a choir procession, the members in black cassocks covered with white cottas (symbolizing forgiveness over sin) and a minister "vested" in a surplice or black gown. Members were invited to "kneel for a moment and offer prayer alone with God," while the organ played softly behind—the old in service of the new.[71] Though the new building of the congregation in Kalamazoo, Michigan, that was dedicated in 1928 looked like a medieval cathedral, the church's leaders insisted that the spirit behind it was "revolutionary." "We have gone back to the Cathedral-like temple from which [the Puritans] fled in fear," the anniversary booklet declared. And why not? "We are more widely educated, we are enjoying more fully the fruits of culture, and we are more world-conscious." Though "economic necessity" drove the austere aesthetics of the first Congregationalists, for whom "beauty was a vanity because it was costly," this was not necessary in a modern, more affluent age. The Kalamazoo church was to be a "sermon in stone," complete with memorial windows, juxtaposing Mary with the coat of arms of the state of Michigan, and Saint John with the coat of arms of the United States of America.[72]

Large, expensive Gothic-style churches were the height of Protestant fashion in the early twentieth century, symbolizing for some the permanence of Christianity in a world going astray. But for Congregationalists, at least, those medieval churches demonstrated to the world their modern freedom from old restrictions. They were in effect exchanging one past for

First Church, Kalamazoo, from *Our Church: It's [sic] History, It's Buildings, It's Spirit* (Kalamazoo, Mich., 1928)

another by a simple act of religious architecture. As Detroit pastor William Davis explained, "We have come . . . to a larger liberty in the interpretation of our historic symbols."[73]

Many of the turn-of-the-century celebrations, like those half a century or more earlier, did include remembrance of the dead. The lengthy memorials address at the Detroit celebration included fond portraits of deaconesses, Sunday school superintendents, and pastors. But Henry Barker, the deacon who gave the address, did not pause to speculate, as had previous generations, about the spiritual continuities and the continuing presence of those departed. "Can they hear our sighs of weariness, our groans of pain?" he wondered. "Do they have knowledge of our forbodings [sic], our alternating hopes and fears, as we vainly scan the future's horizon to guess what shall be for us and those we love on the morrow?" Likely not, said Barker. "There comes back to us neither token nor utterance from those who have gone, and none returns to tell us of the wonders of the Land beyond the Unknown Sea." Comparing the losses of the congregation to personal loss of a friend or family member, Barker spoke of emptiness that "takes many a long day to remove" and "an ever-present sense of lonesomeness haunting our steps."[74]

Perhaps not surprisingly, by the end of the 1920s even Congregationalists were becoming a bit weary of Pilgrim spectacles. The reasons behind this are rooted partly in denominational politics, partly in the seriousness of the crises facing the nation and the world during a time of economic collapse and world war. Certainly, after decades of pilgrimages and tableaux and lavish pageants, the old Congregational tradition was beginning to look a bit timeworn, even trivial.

The year 1930 presented one more opportunity for Congregational celebration, though more muted, with the tercentenary of the founding of Massachusetts. In contrast to 1920, this one was far more secular, aimed at celebrating Massachusetts rather than Puritanism per se. Throughout the summer of 1930, towns across the Commonwealth held "old home weeks," historical pageants, and tours of "ancient houses," all designed primarily for the new wave of car-driving tourists.[75]

The major event for Congregationalists that year was being held in Great Britain, not New England, at the International Council in Bournemouth, England. In 1930, some 500 Congregationalists crossed the Atlantic to attend the International Council, landing first in Glasgow and then continuing on to Bournemouth. The *Congregationalist* dubbed this a "Goodwill Pilgrimage" because it involved not just denominational solidarity but issues of world peace. "The larger significance of this Congregational Pilgrimage is found in the fact that President Hoover recently summoned to the White House a group of our official leaders to whom he gave a message to convey with the Pilgrimage to Great Britain," the *Congregationalist* boasted.[76]

The trip began on a serious note and continued on in a similar fashion. The *Adriatic* left New York on 14 June in a thick fog that did not lift for days; the crew ordered the passengers to undertake a safety drill. The first Sunday on board was Father's Day; after a morning Church of England service, the pilgrims gathered for an afternoon of hymn singing and preaching and an evening service of more singing and more sermonizing. The evening included serious addresses by three prominent women, including the "celebrated Negro educational leader" Charlotte Hawkins Brown. "Conferences, seminars, and lectures do not, to be quite frank, seem particularly attractive to one contemplating the rest and change of an ocean voyage," the editor of the *Congregationalist* admitted. But this group filled every room to capacity, especially as the week progressed with lively missionary lectures on Turkey by James Levi Barton and an address on India by educational leader Professor J. V. Chelliah.[77]

From the start, the pilgrims of 1930 were a far more serious group than those who left in 1896. Every morning of the six-day voyage began with seminars in theology, intended to provide an "exchange of ideas by ministers from many sections of our country" but also attended by interested laypeople. The ministers discussed general topics—why theology was the queen of the sciences, for example—but they also took on a new book by neoorthodox theologian Emil Brunner, entitled *God and Man*. Led by Douglas Horton, then a minister in Brookline, Massachusetts, the discussions on "theology in crisis" had a deep impact. Before landing in Scotland, the seminar participants put together a six-point summary of their conversation, the longest section dealing with sin and forgiveness— also a topic rarely discussed in 1896.[78]

The International Council itself was a formal, rather serious affair. King George V sent a personal message through his representative, Major General the Right Honorable J. E. B. Seely, Lord Lieutenant of Hampshire, who delivered a genial but, in the end, forbidding message of warning. He stressed the "continued dangers of war," which he saw as a certainty for the future, promising to "'send down into the abyss millions of people who are now raising their standard of comfort." Major addresses by leading British Congregational statesmen were inspiring but also rattled more than a few swords. The Reverend J. Morgan Gibbon delivered a "vigorous defense of Protestantism and arraignment of its critics," taking particular aim at Roman Catholics and High Anglicans. Dr. Ferdinand Q. Blanchard organized his remarks around a recent article in the *Atlantic Monthly* decrying the "failure of Protestantism."[79]

Clearly, Congregationalism had changed considerably between 1896 and 1930, taking on a much more serious ethical tone. The Goodwill Pilgrims of 1930 visited a few historic sites in England and posed before a plaque or two but other than that spared relatively little sentiment for their historical forebears. Within another few years, they would have even more serious issues to address, with the sudden arrival of economic depression and world war. The years ahead would prove the most transformative in the denomination's history and mount the deepest challenges to its sense of connection with the Pilgrim past.

CHAPTER SEVEN

The End of One Epoch and the Beginning of Another

Published in 1935, *The Last Puritan* is an elegiac novel written by the philosopher George Santayana. The title character, Oliver Alden, is a wealthy New Englander coming of age during the early twentieth century and caught between the competing demands of the past and present. To Santayana he is a representative puritan traditionalist, a man dedicated to "hatred of all shams, scorn of all mummeries," taking "bitter merciless pleasure in the hard facts." But he is also a man of means, rich, comfortable, and aimless. The novel paints Oliver as fundamentally out of sync with his time and place, unable to live according to his own high standards and equally unable to accept the irrationality of modern life. The last puritan would end his days in genteel obsolescence, an antique figure in a rapidly changing world.[1]

That sense of leave-taking with the past found an echo among Puritanism's other descendants as they lived through the harrowing days of the Great Depression and looming world war. Congregationalists approached their national gathering in 1934 with sharp uncertainty. "We meet in Oberlin not at the end of a depression but at the end of an epoch," the *Advance* declared. "There must be a new world order—or all which passes for civilization will perish from the earth." The message was clear: the General Council meeting of 1934 promised to be one of the most "fateful" in the entire history of American Congregationalism.[2]

The *Advance* spoke truer than anyone could have known at the time. The Oberlin meeting set in motion a chain of events that would permanently divide the Congregational rank and file, the first time the denomination had ever experienced a schism of this magnitude—in many ways more fundamental than the Unitarian departure in the early nineteenth century. These conflicts would persist for decades and eventually result in an angry division over a proposed ecumenical merger in the 1950s, a story told in Chapter 8.

At the core of these disputes was a question about "Congregational principles," first raised at the Boston Council in 1865. What did it mean to follow historic Congregationalism? Were some paths more "legitimate" than others? In 1865, a visit to Burial Hill smoothed over the most fundamental disagreements over polity and belief, as Congregationalists rallied together around their common allegiance to the Pilgrim fathers. This time, however, the matter was not so easily resolved. After years of consensus building around a broad and sometimes blurry definition of Congregationalism, the denomination was suddenly on the defensive. The wide-ranging arguments of the 1940s and 1950s pitted fears of communism and antagonism to the New Deal against aspirations for social witness and Christian unity, each side invoking history in their defense.

The catalyst was the formation of the Council for Social Action (CSA), established at the Oberlin meeting of 1934. Its stated purpose was to provide information for laypeople about the social problems of the day—including unemployment, racism, and militarism. At the time, few Congregationalists objected, seeing little harm in what looked to be a primarily educational effort. In fact, historian Robert Moats Miller has described the CSA as "the sanest, least biased, and certainly least doctrinaire of almost all the church social agencies" of the early twentieth century. It was, for the most part, "sanely, pragmatically, tolerantly liberal."[3] But just months after its formation, the CSA was the center of a controversy fueled by a toxic mix of anger and suspicion.

The presenting issue was the organization's right to speak on behalf of local churches, and more specifically its power to decide what issues to address and how to address them. Critics of the CSA, who formed organizations with names like the League to Uphold Congregational Principles, warned that the denomination's core tradition of local independence was under threat from a small group of self-appointed, power-hungry radicals. If the churches did not wake up and defend their centuries-old polity, they would be courting its destruction. Supporters of the CSA argued the opposite (though less stridently), pointing out the denomination's long history of corporate social witness, from women's rights and abolitionism to the twentieth-century Social Gospel.

The 1930s and 1940s were a turning point in the Congregational churches' long engagement with their past, as a century of sentimental pride over the Pilgrim and Puritan legacy ended and history became a tool of angry people locked in a sectarian dispute. Certainly, the vocabulary of the day—anticommunism and aggressive patriotic pride in American values—persuaded many Congregational laypeople to see a conspiracy at work. And there is no doubt that an overpowering sense of living in unprecedented times made it feel that, as one Congregationalist said in 1938, "the ice-cap of accumulated tradition" was melting "under the heat of contemporary events."[4] But these provided a language and an emotional intensity to a question that, as the previous chapters have shown, was already familiar in Congregational circles: What authority does the past have over the present?

By 1934, the past itself was something far different from what it had been in 1871, when Congregationalists first formed their National Council. In the broader culture of the 1930s and 1940s, history was still durably popular, a ready source of unifying symbols to an America proud of its past and grounded in the heroism of minutemen and founding fathers. During this time, Americans began flocking to colonial Williamsburg and Henry Ford's detailed recreation of Greenfield Village. Colonial New England, in fact, played a central role in the midcentury nostalgia for simpler, more cohesive times. This was the era of New England poet Robert Frost and the rise of *Yankee* magazine, both burnishing the region's image as the land of self-reliant and plain-speaking people in a world gone awry.[5]

In other ways, the past, or particular versions of it, became useful. In Michael Kammen's words, "the interwar years gave Americans splendid memories and star-spangled amnesia." Under Franklin Roosevelt, the government began to play an ever-larger role in preserving documents and historic places; when the United States entered the war in 1941, Roosevelt acceded to the request of prominent historians and ordered executive agencies to store and document their role in the war effort. Even more than that, Depression-era programs sponsored researchers and writers, the building of monuments and museums. The National Park Service began to take an active role, for the first time, in preserving and staging historic battlefields and monuments.[6]

The historical profession was also enjoying a new heyday, this time of greater specialization and emphasis on research. Between 1925 and 1930, historian Robert Townsend writes, the number of doctorates in history more than doubled, from 61 to 141, and it grew another 24 percent by 1940. Professional associations also began to multiply by the late 1930s, each with its own field of expertise and stable of star scholars. The 1930s also saw the beginning of renewed interest in Puritanism: Perry Miller's seminal work, *The Puritan Mind*, appeared in 1939 and set off a wave of scholarly interest in New England and its complex role in American culture.[7]

Church institutions, however, did not directly benefit from any of these initiatives. In fact, by the mid-twentieth century, history had becomes a far weaker tool of religious self-understanding than it was for previous generations of Congregationalists, or Protestants in general. The new past served secular interests more than spiritual ones, whether academic advancement or national pride. During the 1930s and 1940s Congregationalists entered into fervent arguments about the past with a smaller and smaller purchase on their own story.

CONGREGATIONALISTS AT MIDCENTURY

No one traveled to the Oberlin Council meeting in 1934 spoiling for a fight. In fact, on the whole the early twentieth century had been a prosperous time for the northern white denominations, Congregationalists not least among them. In short order, they repented the excesses of patriotism during World War I, made public in Ray Abrams's searing critique of religious "warmongering," *Preachers Present Arms* (1933).[8] The two great causes of the era, ecumenism and the Social Gospel, had made steady progress, broadening into a unified Protestant effort to bring about the kingdom of God on earth. By the 1920s, the Federal Council of Churches, working as an ecumenical and socially progressive coalition of Protestant denominations, served as an "informal national establishment," presiding over a vast network of cooperative efforts for foreign missions, social reform, and religious education. And the mainline denominations themselves were at the peak of their cultural power, providing a regular supply of college presidents, congressmen, and prominent writers and editors.[9]

The "average Congregationalist" was not a fighter either. Congregationalists tended to be leading citizens of their communities—according to the national census of 1926, almost 70 percent of the membership lived in towns and small cities—but more by virtue of professional or business expertise than material wealth. They were doctors and bankers and businessmen, recognizable figures in the social hierarchy, not big-city intelligentsia or tycoons of industry.[10] For the most part, Congregationalists were quietly and judiciously socially progressive. As Albert Parker Fitch wrote in 1922, describing his denomination to the readers of the *Christian Century*, "I should not expect to see the Congregationalists the heads of great popular movements in the future, but I should expect to see them a small, powerful body still in the vanguard, accomplishing by the quality of their work achievements which popular understanding would never adequately appreciate."[11]

Up through the 1930s, the denomination's leading figures mirrored this profile. They were men like S. Parkes Cadman, pastor of the Central Congregational Church in Brooklyn, whose cultured British voice and easygoing style made him a popular figure in the pulpit and on the radio. In an age when radio religion often meant fundamentalist and Pentecostal preaching, Cadman was a dignified everyman with a broad national appeal—his Sunday afternoon programs were said to have "emptied the golf courses" all across the country. Some estimates put his audience at five million listeners, many of them, as the *Congregationalist* allowed, more "among the 'better classes' than any one would suppose."[12]

Congregationalists also admired Roger Babson, a businessman and self-described "hard-boiled statistician." Ever the pragmatist, he urged the clergy to "declare a moratorium on theological preaching" and work on shoring up declining membership and finances. Babson was not necessarily opposed to liberal theology—he just thought it a waste of time and energy. The wise minister, he said, would stick to the facts and "omit the questionables." To Babson the best religion had market value: a non-churchgoer should be able to "absolutely trust" a Congregationalist with his wallet. In fact, in his view, the formula for success was simple: "Never allow anyone to lose a dollar through a church member."[13] Babson had no love for "Wall Street's house of cards" and cautiously supported the New Deal reforms but in the end believed that only the right kind of religion would end the Depression. "What our country most urgently needs," he declared in 1934, "is not water power or electrical energy as much as higher powers and spiritual energies. Nations as well as individuals will find their real Balance Sheet is one of spiritual Assets and moral Liabilities!"[14]

Los Angeles pastor James Fifield added a celebrity twist to Babson's formula. A vigorous entrepreneur with a talent for organizing and motivating people, he cultivated friendships with Hollywood luminaries like John Wayne, Dale Evans and Roy Rogers, and Charlton Heston and rubbed shoulders with presidents, Nobel prize winners, and captains of industry like Albert Sloan, chair of General Motors, and J. C. Penny. Like Babson, Fifield combined a passionate faith in capitalism with a libertarian political philosophy and intensely practical spirituality. He formed his own organization, Spiritual Mobilization, in 1938, on the conviction that "we can only enjoy freedom UNDER GOD, not aside from God and not by ignoring God."[15] Fifield always insisted that he had no political agenda, only a desire to return the United States to its spiritual heritage of freedom and "to inspire each American to do his own thinking." During the Depression, Fifield said,

James Fifield (Courtesy of Congregational Library)

"controls were springing up everywhere. It seemed that people could not do anything without asking the government."[16] At its peak, Spiritual Mobilization sponsored a newspaper column published in 215 newspapers and a radio program on 525 radio stations and comprised a broad constituency of some 125,000 clergymen. It was, in other words, an enormous power base for a single pastor and, not surprisingly, would allow Fifield a high degree of visibility in the looming denominational controversy.[17]

In the meantime, the Social Gospel generally flourished among Congregationalists. In 1913, the denomination had its own Commission on Social Service, with an independent budget and permanent staff. The National Council itself issued a regular stream of statements in accord with the Social Gospel ethic, pledging in 1919 to work toward a social order that promised a decent wage for hard work and denied privileges to the idle rich. Moreover, by the time of the Great Depression, the National Council had adopted a number of measures that clearly signaled dis-ease with capitalism. One of the most important was a "Statement on Social Ideals," issued in 1925, declaring support for racial equality and for an American economy that upheld "the supremacy of the service rather than the profit motive." Though private ownership was not wrong, it was a "social trust," and the true purpose of individual wealth was service to others.[18]

Congregational laypeople rarely weighed in directly about these measures, but their silence did not necessarily signal unanimity. This much was evident when, in the months before the Oberlin Council, readers of the *Advance* began debating the case of Hugh Magill, a highly regarded churchman who was both head of the International Federation for Christian Education and president of the American Federation of Utility Investors, an anti–New Deal lobbying group with a dubious reputation. The *Advance* went on the attack, denouncing Magill for condoning the "ruthless exploitation" of the American people by the utility companies and insisting that he resign.[19] Many readers agreed, praising the editor for his "sound, sane, and timely" work. "More strength to your pen!" a Wyoming man declared, and a Washington, D.C., reader declared that "the mass of church leaders are with you." But others were equally, if not more, angry at the editor's summary treatment of Magill. A Michigan man declared the article "so childish and so full of naïve ignorance that it could not be answered in a single letter." "I do not claim to be one of the 'socially alert' people of America," a sarcastic reader from Connecticut rejoined, "but I do consider that the individualism that has made the US of A what it is today will continue to make our country the grandest in the world." Others responded in a similar vein: the editor of the *Advance* had no right to be pushing "socialism" on "all those of us who help pay your salary."[20]

FOUNDING THE COUNCIL FOR SOCIAL ACTION

The *Christian Century* heralded the formation of the Council for Social Action as an entirely "new frontier" in American church life, the first time any denomination had created an entire department aimed at changing the world. Yet in many ways, the CSA embodied the kind of prudent sense that the Roger Babsons of the world admired. By the early 1930s, the denomination's Social Service Commission looked too small and haphazard to meet the humanitarian emergency brought on by the Great Depression. Simple "public-mindedness" was no longer enough, said Arthur Holt, a former head of the commission. He proposed that the Department of Social Relations become fully integrated into the organizational structure of the Congregational Christian churches, with a status equal to the foreign and home mission boards. With its own board of directors and staff of trained specialists, the new commission would work on educating and mobilizing the church on four major issues: rural–urban conflicts, problems of church and state, disputes between capital and labor, and racial justice.[21]

In the months leading up to the Oberlin meeting, scheduled for late June, Holt's proposal encountered little opposition. Many laypeople responded positively to the prospect of "expert, objective information" on complicated social issues like race and poverty.[22] "If there is anything to the Pilgrim traditions of our order," said a Massachusetts layman, "we must be prepared to justify them by living adventurously." "We need this new arm of the Christian social conscience," Chicago churchman Ernest Graham Guthrie agreed, "to radically transform the anti-social character of the Church's own tribal formations."[23] The main public opposition came from functionaries on the existing boards, who perhaps rightly feared that the CSA would further divide a dwindling supply of funding. No doubt, said critic George Cady, the denominational bureaucrats sitting in "swivel chairs in Boston and New York" were happy to open up some employment opportunities for their peers, but without its own separate source of funding he thought the CSA was doomed to failure.[24]

Cady's prophecy—which turned out to be substantially correct in terms of financial support—found few open ears. When the General Council took up the Holt proposal in July 1934, even the remaining opposition from the mission boards had dissipated. The measure passed with an air of celebration and hope, generated in no small part by the ringing text of the resolution itself. "Stirred by the deep need of humanity for justice, security, and spiritual freedom and growth," Congregationalists declared, "aware of the urgent demand within our churches for action to match our gospel, and clearly persuaded that the Gospel of Jesus can be the solvent of social as of all other problems," the CSA would help the churches with "research, education, and action." The council was to be "impartial, its only bias being that of the Christian view of life." The scope of the call for action was less clear, however, indicating only that that "the Council may, upon occasion, intercede directly in specific situations"—a small phrase that would later bring very large problems.[25]

Two days after the vote establishing the CSA, another initiative came to the floor, this one far more problematic and far-reaching. The resolution on the "Social Gospel and Economic Problems" committed the Congregational churches to work toward abolishing capitalism by eliminating both the "legal forms which sustain it, and the moral ideals which justify it."

Not only that, the resolution called for the end to private ownership wherever it "interferes with the social good."[26]

In some respects, the resolution was not surprising: in the depths of the Great Depression, many Americans, both middle class and poor, asked with good reason whether capitalism had run its course. After all, as they looked abroad they could see the collective farms and industrial centers of Stalin's Russia apparently thriving while capitalist nations starved. Socialist and communist groups edged surprisingly close to the political and cultural mainstream during those desperate years. Indeed, the postwar generation of the 1950s would remember the 1930s as the "Red Decade," when many leading American intellectuals—and the general public—used a Marxist vocabulary to condemn greed and selfishness and to uphold "the values of community, justice, and cooperation." Just months after Congregationalists debated in Oberlin, the 1934 election brought in a surprisingly left-wing group of new politicians, all promising to redistribute wealth along more equitable lines. The radical campaigns of Louisiana senator Huey Long, economic activist Francis Townsend, whose "Townsend Plan" prefigured the establishment of Social Security, and the popular "radio priest" Father Charles Coughlin enjoyed enormous followings during the mid-1930s, among the middle classes as well as the poor and disenfranchised.[27]

Moreover, compared with the left-wing politics within other Protestant denominations, the profit resolution was actually fairly tame. By the mid-1930s, northern Presbyterians, Methodists, and Baptists, and to a degree their southern wings, had all established social action commissions; most had issued statements critiquing materialism and urging economic justice. In 1932, a year before the beginning of Franklin Roosevelt's New Deal, the Northern Baptist Convention issued a statement calling for "sweeping economic and social equalitarianism," an initiative described by historian Paul Carter as "frankly Marxist" in spirit.[28] In 1934, the Presbyterian General Assembly denounced "money-making and self-interest" and endorsed "rational planning" of economic resources to serve the "public good." The Presbyterian Fellowship for Social Action urged social reform, but as Robert Moats Miller writes, "for some of the officers this meant the abolition of capitalism." Even the Episcopalian *Churchman* pronounced the American economic system "rotten to the core."[29] No one outdid Methodists, however. In 1934, the attendees at the National Council of Methodist Youth received "decision cards" declaring "I surrender my life to Christ," as well as "I renounce the Capitalistic system based on economic individualism and the profit motive and give myself to the building of an economic order based on co-operation and unselfishness."[30]

Even so, the profit resolution was far to the left of anything Congregationalists had considered before. And it passed quickly—to some mysteriously so. The measure came to the floor on the final Wednesday afternoon of the council meeting, a time when most weary delegates had left or were about to go home. It received only 130 votes in favor—about one-quarter of the total number possible—with only 17 opposed. Even more alarming in retrospect, another full week passed before a copy of the resolution appeared in the denominational press. In the to-do that followed, critics as well as supporters assumed that the anticapitalism resolution was simply step two in a well-planned plot by the supporters of the CSA, an effort to win by stealth what could not be approved in a full public meeting.[31]

The loudest voices in the fray were those of Congregational laymen, already frustrated by what they believed was a paltry role in denominational decision making. Only about a third of them were active delegates and the rest were, as one said, only "interested spectators," attending the meeting to provide transportation for their ministers. After a few days of sitting through speeches, the men began grumbling openly about their lack of power.[32] "Why should there be but forty-eight lay men at a great church Council meeting of 1300 delegates and associate delegates?" asked Douglas A. Adams, at a luncheon organized for laymen. The grumbling filtered upward and became a matter of discussion on the floor of the National Council. In response, the 1934 council adopted a resolution to "make mandatory a suitable proportion of unordained men, as it does now of women, in the voting membership of the General Council."[33]

Congregationalists were not used to gender politics, however. In the late nineteenth century, while all of the other Protestant denominations endured national controversy and division over women's ordination, Congregational polity allowed local churches to decide on their own whether to choose a female pastor. Few did, of course, and by 1919 barely 1 percent of ordained Congregational clergy were women—praised, nonetheless, by the denomination for their "quiet, inconspicuous service."[34] Women also voted in local churches and were appointed as delegates to ecclesiastical councils and local conferences, noteworthy only because few commentators could identify any moment when old policies had changed. Most simply put it down to the development of "usage" over time.[35] The relative lack of institutional structure also meant, of course, that few women would breach the denomination's informal monopoly of power by "grand old men" and pastors of tall-steeple churches: in many ways, the debate over the CSA was the closest Congregationalists would ever come to an open confrontation between men and women. But it was men, not women, who provided the emotional energy behind the widening controversy. The mobilization of Congregational laymen in the wake of the Oberlin Council soon became a vehicle of masculine resentment against higher forces beyond popular control.

The profit motive resolution was the last straw. In the weeks and months that followed the Oberlin meeting, mutterings about communism and the Council for Social Action escalated and threatened to become a groundswell. Hoping to forestall an argument, CSA leaders Hubert Herring and Allan Chalmers began traveling around to laymen's groups, with the aim of winning at least a few supporters. A meeting that fall in New Jersey should have served as a warning, however. After Herring and Chalmers ran through a simple description of the CSA's work, one of the men in the audience abruptly stood up and began to read the text of the profit motive resolution. "You could feel the atmosphere grow tense as he proceeded," eyewitness Will Patton wrote. "When he had finished he asked whether that was the charter for the CSA. He very definitely stated that he believed it was, because the resolution creating the CSA and the resolution condemning the profit motive had been passed by the same body." Chalmers and Herring tried to explain that the two came from separate groups, but "their efforts were of no avail." The laymen could not see the resolution as "anything but the charter for the CSA." Even more troubling, they clearly believed that Chalmers and Herring "had tried to conceal something from the meeting, and that the man who had produced from the floor the resolution on the profit motive had uncovered it."[36]

Others squared off on more fundamental questions. Did the Congregational tradition legitimize social radicalism, especially the kind apparently advocated by the CSA? Or was this a dangerous departure from founding principles? For some supporters, the answer was obvious: a layman writing in to the *Advance* thought the Oberlin Council was thoroughly consistent with the general spirit of social idealism embodied by the Congregational men and women who stood against slavery: "Can we, after all, ask for anything better in our day than the spirit and directness of action with which the Amistad incident aroused the Christian conscience of those who founded the AMA [American Missionary Association]?" The CSA was Congregationalism at its best.[37] A California minister agreed that the creation of the CSA was the right step. The CSA "belongs to the genius of our church," reflecting its inherited tradition in its simplest, purest form. "See what we have done with theology," he reasoned. "Have we not with scrutiny and discernment plucked out most of our inherited beliefs and then diligently tended and nourished the balance into healthy growth? Now we have in the end a faith that can stand, or so we . . . think." The same would be true for the Congregational tradition of social action.[38]

Others, who looked only to the founding principles of Congregationalism, not their development over time, believed that the church was taking a new and alien direction, seemingly into the arms of Russian communists. "I am shocked beyond expression," wrote South Dakota layman Doane Robinson, "to learn the church I have loved and supported all my life— the church for which two centuries has carried high the banner of human freedom, apparently, so thoughtless—has seized this first opportunity to align itself with the most dangerous political philosophy yet devised."[39] In a similar vein, a Wisconsin reader worried that Congregationalism was now "committed to the social and industrial goose step." "I want to know what is the matter with the laymen of Congregationalism!" he declared. "Are they dead north of the neck?" What had become of that love of local independence "which made Congregationalism historic and effective in a day of former dictators?"[40]

FINDING "CONGREGATIONAL PRINCIPLES"

From a larger perspective, all the talk about Congregational principles was more out of denominational character than the progressive agenda of the Council for Social Action. The spirit of the times leading up to 1934 was emphatically nondenominational, with a willingness to avoid talk of Congregational distinctives for the sake of ecumenical cooperation. Even a proposal in 1919 for closer union between Congregationalists and Episcopalians raised little in the way of alarm. To some readers, the ancient creeds and symbols of the Episcopal Church were no threat to freedom, especially under the "liberty of interpretation" that most modern Protestants employed. "We shall not honor the last three hundred years of our past any the less," a Vermont reader opined, "if we put a little more emphasis upon our identity with the church which preceded the Pilgrim Fathers."[41] In the early twentieth century, Christian unity was uppermost in the minds of Congregational leaders, and they fervently believed that their decentralized and noncreedal polity made it the most viable model for the future. They valued their tradition and believed it worth preserving largely because its boundaries were so permeable to outsiders. "The fact of the matter is," the *Congregationalist* declared in 1924, that those "who are most intense in their undenominationalism" are the ones "disposed to be the most intense in their denominationalism."[42]

This spirit was certainly evident among the founders of the CSA. In 1914, Hubert Herring declared Congregationalism at the forefront of modern Christianity, a denomination that "has perceived the demand of the time and sought to meet it." After all, he said, it has "the minimum of shibboleths"; it was willing to lose members and prestige "in order to be fraternal"; and its loose form of organization had made possible a "quick response to the opportunities of cooperation." "Most of all," said Herring, "it has been willing to co-operate with other bodies without asking too many questions about credentials."[43]

By the 1930s, enthusiasm about Congregationalism's unique contribution to ecumenism was widespread across the denomination. As the *Congregationalist* editorialized in 1924, the Congregational faith "is to us nothing more than a gateway to Christian liberty and service." In an analysis of Congregational polity, written for the World Conference on Faith and Order in 1939 (the precursor to the World Council of Churches), George Richards declared that Congregationalism was the polity all other churches were searching for, the goal that all of Christian history was moving toward. Only Congregationalism would allow other traditions the freedom to hold their own forms and also "permit a maximum of freedom in Christ." It was "key to the ecumenical future."[44] "I see in Congregationalism the ultimate solution of the Christian unity problem," a Los Angeles layman agreed, "for we cannot look forward to a time when all Christians will think exactly alike." Only a decentralized polity would allow both freedom and unity.[45]

That spirit of openness even applied to the word "Congregational." We are not "at all concerned about the Congregational name," as an Illinois churchman wrote in 1923. In fact, in 1927 the National Council declared its willingness "for the sake of promoting the larger unities which our churches earnestly desire even to surrender its historic name," or to return to the older Puritan practice of simply naming themselves the "Churches of Christ" in a particular locality.[46]

Blurred boundaries proved a strategic advantage when Congregationalists successfully united with the Christian Church in 1931. This merger caused barely a ripple, partly because the Christians were a small, mostly rural denomination with a similar congregational structure and shared history of aversion to creeds. Their own *Herald of Gospel Liberty* declared it "the most natural thing in the world for Christians to become Congregationalists and for Congregationalists to own the name of Christians."[47] In fact, the two governing bodies, the National Council of Congregational Churches and the General Conference of Christian Churches, simply became the General Council of the Congregational and Christian Churches, a long and cumbersome name they tolerated under the expectation that it would soon change when other communions joined them.[48]

Even so, in 1934 the General Council requested its executive committee to come up with something shorter and easier to say, prompting a round of friendly discussion about alternatives. One suggestion was the "Pilgrim Church," which to Congregational ears at least sounded fairly generic. John Scotford, soon to be editor of the *Advance*, noted that the word "Congregational" was "not particularly melodious, and to the man on the street it suggests something having to do with a Congressional investigation rather than religion." Why not pick something "inclusive and forward-looking?" he asked. "The day of denominationalism is done," so "why not change it?"[49]

Congregational laypeople jumped to the challenge. A Connecticut woman who worried that "Pilgrim Church" somewhat excluded the Christian churches suggested "Fellowship Church" as one that "invites and does not antagonize."[50] A Kansas reader wanted a name "so simply as to be childlike," the "Jesus Way Church." Another Michigan layman, who was concerned about confusion with the Pentecostal Pilgrim Holiness Churches, offered that "If we swung the name around, we might get by with it," he wrote. "'Church of the Pilgrims' would be longer but would mean the same thing."[51]

But the tides were shifting toward greater denominational self-consciousness. One major source of change came from abroad, from leading voices in the British Congregational churches, who had over the years reestablished ties with their American cousins in regular meetings of an International Council. In the 1930s, a debate among British Congregationalists spilled over into the American churches, an intense disagreement about the meaning of their common historic tradition. On the one side was Albert Peel, editor of the British *Congregational Quarterly*, and his book entitled *Inevitable Congregationalism*. The argument of Peel's book was contained in its title, that all church life will "naturally and inevitably" fall into the tolerant decentralized pattern embodied by modern Congregationalism, echoing the hopes of many ecumenically minded Protestants in the United States. On the other side was Nathaniel Micklem, principal of Mansfield College, the Congregational foundation attached to Oxford University, whose book was entitled *Congregationalism Today*. Micklem, in sharp contrast to Peel, insisted that the future of Congregationalism required people willing to fight for its survival—an argument that certainly reflected the broader peril of Britain itself in the face of German fascism but also the theological edge of neoorthodoxy. To Micklem, the tradition would not survive without a firm grounding in solid ideas like "covenant" and the ethics of liberty, order, and discipline.[52]

Micklem's argument hit a nerve in the American churches. Theodore Hume, the American reviewer in the *Advance*, denounced Peel as sadly outdated, a "voice from the remembered past" with little to offer amid "the harsher realities of today." American churchmen wanted something with backbone and grit. Indeed, to Hume the most urgent questions facing the denomination in 1938 were about tradition. Could the trend toward centralized bureaucratic structures, "required by the conditions of American city and national life," be reconciled with "the principle of the God-guided autonomy of the local church"? Independence was, he warned both the source of its "historic strength" and its "present weakness."[53] In the months that followed, Congregational leaders began meeting in study groups aimed at "re-thinking Congregationalism," and their opinions circulated through a series of articles published in the *Advance*.[54]

But the conversation was only just beginning. In the 1940s and early 1950s, Congregationalists would be guarding their historic identity, and their denominational name, with furious intensity. Genteel conversations about tradition and the virtues of ecumenism would give way to a fervent and often ad hominem campaign to preserve "Congregational principles" at any cost.

THE FIGHT FOR CONGREGATIONAL PRINCIPLES

Once again the Council for Social Action provided the focus for dispute. Many Congregationalists assumed its mandate was strictly educational, and certainly the CSA more than fulfilled this. Its Rural Life Committee provided unstinting reports about the poverty of sharecroppers, the struggles of small farms, and the social injustices causing them; the Industrial Committee gave information about labor unions and working conditions. The CSA's monthly journal, *Social Action*, provided in-depth analysis of race relations, civil liberties, and labor legislation by leading scholars and activists—among them, the historian Charles A. Beard and sociologists Liston Pope and Paul H. Douglass. All of this analysis was thoroughly in advance of anything available to the general public.[55]

In the late 1930s, the CSA also took on a far more active lobbying campaign than most laypeople had envisioned in 1934. In one case, CSA staff offered testimony to the United States Senate about a labor riot in Chicago, the so-called Memorial Day Massacre that killed ten strikers and left over a hundred wounded. Other testimony involved federal aid to education and support for compulsory health insurance.[56] These activities attracted relatively little notice, however, until 1948, when a quiet change in denominational bylaws ignited a firestorm.

The change had to do with the CSA's representation within the General Council; by any objective measure, it was a routine, if not mundane, move toward bureaucratic symmetry. All the other denominational boards, including those dealing with home and foreign mission, had such representation already, and in 1948 the General Council simply agreed to widen it to include the Council for Social Action. Thus, 250 CSA "associates" received voice and vote in all matters affecting their organization.

In the late 1940s, however, even the appearance of centralizing power for a left-wing cause was enough to incite alarm, and for this reason the bureaucratic change in the CSA's status was cause for continuing trouble.[57] Opposition began to form within small local groups of laymen, first in Minneapolis and St. Paul, Minnesota, in 1949. Most of the members of these groups were white-collar businessmen, including an executive of a large Minneapolis real estate firm, president of an automobile agency, a utility conglomerate, assorted lawyers, and the executive editor of the *Minneapolis Star-Tribune*.[58] They were not angry reactionaries. The group also included former missionary to China, leading anticommunist, and Minnesota congressman Walter Judd as well as Ellis H. Dana, a lay leader in the Wisconsin Council of Churches who had written a thorough, even-handed analysis of "Congregationalism as a Social Action Pioneer."[59]

Although some of the rhetoric was fiery, for the most part these early critics of the CSA avoided ad hominem attacks, insisting that their main purpose was to "study" the CSA and its work. The Minnesota group emphasized its general support for the Social Gospel and "the application of religious convictions to the solution of contemporary problems." But in their view the CSA had strayed beyond its original purpose, which was simply to "challenge Congregationalists repeatedly and on every major issue with a fair and fearless presentation of the facts." The Minnesota laymen did not believe the council was "communistic," but they did find it "intellectually flabby, arrogant and bureaucratic," so caught up in political maneuvering that it had lost its original goal of "bringing about the kingdom of God on earth."[60]

Not surprisingly, "big-steeple" pastors like James Fifield and Howard Conn, minister of the Plymouth Church in Minneapolis, played a leading role in the dispute. As pastor to most of the laymen organizing in his city, Conn tried to be clear that he was a firm supporter of the Social Gospel but not of direct political action. More than lobbyists in Washington, he said, the denomination needed unbiased information about social issues and a broad-based effort by individual laypeople to bring about needed social change.[61]

Los Angeles pastor James Fifield was less nuanced. In 1951, he formed a study group and employed a full-time researcher, John Payne, to build a case against the CSA. The Southern California Committee for Inquiry into the CSA raised a new round of pointed questions about the fundamental legitimacy of any kind of social or political efforts by the Congregational Christian Churches—and about the possibility that the CSA was "giving aid and comfort to Communists and others who advocate the Socialist State." "Christians cannot be neutral in the battle against Marxism and all forms of tyranny," the Californians declared. "We should initiate and carry forward vigorously a program for creating belief in the virtues of Congregationalism and Americanism, such as freedom of belief, local self-government, [and] opportunity for individual enterprise." At bottom, the Committee for Inquiry insisted that legitimate social action was personal and individual, not through legislative process or political pressure.[62]

The Committee Opposing Congregational Political Action (COCPA), formed in 1952, charged the CSA with violating fundamental Congregational principles and, worse than that, advocating a solution to social problems that was "basically materialistic and immoral."[63] Members of COPCA insisted that individual freedom was the true heart of their Congregational tradition and that any form of political involvement obscured the "true light of the Gospel." Even more to the point, they identified a fatal flaw in the CSA's original charter, making it accountable only to the General Council and not to the whole membership within the churches. In other words, eighteen people were attempting to speak for over a million fellow Congregationalists. A pamphlet issued in 1952 declared in urgent black-and-white graphics that "They're Using Our Church" to promote a radical social agenda, even to the point of opposing all efforts to fight communist subversion and participating in communist fronts. "We know that there are men in this world who want to plan other's lives," the pamphlet read in large block letters, "who want to govern others [*sic*] thoughts, and to speak for them. We've fought two wars about that lately. Yet here, *in our own fellowship*, is a group that wants these things done."[64]

The General Council agreed to conduct a review of the CSA, hoping to moderate the increasingly hostile interchanges between the supporters of the two sides. The Review Board's verdict, issued in September 1953, was generally supportive of the CSA, though it recommended steering its work toward broad-based education on social issues rather than direct lobbying efforts.[65] But the action did little. While the COPCA named communist sympathizers and accused the CSA of a left-wing stealth campaign within the denomination, supporters of the CSA published lists of "errors" in the infamous "black book" and charged its opponents with the same kind of agenda-driven bullying of the Congregational rank and file as they'd been accused of perpetrating.

In the meantime, the League to Uphold Congregational Principles, organized in 1953, moved the debate to a new plane, from simple denunciation of the Council for Social Action to a broader championship of the historic tradition, now defined as "fellowship without ecclesiastical control." The shift from political theology to history did not go without notice. Herman Reissig, a member of the CSA board, wrote to his colleague Russell Clinchy in April 1952, noting the "increasingly frequent use of the words 'Congregational' and 'unCongregational.'" To Reissig, this was both surprising and disconcerting. "I had thought that most laymen in our fellowship were somewhat impatient with a denominational approach to religion," he wrote. "Quite suddenly now, laymen critical of the C.S.A. seem to be giving a sacrosanct character to 'the Congregational Way,' or to a particular definition of it." "I do not quite know what is going on here," he confessed to Clinchy, "Can you help me?"[66]

In fact, Clinchy was well positioned to provide the answer. In the 1930s and early 1940s, he had been well known for his solid liberal credentials, even to the point of presiding at the wedding of New Dealer Harry Hopkins in 1942.[67] Clinchy was one of the CSA's earliest supporters, but under the rising threat of totalitarianism and the shadow of the Cold War, his views began to shift. In 1947, he published a collection compendium of lectures under the title *Faith and Freedom*, tracing the decay of liberalism and calling for vigilant defense of individual freedom against the powers of evil.[68] By that time, Clinchy had not only renounced his earlier support for the CSA but began to lead the campaign against it.

His argument went beyond simple fears of communism or support for the profit motive; by the early 1950s, Clinchy had developed a lecture outlining his opposition to the CSA within a broad historical framework, beginning with the earliest days of Christianity and continuing on through the development of American Congregationalism. His analysis of the "Congregational Way" argued that denominational entities had no right to speak for the whole: "no corporate majority of any agency, association, conference, or council can speak in the name of even one Christian without the express consent of his personal conviction."[69]

CONGREGATIONAL DEMOCRACY

Of course, behind all of the arguments about Congregational principles was the reality of Congregational polity itself. In remarks to Connecticut ministers, Hartford Seminary president Russell Henry Stafford admitted that despite their primary loyalty to laissez-faire capitalism, the critics of CSA did have a point. The denomination really did need an educational commission, "to speak not for Congregationalists, but to Congregationalists, to tell us not what we must think, but that we must think, and what we must think about." In his view, which he set down in a confidential memo, the real and much deeper problem was the way the General Council itself conducted business. By the 1950s, its meetings had "the atmosphere of a mammoth rally"; reasoning that "the bigger the crowd, the more democracy there would be," the denomination had increased the number of delegates to over a thousand. The resulting hubbub and lengthy and dull platform wrangling, said Stafford, tended to keep "sane and sober" people away and leave the actual business of the council to an ever-fewer number of full-time bureaucrats who alone understood the complexities of the issues brought before it. "In practice, as any reasonably sophisticated adult will realize, the bigger the crowd, the less the democracy"—and the greater the perception of "would-be czars . . . putting things through by sleight of hand and surreptitious pressure." The real solution for embattled Congregationalists, Stafford argued, would be to cut representation to the General Council in half and restrict the floor to voting members only.[70]

But by then, even if participatory democracy had ceased to exist in the Congregational churches, it did not matter. The exact nature of "Congregational principles" was the subject of furious debate between people who neither liked nor trusted each other. Chapter 8 tells the story of the denomination's complicated steps toward the merger that created the United Church of Christ in 1957, one in which seventeenth-century history would become both a spiritual and legal point of contention. Members of the League to Uphold Congregational Principles generally insisted that they were not "categorically opposed to the merger" and denied any direct connection between the two campaigns. But as one observer pointed out in 1952, they "did have a closely related personal backing" and similar tactics of "legal and financial pressures."[71] Certainly, both controversies resonated around the same question of historic Congregational polity and insisted on faithfulness to the original tradition. And both would prove equally impossible to resolve peacefully.

CHAPTER EIGHT

History and the Politics of Merger

Thank goodness, the editor of the *Congregationalist* thought to himself as he strolled home across the Boston Common on a quiet Sunday evening in 1922. He had spent the day in two of the city's largest Congregational churches, Old South and Park Street, representing the "opposite poles of liberalism and conservatism" in the religious thought of the day. In the first, George Gordon presided as a quintessential liberal, urbane and broad-minded, and a few blocks away, the irascible A. Z. Conrad ended his sermons with an altar call for sinners. Both churches were thriving in their own separate ways, with none of the rancor dividing Baptists and Presbyterians, who were then both deeply mired in fundamentalist controversy. The editor's primary feeling was "pride and gratitude" for a Congregational fellowship "broad enough and free enough to include within its circle men of different types, and views, and temperaments, with the common denominator of earnestness and a fervent message." All Congregationalists should rejoice, he said, "in the variety of religious life that our freedom makes possible" and the inclusive spirit that distinguished their denomination from all others.[1]

How could he have predicted that just a few decades later Congregationalists would be slogging through one of the most prolonged and painful disputes in their long history? Behind all of the high-decibel name-calling, however, this case was different in one important way: the fundamental disagreement was not about doctrine or the Bible, nor was it about church polity or personalities. Congregationalists were arguing full tilt about the Pilgrims and Puritans, about the meaning of the past and the purpose of tradition.

The intensity of the conflict, fueled by disputes over the Council for Social Action, was uncomfortably out of character for a denomination long unused to heresy trials or doctrinal splits and with no institutional forum for airing and repairing disagreements. Indeed, the controversy over "true Congregationalism" had all the earmarks of an all-out fundamentalist-modernist conflict, proving as visceral and dogmatic as anything biblical literalists had to offer, and ending with a denominational schism. Each side claimed the correct exegesis of the past, a small dissident group insisting on absolute fidelity to the "Genesis account," in this case the actual forms of church order bequeathed by the Pilgrim fathers, and on the other side an embattled majority with a more open-ended view of history and its power over the present.

The common wisdom about ecumenical mergers is that they are a sign of weakness, a step by indifferent people down the path toward generic religiosity. "The most vigorous, growing, and significant organizations," as some critics have argued, are those with a clear sense of their own distinctiveness. They are never attracted by ecumenical rhetoric— the call for unity attracts only those already weakened by a fuzzy polity and watered-down theology. And so, the argument goes, ecumenical movements, however well intentioned, are simply "doomed" efforts to stave off the inevitable.[2]

The disputes among Congregationalists in the 1940s and 1950s, however, were much more than a disagreement between some people who cared about denominational distinctives and others who did not. As one layman commented, the "merger matter" is "making us think about Congregationalism more seriously than we ever have before in this generation."[3] In fact, Congregationalists were resuming a conversation about the Pilgrims and Puritans from many decades before, at the Boston Council of 1865. At the time, the questions were broad and challenging: Did historical continuity require all Congregationalists to remain Calvinists? What innovations to the original church polity of the Pilgrim fathers were permissible? The questions remained unanswered in 1865 and were largely tabled in the years following, as Congregationalists found other ways of identifying with their New England ancestors, some profitable, some intellectually challenging, and others just plain fun. But in the 1940s and 1950s, the questions became far more narrow and urgent. The Pilgrim and Puritan fathers were not so much flesh-and-blood ancestors as abstractions, boundary markers separating the "true" Congregationalists from the false.

This chapter, like the previous one, is about denominational politics. We pick up the story in the middle of disputes over the Council for Social Action, now growing into a full-scale libertarian protest against ecumenism, and follow it through to the merger itself and its immediate aftermath. This is a narrow angle of analysis, of course, with relatively fleeting glances at major historical events and social trends of the 1940s and 1950s. It deals with old fights, semiobscure people, and bureaucratic structures whose value might be lost on outsiders without a stake in the outcome—but it is worth picking through the details. This is an arena where the hopes and fears of laypeople met the concerns of leaders and thinkers; it is also the right scale for understanding the sharp inward turn of a broad and long-standing conversation and the contentious and painful role of history and tradition in the mid-twentieth century.

A HISTORICAL SOCIETY, AT LAST

Post–World War II Protestants have been described as "the bland leading the bland," a happily patriotic group content with a vague form of "faith in faith." This was, after all, the era of Norman Vincent Peale and *The Power of Positive Thinking* and the revivals of Billy Graham, when no one seemed to mind when the United States Congress added the phrase "under God" to the Pledge of Allegiance. All across the country churches were full and denominational budgets soaring and strong.

Although true in some respects, the stereotype obscures a deep and growing intellectual interest in religion. One sign was a revival of theology, which in the wake of the fundamentalist controversies of the 1920s and the social radicalism of the 1930s had mostly dropped from public conversation. In the 1940s and 1950s, when a theologian like Reinhold Niebuhr could end up on the cover of *Time* magazine, no scholar or intellectual worth the name could plead indifference to religious thought.

The other sign was a deepening curiosity about the history of religion in the United States, to the point that in 1959 historian Henry May declared the subject in full recovery. "A vast and crucial area of American experience," he wrote, "has been rescued from neglect and misunderstanding."[4] The recovery, which began in the 1930s with the seminal work of H. Richard Niebuhr and Perry Miller, reached the scholarly mainstream in the 1950s in the writings of Arthur M. Schlesinger Sr. and rising stars like Sidney Ahlstrom, William McLoughlin Jr., and Timothy L. Smith. The revival of religious history was also, to a great extent, a reinvigoration of interest in Protestant denominationalism as a social phenomenon, not necessarily non-Christians or even Roman Catholics. The *Great Tradition of the American Churches*, as Winthrop Hudson titled his influential book, published in 1953, was primarily the story of the mainline Protestant churches. Serious study of other "nonmainstream" believers was still decades off.

The revival also marked the emergence of church history as a field of study, a bridge between secular scholars in university departments and their counterparts teaching in theological seminaries. During the postwar years, as May observed, "to draw a line between believing 'church historians' and 'positivist lay historians' had become impossible. . . . No one could say with precision where in religious terms, the best new writing was coming from."[5]

Without a doubt, this invigorated the efforts of denominational historical societies, many of them established in the late nineteenth century and mostly moribund in the early twentieth. In 1958, the American Baptist Historical Society, for example, closed down the old *Chronicle*, a small and fairly dull journal devoted to biographies of obscure ministers and long-forgotten missionaries, and replaced it with *Foundations*, an academic journal with a full array of seminary professors on its masthead: leading Baptist church historians like Robert Handy, Winthrop Hudson, and Edwin Gaustad were regular contributors. The primary audience of *Foundations*, however, was not the academy but the rank and file in the churches. "We live in a time," the opening editorial declared, "when Baptists, like the other great bodies of Christians in the world, are asking themselves what is their peculiar witness to bear before the world." During a "time of transition," when "many landmarks are barely recognizable" and "nothing can be taken entirely for granted," history would provide them with an anchor.[6]

Northern Presbyterians, still riddled with internal divisions between liberals and conservatives, were more cautious but equally convinced that, in the words of the General Assembly of 1958, "the church must reaffirm and reapply the principles of our Reformed faith to the crucial issues of our time." "To fail to know what we believe, why we believe it, and what it requires in meeting the problems of our day," it declared, "is to forsake our heritage."[7] This was not just talk, for the denomination poured both money and resources into this challenge. In 1960, the Presbyterian Historical Society broke new ground on a facility in Philadelphia, a beautiful building housing an important and comprehensive collection, completed in 1967. Church history was also prominently featured in the popular experimental religious education curriculum of the 1940s and 1950s, the Faith and Life series, and the postwar years also saw a steady stream of academic books rolling off the denominational presses, written by leading scholars like Leonard Trinterud, Lefferts Loetscher, and H. Shelton Smith.

Mortified Congregationalists raced to catch up, forming their first historical society just five years before their separate existence came to an end. Suddenly aware that even their prospective partner, the Evangelical and Reformed Church, had its own historical society with 150 members, two full-time staff, and a close connection with the Lancaster Seminary Library in Pennsylvania, they could not avoid the conclusion that nearly every other Protestant denomination took their historical responsibility far more seriously than they. "How is it," one supporter demanded, "that the one denomination that enters most frequently into the early records of America has for so long a time" had no historical society to call its own?[8]

Though the Congregational Christian Historical Society (CCHS) had the feel of a last-ditch effort—the proposed budget was less than $3,000 with a vague hope of "perhaps a minimum contribution" from the General Council—it aimed high. Indeed, like its sister societies, CCHS was able to enlist some of the most eminent church historians of the time: Reformation scholar Roland Bainton was a vice president on the first CCHS executive council, and in 1966 the Board of Governors included Bainton as well as historians Ford Louis Battles, Arthur C. McGiffert Jr., and George Williams. Enjoying the new prominence of Puritan studies in the postwar era, Congregationalists also had access to a stellar array of scholarly talent: Edmund Morgan gave an address to an annual meeting, while Perry Miller and Sidney Ahlstrom published articles in the *Congregational Bulletin*.[9]

In other ways, however, CCHS embodied a sense of impending loss within the denomination. Instead of beginning with energetic plans for the future, its leaders tended to mourn past failures and missed opportunities. "We have been so deeply involved in the changing conditions of American life" and "the pressure of immediate tasks," said founder Frederick Fagley, that "[we] have left our history too much in the keeping of secular writers" and have become "somewhat complacent towards our heritage." The past years not only had seen local churches "fading away with no record of their unusual service to God and man" and "even their location forgotten," but "countless fine old books on Congregationalism and valuable records" had been sent "to the rubbish bin." Only the CCHS, said Fagley, was holding back the tide of indifference, by providing "asylum for old books of historical value" within the safe and utterly quiet confines of the Congregational Library.[10]

This sense of being badly misunderstood also defined the society's primary activities, correcting "erroneous statements in books and pamphlets" and preparing "fair and accurate statements" for encyclopedias, almanacs, and yearbooks. In fact, CCHS leaders could sound a bit like an exasperated older generation unhappy with the direction postwar American society was headed. In a report issued in 1953, president Arthur Bradford declared the need for a "decent respect for the work of our Fathers" as a means of building the nation's "moral fiber."[11] Fagley echoed the same language in a report issued in 1956, insisting that CCHS "seeks to help individuals and churches to pay due respect to the leaders of the last."[12] CCHS leaders insisted they had no political role in the merger dispute—they included both pro- and antimerger figures—and made a point of focusing on the glory days before the 1950s. "All of us, pro-union and anti-union," said Bradford at the annual meeting in 1960, "cherish the same memories of the past which belongs to us all." The "more we study that past together with the open mind of true scholarship," he said, "the more we shall be drawn together, in mutual understanding and good will, to achieve, at long last, a greater, stronger, more inclusive Fellowship than any we have known."[13]

If anything, the opposite was true, however. History was already a contentious issue, and it would remain one for decades to come. The long battle over the merger enlisted two entirely different interpretations of the Pilgrim and Puritan past, one emphasizing the independence of local churches and the other their interdependence. They were not the first Congregationalists to feel this tension, inherent in their polity from the very beginning. But it would be their generation, the most modern and secular of Congregationalists, who would finally split the denomination over a dispute going back to the days of the Pilgrims and Puritans.

THE RIGHTS AND WRONGS OF ECUMENISM

Enthusiasm for Christian unity reached a peak after World War II, in a wave of determined optimism after years of destructive conflict. The World Council of Churches met for the first time in 1948 and was the largest and most visible of many other mergers, unions, and international meetings that year. The signal achievement was the new Church of South India, bringing 1.1 million Anglicans, Methodists, Presbyterians, and Congregationalists into a single body. All across the world, other denominational families began taking steps toward greater harmony. In 1948, the Lutheran World Federation met in Lund, Sweden; the Baptist World Alliance in Copenhagen; the Methodist Ecumenical Conference in Springfield, Massachusetts; and the World Convention of the Disciples of Christ in Buffalo, New York. Zeal for large international meetings, in fact, knew no bounds: 1948 also saw meetings of the World Conference of Christian Youth, the North American Interseminary Conference, the International Missionary Conference, the International Council on Religious Education, and the Home Missions and the Foreign Missions

Douglas Horton
(Courtesy of
Congregational Library)

Councils of North America. These efforts enjoyed wide public support—a Gallup poll taken in 1950 found half of those surveyed in favor of a single Protestant church in the United States.[14]

American Congregationalists were enthusiastic and often leading participants. They convened their own International Congregational Council in Wellesley, Massachusetts, in 1949, drawing delegates from the United States, the British Isles, as well as Canada, India, and the Philippines. Douglas Horton, who was then minister and secretary of the Congregational General Council, became moderator.[15]

Not all Protestants were happily on board, however. In fact, what looked like progress to some was outright betrayal to others, especially in denominations with a strong and theologically conservative voice of dissent. "Nothing is more deplorable," a Presbyterian conservative declared in 1948, "than the manner in which organizational unity has been promoted at the sacrifice of Christian truth."[16] The opposition not only disapproved of ecumenism, it took opportunities to block it when possible. When northern and southern Presbyterians were contemplating union in 1948, the ultraseparatist Bible Presbyterians invited skittish southern conservatives to join them. In a veiled reference to the racial tensions delaying the merger, the Bible Presbyterians promised a return to "historic Presbyterianism as it was before the division into Southern and Northern churches."[17]

Already in the 1940s, disagreements over church union began to surface in battles over history, rooted in old disagreements over the role of creeds and confessions but also heavy with symbolic weight. For Presbyterians, the occasion was the denomination-wide observance of the Westminster Confession's 300th anniversary in 1943. Liberals offered cautious praise, emphasizing both the strengths and limitations of the document's authors: though "we may learn to love their courage and their exactness," the *Presbyterian Survey* declared, "[we] may well weep for their lack of patience with the views of others." Though there was "much to learn" from Westminster, the author concluded, they should not "stop there."[18] In contrast, the *Presbyterian Guardian*, the voice of the Orthodox Presbyterians, who had broken with the northern denomination in 1937, celebrated Westminster as the eternal standard of Calvinist orthodoxy. With Protestant principles "largely forgotten or ignored or compromised or trampled under foot," there was "special urgency," the *Guardian* declared, in celebrating the "high principles which brought about a new day of light and liberty."[19]

In light of later battles to come, of course, these disagreements about the Westminster Confession were barely a skirmish. But they point to the continuing importance of history in mainline churches, even during the otherwise peaceful postwar years, and suggest the powerful role that historical disputes could play in denominational politics. In fact, as sociologist Robert Wuthnow has observed of twentieth-century religion, the greater the similarity, the greater the potential for acrimony. Though in one sense the breakdown of old barriers of class, geography, and theology signaled the "end of denominationalism," it also raised the stakes on other more elusive and debatable differences.[20] The splintering of American churches over the past several decades into competing interest groups over issues like abortion, women's ordination, and homosexuality is one obvious example of this process. But it was not the first. A less-known but equally intense symbolic battle had unfolded many years before among Congregationalists, a group that until the 1940s and 1950s had no history of sectarian disputes and apparently little taste for them.

The possibility of joining the Congregational Christian Churches and the Evangelical and Reformed (E&R) Church emerged quietly, right after the General Council meeting in Oberlin in 1934. Officials of the two denominations—Douglas Horton and Truman Douglas on the Congregational Christian side and Samuel Press and George Richards on the Evangelical and Reformed—began holding informal meetings together, recognizing in each other a mutual commitment to ecumenism and social action.[21] Like the Congregational Christians, the E&R was itself brand new, the product of a merger in 1934, carefully crafted on deliberate compromise. The German Reformed churches were an old American Calvinist denomination dating back to the settlement of eastern Pennsylvania in the early eighteenth century, and the Evangelical Synod came from a more recent wave of Lutheran and freethinking German immigration to the central Midwest. By the early twentieth century, historic differences in theology and church polity mattered less to these two groups than their common enthusiasm for ecumenism and social action. Accordingly, the E&R statement of faith included both the Reformed Heidelberg Catechism and the Lutherans' Augsburg Confession, with the explicit understanding that both were equally essential to Christian belief and doctrine.[22]

Negotiations with the Congregational Christian Churches picked up speed in the early 1940s and seemed headed for success. In fact, by decade's end, one observer prophesied that the "proposed merger of the Congregational Christian Churches with the Evangelical and Reformed Church is so far advanced that its completion is probably news for 1948."[23]

History unfolded differently, however. This particular merger was inherently tricky for Congregationalists, far more complicated than their union with the Christians in 1931. Most other ecumenical mergers taking place in the twentieth century had been reunions after historic splits: Southern and Northern Methodists came together in 1939 after separating in 1844 over slavery; Presbyterians worked to unite both their northern and southern branches and smaller regional ones, a process that culminated in the formation of the United Presbyterian Church in the United States of America in 1958. In both cases, polity was not an issue, at least compared with differences over race and theology, and the end goal of full "organic" union rather than a simple federation seemed both reasonable and reachable. As Wilbur LaRoe, the retiring moderator of the Presbyterian Church

U.S.A. declared in 1948, "organic union is a mere engineering problem which we can solve whenever we make up our minds to do it."[24]

But for the E&R and the Congregational Christian churches, organic union proved a near fatal stumbling block. As part of a body organized along presbyterian lines, local E&R churches did not have final authority over doctrinal or financial matters. The regional classis and then the national synod had the power to adjudicate in both areas and to ordain and discipline clergy. Of course, in many ways, the problem was more perception than reality: the E&R was built on flexibility and compromise, and its constitution, according to a denominational insider, was "essentially presbyterian but functionally congregational."[25]

Finding a compromise between these two different forms of polity would have been a challenge but not an impossible one. In fact, Congregationalists also had a long record of flirtation with Presbyterianism, formalized in the Plan of Union but dating back to the seventeenth-century Heads of Agreement, a document championed by leading Puritan ministers Increase and Cotton Mather. In an even more specific sense, Congregationalists of the mid-twentieth century had become far more comfortable with denominational supervision than any of their predecessors would have dreamed. The General Council was no longer the advisory body envisioned in 1871 but had amassed real budgetary and bureaucratic power. Moreover, a major reorganization in 1913 brought all of the independent agencies organized during the nineteenth century—the American Board of Missions, the Church Building Society, the Congregational Sunday School and Publishing Society—under denominational supervision for the first time. During the 1920s and 1930s, the unification continued, beginning with the dissolution of the Women's Board in 1926 and ten years later a broad merger of many disparate church agencies—the American Missionary Association, the Congregational Education Society, and the Publishing Society, as well as the Board of Ministerial Relief and Church Extension boards—into a single legal corporation, the Board of Home Missions. In the early twentieth century, the General Council also exercised firmer control over standards for ministerial ordination. Individual congregations could still call a pastor but not before he or she had been thoroughly vetted by the local association or the state conference. Prospective clergy had to undertake a lengthy process involving licensure and regular supervision before being formally examined for ordination. Recognizing the growing difficulty in supplying pulpit vacancies in local churches, the General Council proposed a national registry of pastors to aid in placement, a step finally authorized in 1946. Many people continued to define the central tenet of Congregationalism as the autonomy of the local church, but by the mid-twentieth century, for all practical purposes, absolute local independence was a thing of the past.[26]

Why, then, did the proposed merger with the Evangelical and Reformed Church create such determined opposition? One obvious answer is the mood of the era itself, especially by the late 1940s, when the Cold War between the United States and the Soviet Union was at its most tense and dangerous pass and the nuclear arms race gathering alarming speed. Among Congregationalists, the atmosphere had already been poisoned by the dispute over the Council for Social Action, and for some it was not a particularly long stretch to interpret the determination of merger supporters as obedience to secret orders from above. In an era given to fears of conspiracy and rumors of spying, anything that looked like a centralization of power was easily suspect, and to those willing to believe, the move toward the formation of the United Church of Christ had all the earmarks of a takeover. The contempt of the prounionists for the Congregational polity was the same as "those who seek for totalitarianism in our political life," one opponent charged. According to Malcolm Burton, pastor of the Second Congregational Church in New London, Connecticut, and a leader of the antimerger forces, the proposal for uniting with the E&R originated with "people who had been indoctrinated with strange and different concepts of the Church." "Ecumenicity," he said, was at heart "a grandiose scheme for unified organization in 'one big church.'" Supported only by bureaucratic propagandists and theological jargon (mostly from European neoorthodox theologians), he warned, this new idea was distinctly un-American, an attempt to return to the old "State Churches of Europe," the original nemesis of the Pilgrim fathers.[27]

Anticommunism was only one of many sources of opposition to the merger, however. Some critics, like Roger Babson and James Fifield, were simply libertarians and objected to any threat of centralized control, communist or otherwise. Others worried about the legalities of merging money and personnel under the new denominational structure and, more prosaically, criticized Evangelical and Reformed "clannishness," their German ethnicity, and their frequent use of tobacco and alcohol at clergy gatherings.[28] Indeed, Minnesota pastor Howard Conn believed much of the antimerger fervor was simply "a cover-up" for "Anglo-Saxon superiority . . . even though many of these people have been on our soil since the days of William Penn."[29] Others objected to the neoorthodox theology of merger leaders like Douglas Horton and their "vague and sacrosanct authority about the 'will of God' and the 'mind of Christ.'"[30] It all looked far too arcane, and far too European perhaps, to pass unnoticed. The "main stream" of Congregationalism, Brooklyn pastor Arthur Rouner wrote, "will follow the wake of the Mayflower and the trails of the Pilgrims rather than the train of Calvin and pages of the Catechism."[31]

Theologically conservative Congregational churches worried about the merger as well, to the point of leaving to form a separate denomination, the Conservative Congregational Christian Conference, in 1948. The problem was not ecumenism per se—anxious to shed their isolated fundamentalist past, many postwar evangelicals hoped fervently for a united and aggressive Christian witness. In the 1940s and 1950s, in fact, Congregational pastor Harold John Ockenga had played a leading role in a "neoevangelical" revival toward a less combative form of fundamentalism.[32] But the specter of a "giant church," as a Nebraska editor called it, with centralized control over individual churches was not what they had in mind.[33] Conservatives, perhaps more than any other group in the denomination, prized their independence and guarded it carefully. "Congregationalism has no universal creed which is obligatory on all members of the churches," Ockenga declared in 1948, even though this meant a range of beliefs from "high Calvinism to extreme Pelagianism." The proposed merger, however, would introduce for the first time, the possibility of liberal ideas imposed on everyone, a situation "intolerable" for Ockenga's Park Street Church congregation in Boston, which voted emphatically against the merger. "We do not say that they would do this tomorrow," he said, "but that it would be true ultimately."[34]

But these were not the fundamental arguments against the union. Anticommunism and fears of centralized control gave urgency and weight to what became the primary charge of merger opponents, that any kind of partnership with the Evangelical and Reformed Church would spell the end of Congregational independence and, even worse, the death of a vital American tradition long (self-) identified with democratic values. In direct contrast to 1931, when denominational labels seemed to matter relatively little, merger opponents in the 1940s and 1950s fiercely mourned the loss of the word "Congregationalist," "a distinctive and significant name," as one declared, "with great traditions."[35] Eliminating that time-honored term, a Connecticut pastor argued, "would cut the line of human tradition." Changing the name to the broad and generic "United Church of Christ" amounted to a fundamental betrayal of history and would spell the end not just of Congregationalism but of the principles of freedom and liberty that it had always fostered.[36] "If this merger is consummated," a Brooklyn pastor and denominational official warned, "the historic fellowship we have heretofore known as the CC Churches will cease to exist. A fellowship with a heritage of three hundred years of consecrated cooperative effort which has made one of the most outstanding contributions of any denomination to religious development in America cannot be treated lightly, nor can its name be lost without the sacrifice of something which thousands have deeply cherished."[37]

In his most insistent moments, Douglas Horton also believed that the merger with the Evangelical and Reformed Church was essential to the survival of Congregationalism. "What makes you think that any of Congregationalism will be sacrificed in the proposed union?" he queried a critic in 1947. "If I thought that we should lose a jot or a tittle of anything that we have stood for in the past by uniting with the Evangelical and Reformed Church, I would be unalterably opposed to it. The fact is, however, that the union will give the Congregational spirit a power in American Protestantism such as it has never before enjoyed."[38] "In union new attitudes and new ideas would be brought to us," he wrote to a colleague in 1952, in "forms of thought" and "ways of worship." Failure would lead to controversy and a dangerous loss of morale, not to mention the next generation of potential leaders. "All of us would have to carry with us the consciousness that we belong to a denomination too weak to carry out its avowed purposes."[39]

Unfortunately, merger supporters did not always allay fears of denominational extinction. When he was moderator of the General Council, Albert Buckner Coe issued a press release calling the church to "go forward in our ecumenical outreach" even though it "may require obedience until death." The Congregational Christian Churches, he said, may have to "offer up some of their accustomed, inherited forms of life" as a "step of faith" toward a greater good. "The perpetuation of the Congregational church or any other church is not the important task of this time," a California reader wrote to the *Advance* in 1948. "What we need is to discover ways of projecting the Christian interpretation of life into as many areas of our world community as possible."[40] An equally ominous promerger brochure published in 1955, "United in Christ," declared it was time for both the Congregational Christian and Evangelical and Reformed churches to "set aside personal wishes, even cherished traditions, in the realization that we are *being called* into this Union . . . to witness that the divisions in the Christian Community can be healed, that the divided groups no longer represent convictions sufficiently central to the Christian faith to justify continuance in their separation." The new denomination would "demonstrate that the power to break down the walls of partition is at work among us," turning "diversity into unity," the "very essence of the power of the Christian faith."[41]

Merger supporters were not on a suicide mission, however. Congregationalists had long prided themselves in playing down their distinctives for the sake of unity—to the point where critics began to wonder what "Congregational principles" really entailed. The promerger forces believed, as did the opposition, that they were carrying Congregationalism most faithfully into its future.

ANTIMERGER

By the late 1940s, the prospect of a United Church of Christ looked dimmer than ever. Merger negotiations had encountered a storm of resistance, one that few denominational insiders expected or were prepared to manage. What had once looked like a simple feat of institutional engineering, bringing two church bureaucracies into one body, had grown into a full-out controversy involving an increasingly alarmed grassroots constituency of local churches, pastors, and laypeople.

Congregational leaders assumed that they could follow the general procedure for ecumenical unions: prospective partners would craft a "Basis of Union," a carefully worded document laying out the terms of the union, and then they would send it out for approval. The document the Evangelical and Reformed and the Congregational Christian churches issued in 1943 was a standard treatment of denominational business, laying out various procedures for uniting bureaucratic structures and pension funds, ordaining ministers and meshing together missionary societies and departments of social justice. Almost instantly, however, the Basis of Union ran into a storm of criticism from Congregationalists. Critics instantly flagged the proposal for a national synod with its own officers and committees and a schedule for regular gatherings—this following a model long established in Presbyterian churches and part of the Evangelical and Reformed heritage. Though the synod's powers were basically advisory and the document as a whole emphatic on the local church as the denomination's "basic unit of organization," the term was enough to rally an alarmed opposition.[42] Undaunted, supporters put together a set of "Interpretations" to clear up points of conflict. This included a specific stipulation that the Congregational Christian Churches "do not go out of existence at the time of the union" and that, "in consummating this union," the two "are uniting without break in their respective historical continuities."[43]

But far more troublesome problems loomed, including the basic question about the procedure for approving the merger. The Evangelical and Reformed Church already had a structure in place: after two-thirds of the members of its General Synod approved it, the Basis of Union would go out to the thirty-four regional synods for a final vote. Everyone had a proper say and the system worked without a major problem. In due time, all but one of the synods accepted the full text of the Basis of Union. The Congregational Christians, however, had no such procedure and faced an ill-defined road ahead. The questions were both brand-new and far-reaching: What would constitute approval? Was a simple majority enough? And who would vote? State conferences, local churches, or individual members?

In the end, the Executive Committee of the General Council decided that a "yes" vote by 75 percent of the state conferences, associations, and local churches would be more than sufficient, and they set 1 June 1948 as the deadline for approval. This was a steep requirement, a generous concession to the opposition and in the end a rash one. For one thing, allotting a vote to each individual church was an advantage to merger opponents: small congregations, which tended to be antimerger, had as much say as large ones. Nor did the procedure stipulate the total number or proportion of churches needed to constitute a fair decision. Even more perilously, the Executive Committee did not have a plan in place if the measure did not pass.

In the end, the Basis of Union received only 72.8 percent of the total vote. The problem was made worse by the extremely low turnout: the vast majority of local churches simply did not vote. In Massachusetts, for example, the vote was 19,000 "yes" and 6,646 "no"—this against a total membership of over 162,000. In Michigan, only about one-fifth of the members registered a vote, and in northern California, barely 4,000 of a total 23,000 participated. African American congregations were even less involved, with 446 of the 19,864 of the "South East Colored" conference voting yes and 842 voting no.[44]

Not surprisingly, by 1949 Congregationalists were headed to court. That April the newly founded Committee for the Continuance of the Congregational Christian Churches filed suit, naming the Cadman Memorial Church in Brooklyn, New York, as plaintiff—apparently overlooking the

Helen Kenyon (Courtesy of
Congregational Library)

irony that the church's eponymous former pastor, S. Parkes Cadman, had
been an enthusiastic ecumenist. The defendant was Helen Kenyon, the
first woman to serve as moderator of the denomination.

The *Cadman v. Kenyon* case ground through the New York court system
for years, beginning with an initial ruling in favor of the plaintiffs, an appeal
by prounion forces, and then a reversal by the state supreme court in 1952.
The presenting issue was Congregational polity, specifically whether the
General Council alone had the authority to effect a union with another
denomination. The plaintiffs argued that no merger would be valid unless
every individual church voted in agreement. In fact, the entire process
was an outlandish imposition on the time-honored Congregational Way,
they declared, to the point that any church voting "yes" would be giving
up its historic Congregational identity. The centralized structure of the
"proposed United Church of Christ," the plaintiff's argument ran, "is and
will be so alien and different in structure and polity that fundamental

congregational usage and practice will be wholly lost and destroyed." This was more than just a theoretical exercise in church government: the plaintiffs further argued that only churches voting against the merger should have legal control over denominational properties, including assets related to all boards, agencies, commissions, and bequests.[45]

The court case itself unfolded as a seminar on seventeenth-century New England church polity. Lawyers from both sides quizzed witnesses about the Cambridge Platform and read aloud long passages from a popular denominational history, *Adventure in Liberty* by Gaius Glenn Atkins and Frederick Fagley. Witnesses established their bona fides with long lists of primary sources. Harry Butman, pastor of the Allin Congregational Church in Dedham, Massachusetts, testifying for the plaintiffs, began his statement with an inventory of the historical texts he had studied: the Cambridge Platform, Williston Walker's *Creeds and Platforms*, William Bradford's *History of Plimouth Plantation*, John Wise's *New England Churches Vindicated*, and George Punchard's *View of Congregationalism*.[46]

The plaintiffs were confident that history was on their side, down to the smallest technical detail. James Fifield, serving as a key witness, emphasized the Pilgrim and Puritan heritage of liberty and democracy. Since its sixteenth-century origins, he said, Congregationalism had been "groomed to render an heroic service to the cause of freedom"; now it was to be "deprived of its birthright and put into eclipse." The essence of the tradition, what Congregationalism had stood for "since the Pilgrim Fathers," was the power of local churches "acting for themselves and in their own right."[47] But historic Congregational polity also addressed more technical aspects of the legal case. Arthur Rouner, at the time pastor of the Cadman church, quoted Puritan pastor Thomas Hooker's "Summary of Congregational Principles" to argue against the form for representation in the Basis of Union—Hooker insisted that churches alone, not state conferences or associations, had the power to send delegates. In fact, Rouner argued, Congregational polity meant absolute freedom on the local level. "Any church may have a creed if it so desires," he said, even if it meant "6,000 different creeds in the 6,000 different churches."[48]

Not to be outdone, the defense called two church historians to the witness stand, Wilhelm Pauck, of the Chicago Theological Seminary, and Henry Pitney Van Dusen, a Presbyterian then teaching at Union Seminary (later its president), to deal with the question of historic continuity. Pauck saw no problem with the merger; in his view, continuity involved the "practices, usages, constitutions, [and] charters" that had developed over time. "That is how any historical process works," said Pauck, and he went on to point out that Congregational practice on local church independence had varied widely, especially among first-generation New Englanders, who "became as insistent upon uniformity as the people in England had been." Congregational polity, said Pauck, "[had] been transformed again and again" by additions designed to "fulfill new needs . . . as they arose in their common life." It was "not static, but . . . capable of evolution."[49]

Van Dusen took pains to emphasize this same point, though with less deference. "I am trying to suggest and I insist upon it," he said, and "if I can help you to become educated on this point it will be a good thing— that the actual progress of Christian unity in the last 25 years" was simply unprecedented in the entire history of the faith. Congregationalists would have to look far beyond their seventeenth-century polity for answers. Van Dusen also dismissed the principle of local church autonomy as "utter nonsense." The churches had been delegating their work, especially in home and foreign missions, to denominational agencies for many years without any threat to fundamental beliefs. The practice of Congregational polity, he said, was "utterly different from what it was at the time of the Protestant Reformation. Why would anybody question that?"[50]

PILGRIMS VERSUS PURITANS

Certainly not Douglas Horton. By the late 1940s, Horton was a seasoned churchman, with a solid scholarly background—he translated major works of Karl Barth into English—and long experience in ecumenical work. He was an established theologian, author, and church leader. Behind the scenes, he fielded a seemingly endless stream of questions, quibbles, and accusations from merger opponents and supporters, with a seemingly endless supply of patience. In public, however, Horton was best known for his speech to the General Council in 1950, "Of Equability and Perseverance in Well Doing," a promerger argument from the writings of seventeenth-century Puritan divines.

Historic Congregationalism came in two different forms, Horton argued. In "Congregationalism A," the distinguishing mark was complete local church autonomy; "Congregationalism B" emphasized "fellowship" and mutual obligation between churches. Neither was completely right or wrong: the difference between the two was a matter of time and changing circumstances. Although the first form may have worked "in the days of an agrarian economy, when the village was the pivotal point of the nation's life," Horton said, modern times required more unity and sophistication, "in order to out-guess and out-maneuver anti-Christian forces which are organized at higher levels than that of the village or local district."[51] The difference was between Pilgrims and Puritans in fact: on the one side were Robert Browne and the Plymouth Separatists with the simple belief that every congregation should be fully independent, and on the other were the true founders of the Congregational Way, the Puritans who remained in England, hoping to reform the English church. The "mighty William Ames," the great Calvinist theologian known for his magisterial *Marrow of Sacred Divinity* (1642), who thought about church polity on a broad scale, recognized the importance of accountability structures and mutual support. He was Congregationalism's true founding father, not John Robinson and his tiny band of Pilgrim Separatists.[52]

The battle was on. In November 1950, the antimerger Committee for the Continuation of Congregational Christian Churches issued a letter and pamphlet arguing that "Congregationalism B" was fundamentally alien to the history of the tradition, which they argued centered on the original polity of Plymouth Rock. "Congregationalism A is the original historic form envisioned by Browne, Robinson and Hooker," a Buffalo layman declared, and Horton's argument was a "distinct departure from first principles." "Dr. Horton chooses to ignore beginnings," a Philadelphia businessman complained. Horton's convoluted argument about seventeenth-century polity amounted to little more than "a stout Presbyterian body under a Pilgrim's cape."[53]

Behind their disagreements, however, the supporters of both Congregationalisms A and B shared two important assumptions: they all believed that history would provide the final answer in the debate, and that the only history that really mattered took place in the seventeenth century. In that sense, the merger debate followed in the grand tradition of Congregational historiography from the early nineteenth century on. All of the important questions were about origins—the "primitive time" of the Pilgrim and Puritan fathers. Almost no one looked to the development of Congregational history in the seventeenth, eighteenth, or nineteenth centuries.

Historian Roland Bainton, who served as an advisor in the *Cadman* case, perhaps summed it up best. "The facts plainly indicate," he wrote to Wendell Fifield (a merger supporter) in 1952, "that throughout the centuries Congregationalism has preserved a fixed continuity in the midst of the flexibility of change. At a great number of points we have plainly departed from the pattern of the founders." Yet, Bainton went on, "History does not settle this question"; it only opened the door into an endless series of philosophical puzzles. "What for example is Christianity? Is any body which is descended organically from the parent stock and considers itself Christian so to be regarded? Or is the New Testament pattern to be taken as a norm?"[54] When all was said and done, history proved itself a thoroughly ambiguous tool, with few, if any, concrete answers to matters of religious belief and doctrine.

USHERING IN THE NEW

The Congregational Christian Churches gathered for one of their last times together in 1956, in a meeting that was fraught with difficulty. Merger opponents were threatening another round in court and, short of that, of employing a range of parliamentary procedures to slow the momentum. In fact, before the delegates could vote to authorize the final steps toward union with the Evangelical and Reformed Church, they sat through an all-night reading of the Executive Committee minutes, covering every meeting from 30 June 1954 to 6 April 1956, in a measure pushed by opponents suspicious of backroom maneuvering. Even after the merger decision passed—decisively but not unanimously—denominational officials on both sides faced another wearying and potentially explosive round of negotiations. The hard task of breaking down and reassembling missionary organizations and ministers' pension funds and all the machinery of church government lay before them.[55]

History would, in fact, have the last word. The address by moderator Albert Buckner Coe echoed a centuries-old tradition of Puritan jeremiads, mirroring the ambivalence of the room. On the one hand, he delivered a lengthy and at times triumphalist survey of Congregational Christian achievements in the ecumenical movement and in progressive social causes. On the other, he offered a frank assessment of the denomination's spiritual and theological failure. "Here and there a bright evangelical light shone abroad," he said, "but by and large our people became weak in the faith, flabby in their profession and cold in their affirmation." The last word for the Congregational Christian Churches had to be one of repentance. "We have all been in error, in each generation. None is blameless." The only hope was Christ, who would "show the way through the darkness of a changing world."[56]

Others saw a more triumphal historical trajectory. Reinhold Niebuhr declared the formation of the UCC a "landmark in American Religious history," opening "hope of order" out of the chaos of pluralism. The *Christian Century* agreed that the world was witnessing a "milestone in our spiritual history," reversing a 300-year trend of division.[57] To Henry Van Dusen, the denominational union was a major victory against 2,000 years of acrimony, division, and schism. "It is as though the powerful surface currents" which had caused Christians to drift apart, had given way to "deep under-surface tides" of unity. At that signal moment in 1957, Christianity was "more fully one" that at "any previous date in its history."[58]

Indeed, the past had lost its power. Carl Schneider, professor emeritus of the Evangelical and Reformed Church's Eden Theological Seminary, rejoiced that in the UCC merger "faith was taking prescience over history." At its core, the ecumenical movement, he said, "challenges the denominations of our day to justify the perpetuation of their cherished traditions— however hallowed they may have become." "We therefore eagerly listen," he said, "for the overtones of faith to drown out the lingering undertones of history that disturb the free rhythm of the eternal Spirit."[59]

Others saw an important line of continuity shattered. In June 1957, the League to Uphold Congregational Principles called for a meeting "to make an act of contrition and rededication." "We shall recognized that our historic faith and practice have been too much neglected and too little understood among us," and our "loyalty to it has been too faint and too intermittent." A Litany of Re-Affirmation distributed to the dissenting churches took the form of a covenant, with promises to "bear witness to freedom under God in voluntary fellowship with others in the church local and in the church universal," and to follow after the example of "the apostles, martyrs, saints, and reformers who thought it good to count all else loss that they might proclaim the infinite riches of a free faith in a Father God."[60]

The Evangelical and Reformed and Congregational Christian churches finally consummated their union in 1957, convinced that they were beginning something entirely new in the history of Christianity. God not only had "appointed [them] for a special witness in this day," the leaders of the Uniting General Synod declared, but had summoned them to "outdo [their] past in every ministry of worship, of Christian nurture, and of dedication to the broadening and deepening of God's kingdom." The union of two denominations had brought together "treasures old and new." The old, "we intend to conserve," but the new was a source of "limitless anticipation," a moment of new beginnings. Fittingly, the editorial cartoon in the *Cleveland Plain Dealer* pictured the occasion as a "blessed event," with a brand new baby swinging peacefully from the beak of an arriving stork.[61]

What would history mean in the years and decades after 1957? In 1960, with much fanfare, Pilgrim Press (by then an arm of the UCC) reissued historian Williston Walker's *Creeds and Platforms of Congregationalism*, this time with an introduction by Douglas Horton. Tellingly, the book had been out of print since 1925, and no doubt it deserved reintroduction (1960 was the centennial of Walker's birth), but the new version was an awkward hybrid of new and old. Oddly, the reprint retained the same nineteenth-century typeface and dense Victorian prose of Walker's commentary, an exact duplicate of the original published in 1893. Even more paradoxically, the text focused heavily on early sixteenth-century Separatists, the heroes of merger opponents, and ended inconclusively with a "Commission Creed" cobbled together in 1883. In other words, it offered little historical justification for Congregationalism's more ecumenical twentieth-century path.

An even stranger mystery surrounded the republication of the short, upbeat account written by Gaius Glenn Atkins in 1947, popularized as *An Adventure in Liberty* and issued with a picture of two Pilgrims on the cover. Atkins's final paragraphs were a paean to the "liberty of the common man" and the danger of "ecclesiastical machinery," and not surprisingly, the book found its most loyal readership among merger opponents. "To me," Malcolm Burton wrote in 1978, "this statement by Dr. Atkins stressed the same kind of permanent values in Congregationalism that we tried to set forth" decades earlier. Burton even professed to remember Atkins, saying he wrote the book "as [his] lick against this—merger." ("It is in contrast to the beautiful language that usually came from the pen and lips of Dr. Atkins, but it probably showed his very deep feeling in the matter," Burton explained.) But subsequent editions published in 1950 and 1961, both by Pilgrim Press, mysteriously omitted that final ringing paragraph; closer inspection revealed that other smaller redactions supported Douglas Horton's view of Congregational polity, not Gaius Glenn Atkins's. To complete the outrage, the 1961 edition ended with a paragraph in praise of the United Church of Christ, described as the "crown" of all other twentieth-century achievements.[62]

Though history seemed to create as many problems as it cleared up, the past still held significant power for both sides of the merger dispute. In fact, in the years ahead, in both the dissenting National Association of Congregational Churches and the United Church of Christ, the past would fill an important role, but an ever more complicated and contradictory one as the years unfolded.

CHAPTER NINE

History and Mainline Protestants

The United Church of Christ Comes of Age

The 350th anniversary of the Pilgrims' landing in New England, observed in November 1970, was a telling moment for the two denominations that claimed their legacy. The *United Church Herald* of the UCC ran one brief article in its November issue, describing the Plymouth event as a "steppingstone." Reflecting a changing cultural awareness of the racial politics behind the first Thanksgiving, the *Herald* downplayed the role of northern Europeans in the settlement of New England, emphasizing that the Pilgrims' arrival in 1620 was one in a string of visits to the region's shores, beginning with the Native American crossing of the Bering Strait some 20,000 years before. The next notable event was a visit to Cape Cod by Thorwald Erickson (Leif's less famous and apparently more directionally challenged brother) in 1004 and then the discovery of Plymouth harbor by Spanish explorer Estevan Gomez centuries later. When the Pilgrims finally arrived in 1620, they came as "victims of intolerance" intent on establishing a community that "practiced democracy, independence and congregationalism [even] before they had been defined." The tone of the article was lively and earnest enough for a more tradition-minded church audience, but the artwork was hip and evocative, featuring woodcut images of sailing ships, bears, codfish, wild turkeys, and tall hats with buckles.[1]

The National Association of Congregational Christian Churches, formed in protest of the merger, began its celebration in February, at its midwinter meeting in Racine, Wisconsin. There the closing banquet was served by waiters and waitresses dressed in Pilgrim garb, the men in neck ruffles and tall hats of various shapes and the women in white caps, kerchiefs, and aprons. As the year unfolded, the editors of the *Congregationalist* emphasized over and over their denomination's role as the true keepers of the Pilgrim way. Over the months, they suggested to their readers various acts of observance: reflecting on the Mayflower Compact (noting defensively that "in this juvenile age of ours it is customary to scoff at the efforts of our ancestors, if indeed, we are even aware of them"), studying church bylaws to make sure they conformed to historic Congregational polity, and singing the reprinted tercentenary hymn based on the immortal words of John Robinson, "More Light Shall Break Forth from Thy Word." When November rolled around, the *Congregationalist* devoted its entire issue to unbarred praise of the Pilgrim heritage.[2]

The contrast between the two denominations suggests that perhaps the antimerger critics had been right all along: history did not survive in the United Church of Christ. After 1957, it appeared, Congregationalists' new life within the UCC allowed them to forget their Pilgrim past, even as the National Association's continuing unity required deeper allegiance to the rhetoric and symbols of the tradition.

But the problem was not the merger itself. If anything, as we have seen, the disputes of the 1940s and 1950s brought history emphatically to the forefront; by 1957, the Congregational churches were more acutely aware of their historic tradition than ever. Moreover, Congregational identity of a sort lived on in the UCC many years after the merger, though often in a truncated and defensive fashion. At the denomination's twenty-five-year anniversary in 1982, Martin Bailey, editor of *A.D.* magazine (then the main UCC periodical), noted ruefully that in New England, "it's a rare congregation that has actually changed its name." Most continued to identify themselves on signage and stationery as simply "Congregational."[3] Another twenty-five years later, when the UCC celebrated its semicentennial, little appeared to have changed. In fact, the *United Church News* featured a heated exchange about the "Often-Hidden, Sometimes-Missing, Parenthetical 'UCC'" among Congregational churches in the Northeast. "My thanks to the editor for having the guts, after 50 years, to point out the refusal of the Congregational side of the UCC" to fully accept the merger, a retired pastor griped. "As a member of a former Evangelical and Reformed church," a Minnesota laywoman agreed, "I resent Congregationalists hanging on to their names. Is it so important to be differentiated from the rest of us? . . . After 50 years," she said, "isn't it about time to change?"[4]

The names, of course, were symbols of continuity in churches that had traveled many spiritual and theological miles from their Puritan origins. In the twenty-first century, that staid white church on the town common was proudly multicultural, welcoming all races, all genders, and all sexual orientations. Perhaps even more tellingly, its members celebrated Lent and Advent with liturgies and printed prayers within sanctuaries complete with stained glass, a choir loft, and an altar rail. All this suggests not so much an abandonment of history, however, as a fundamental confusion about its role and purpose—a problem broadly true of most mainline churches today but particularly acute within the United Church of Christ, coming of age in unusually confusing times.

FIRST STEPS

It is tempting to write the history of the United Church of Christ as a series of bureaucratic problems and their solutions. Many of the church's official histories do just that, and perhaps rightly so. Though the denomination made a name for itself in public controversies over racial integration, women's ordination, and gay marriage, many of its most hotly argued controversies have been internal, as often as not about plans for institutional restructuring. The UCC comes by this preoccupation honestly, reflecting its origins as a complicated denominational merger and the enormous task confronting its first generation of leaders, creating de novo all of the mundane but necessary documents—constitutions and statements of faith as well as Sunday school curricula and ministers' manuals—that other Protestants had long taken for granted.

Not everything was brand new, of course. In the 1950s and early 1960s, as all the disparate pieces fell into place, the first denominational leaders were careful to place themselves within the line of Christian tradition. History loomed large from the start, in fact, in the very deliberate way the denomination selected its leadership and began to build its bureaucratic structure. The first go-round instituted two copresidents, Fred Hoskins and James Wagner, representing the Congregational Christian and Evangelical and Reformed churches, respectively; the twenty-four members of the Executive Council mirrored the same symmetry. Two ad hoc commissions, one to prepare a constitution and the other a statement of faith, also contained equal representation from both sides of the denominational union. Such visible markers of continuity were important. As Hoskins explained to the delegates at the Third General Synod in 1961, the UCC "is not so much a new church as it is a renewal, in unity, of the combining communions." The merger was not a disruption or end of denominational histories but a logical and faithful step forward.[5]

This spirit of consensus guided one important early decision. Instead of taking up the contentious question about the autonomy of local churches, UCC leaders shifted focus from polity to theology; the first task would be drafting a common statement of faith. The committee set to work in late October 1957, while the ink was barely dry on the merger agreement. In his preliminary statement, copresident James Wagner charged the members of the commission to create a standard "which all of us in the United Church can affirm to each other and to the world," and in "language which shall be sufficiently contemporary to speak to our present-day human condition and at the same time reflect so far as possible in its phraseology the great formulations of Christian faith and doctrine." Ancient Christian tradition would provide the grounds but not the limits of modern faith.[6]

The members of the commission worked through the witness of the past carefully and systematically. One of the participants, Mary Ellen Lyman, later recalled "how long a time the Commission spent in the study of history before it began its work of formulating a more modern statement." "Fully realizing that changes were needed if the new statement were to speak to our present age," she said, "we were guided to acknowledge our debt to the past." The statement of faith was to stir the emotions as well as the intellect, echoing the familiar language of the Bible, the "great utterances and prayers of the saints of the past," and other documents like the Book of Common Prayer.[7] Each member of the commission came to the first meeting having read the three-volume *Creeds of Christendom* by Philip Schaff, an exhaustive and annotated study by a nineteenth-century religious historian with roots in the German Reformed Church. They listened as seminary professors Roger Shinn, Walter Marshall Horton, and Elmer Arndt provided historical background of all the major Protestant creeds, from the Lutheran Augsburg Confession to the Reformed Heidelberg Catechism. The members also studied contemporary statements, including the Barmen Declaration of the German churches, written in protest to Nazi ideology, and the Batak Creed from Christians in Indonesia.[8]

Some voiced concerns about "conformity" and worried that these existing creeds would be a "limiting factor." But on the whole the vision was broad and deep. The goal was a theologically expansive platform that would not only appeal to UCC laypeople but would leave the door open for future ecumenical mergers. The UCC was to be both a "united and a uniting church," as Wagner and Hoskins wrote to Everett Parker, one of the participants. "We believe our present union, bringing together communions which represent two of the historic ecclesiastical polities, has changed a course which will be useful in further breaking down of the walls of denominational separation." Rather than act like "a little sect," another participant agreed, the UCC needed a creed which would "appeal to ecumenically minded people.[9]

This language would have been familiar to most of the people on the task force, especially those with connections to the broader ecumenical movement. In the aftermath of World War II, history and tradition were more important in the religious world than ever, but not in the usual way. In light of the spiritual challenges facing Christians—"acute, urgent, and desperately difficult," in historian Albert Outler's description—narrow denominational histories were an unaffordable indulgence. The day of "comparative ecclesiology," he declared, was long past.[10] What the world needed far more was broad understanding of the Christian tradition, as it had grown across geography, culture, and time. Accordingly, the Third Faith and Order Conference of the World Council of Churches, held at Lund, Sweden, in 1952, set two study groups to work, one European and the other North American, to take up the question of historic Christian unity. The Europeans focused primarily on doctrinal statements, but the American and Canadian group, populated largely by historians of religion, addressed Outler's challenge, calling for a bigger, more inclusive story of "God's actions in His world in calling together and building up a covenant-community." Only this way would Christians be able to put aside their old differences, to "overcome history by history" itself.[11]

With this goal in mind, the UCC commission spent nearly two years composing the statement of faith, much of the work done in a cramped hotel room near the Pittsburgh airport. When the finished product finally appeared in March 1959, Fred Hoskins praised its respect for Christian tradition. "All through it one hears the voices of the faithful through the ages chanting the historic confessions of the 'Faith delivered once and for all.'" John C. Bennett, dean of Union Seminary, praised its contemporary feel, "a positive affirmation of 'Biblical faith' in the modern era."[12] Secular news reporters attempted to follow suit. "It upholds most of the traditional doctrines of Christianity," the Associated Press declared, "but does so in up-to-date terminology rather than the customary language." The Baltimore Sun, not quite sure what criteria to use in evaluating the new statement, reported that at 231 "mostly one-syllable words," it was at least twice as long as the Apostles' Creed (111 words) and just 4 words longer than the Nicene (227).[13]

The churches responded with enthusiasm, affirming the statement unanimously at the Second General Synod, held in Oberlin, Ohio. The writers were very clear that the new statement was not "a substitute for the ancient creeds, covenants and confessions" but was meant to "underscore the continuity of the faith held among us," said the United Church Herald, the new denominational journal. "The use of this statement does mean that the United Church of Christ does take seriously the task of expressing the historic faith, which we share, in our own words and, we trust, in words that will speak to the hearts and minds of our contemporaries."[14]

Letters to the editor show that laypeople and clergy were clearly moved by the achievement: "I have clipped out the new proposed Statement of Faith," a Pennsylvania churchman wrote. "Each time I have read it carefully, only to wonder again at the beauty of its language and the perfection of its message. It is a most remarkable piece of work." "I read it again and again," a denominational official from Florida confessed. "I spoke it aloud, imagining myself part of a worshiping congregation. The spell was not broken. Rather the charm deepened: how could such plain-spoken truths be so liturgically satisfying, how could prose be so poetic?"[15]

The new denomination's next hurdle was more prosaic, however. Drafting a constitution was going to be a complicated and messy task, threatening to reignite painful memories of the merger battles.[16] Not surprisingly, then, Fred Hoskins encouraged the commission on the constitution to look ahead rather than behind. "Our situation is similar to that of the children of Israel," he said, "who when brought to the river Jordan by Joshua were told, 'you have not passed this way before.'" In short, the United Church of Christ was "one of the most significant events in American Protestantism . . . to occur thus far in the twentieth century."[17]

Indeed, the constitution's most significant success was laying to rest, for a time, the central controversy of the merger years, prohibiting any attempts to impair "the autonomy of any congregation or local church in the management of its own affairs." This was enough to satisfy most critics at the time, though the subtle ambiguities of these statements would surface in the future. As historian Barbara Brown Zikmund wrote on the occasion of the UCC's twenty-fifth anniversary in 1982, "It was not clear when we came into being in 1957 how our *presbyterian* delegated powers and our *congregational* local church autonomy could mix," and now, decades later, "it is still not clear how patterns of authority and freedom will continue." Quietly, decades of passionate argument and centuries of tradition had faded into general acceptance of ambiguity.[18]

Up through its first decade, then, the UCC cut a strong profile as a mainline Protestant denomination with ecumenical goals and an active social conscience. One of the founding convictions of the UCC's constitution was the sin of racial segregation, which meant in practical terms dismantling the old Convention of the South, home since 1931 to all black congregations from both the Congregational and Christian side of the denomination. "It is crystal clear that the UCC does not and will not bless racial discrimination in any form," copresidents Fred Hoskins and James Wagner informed the E&R Synod presidents and Congregational Christian conference executives.[19] In 1963, the synod voted on a resolution proposed by Board of Homeland Ministries president Truman Douglass to withhold all financial aid to churches and related institutions with segregated memberships. After four hours of angry debate, the resolution lost by a vote of 232 to 204; it took another impassioned plea by UCC president Ben Herbster for the measure to pass, finally, by a vote of 308 to 129.[20]

On the whole, however, the early years of the UCC saw relatively little internal drama, especially compared with decades previous. Without a doubt, the new denomination was liberal both socially and theologically but not combatively so. Early issues of the *United Church Herald* bordered almost on the prosaic, with regular features on work camps in inner cities and cross-racial friendships, the fund-raising projects of women's organizations and new materials for Sunday schools. In many ways, UCC laypeople were quintessential "golden rule" Christians, living by a simple ethic of "doing good to others" and far more interested in concrete church and community projects than personal piety or evangelism.[21] In 1958, for example, a story about laymen's study groups praised their "informal and relaxed" approach to "the religious problems of today." The article described the practical issues the men of Butler, Ohio, found interesting, most of them, not surprisingly given their rural location, about agriculture and industry: "Does a farmer have a right to cut production below his ability to produce? Does the factory worker have such a right? Is a 'slow down' ever morally justified?" In Pittsburgh, where the men's group included several realtors, the members addressed a current social issue head-on, trying (ultimately unsuccessfully) to settle a black family in a white neighborhood. In Seattle, the men were interested in "ideas about God," that is, where they came from and whether they "pass through the same evolution or development which we find taking place in the Bible."[22]

A NEW NARRATIVE

The UCC Statement of Faith proved immensely popular with laypeople, who quickly adapted it to a variety of forms. Some set it to music, while others incorporated it into devotional reading; the Statement of Faith also wove its way into countless sermons and seminary student papers. In fact, in 1971, a church youth group in Florida decided to rephrase it into "language more familiar and meaningful to youth"; the updated results were read out loud alongside the original at the synod gathering. Thus, the original—"We believe in God, the Eternal Spirit, Father of Our Lord Jesus Christ and our Father, and to his deeds we testify"—became "We live by God who we cannot define, put in a box or circumscribe. He is the Father of Jesus Christ, our brother, and regarding his deeds, we tell it like it is." And continuing, further down, the original, "He judges men and nations by his righteous will declared through prophets and apostles," was paraphrased as "Some good guys long ago gave us some fine rules which still help men and nations to know when they are with it." Instead of "Blessing and honor, glory and power be unto him. Amen," the statement concluded with "God is far out! Right on! Amen."[23] This was likely not a version the scholars holed up in the Pittsburgh hotel room some ten years earlier would have envisioned—but by 1971 the United Church of Christ was in the midst of a rapid and profound transformation.

Indeed, the entire world was changing. During the 1960s, as sociologist Hugh McLeod writes, "history moved faster," and old institutions and traditions found themselves powerless in its wake, with less and less to offer.[24] Anthropologist Margaret Mead has described the generation of the 1960s as the "firstborn in a new country," living in a technological and social world their parents struggled to comprehend. Not only were they far more educated—85 percent of the 1960s generation had completed high school, compared with 38 percent of their parents, and half of them would go on to college—they also experimented with behaviors unthinkable to people raised during the Depression and World War II.[25] Between 1969 and 1982, over barely more than a decade, the percentage of Americans who approved of premarital sex grew from 24 to 62 percent.[26]

The same was true of the nation's religious infrastructure. From historically high levels of church participation in the 1950s, when 75 percent of Americans agreed that religion was "very important" to them personally, the pews were becoming empty. In eleven years, between 1958 and 1969, weekly attendance dropped from 49 to 42 percent, "by far the largest decline on this measure ever recorded in such a brief period."[27] To a profound degree, the shift was generational. Among Americans over age fifty, the decline in religious observance was minimal; yet among those aged eighteen to twenty-nine, the change was dramatic. By one measure, for example, weekly church attendance among young adults fell by half between 1957 and 1971, from 51 to 28 percent. Even though over time those baby boomers inched back into church, they would never come close to matching the religious loyalties of their parents' generation.[28]

The suddenness and scale of these changes defy any simple explanation. There is no "master-factor," says McLeod, that will explain the "momentous and mysterious" forces at work. Certainly, a combination of events—the affluence of the post–World War II era, the civil rights movement, the Vietnam War, and Vatican II—contributed to the scale and pace of change, as old invisible lines separating proper behavior from improper suddenly collapsed. McLeod describes this "short and sharp cultural revolution" as a turning point in Western history when for the first time Christianity no longer provided people with a sense of self or a collective identity. In fact, no other institution, political or economic or cultural, rose to take its place. The "end of Christendom," as British sociologist Callum Brown calls it, signaled a broad and permanent shift toward an ethic of individualism and self-realization.[29]

The history of the United Church of Christ, especially after 1963, unfolded within this framework. On the one hand, the new social freedom of the era provided ample room for the new denomination to make its mark. Unlike many other Protestant denominations, the UCC simply had no "old guard" protesting that "we've never done it this way before." This made it possible, for example, for a Maryland church to celebrate its anniversary in 1971 with a "community dialogue on urban problems" led by a visiting German sociologist. The congregation also awarded $1,600 in prizes for a "nationwide contest to create new church music."[30] On the other, however, the new world of the 1960s left many people simply puzzled, confused, and in the end alienated from their own churches. "Why all the interest in way-out worship and hippie-style sessions at the church conferences?" a layperson wrote in to the "Ask the Pastor" column in the *United Church Herald* in 1969. "Why is church money being spent on pornographic films and plays?" another wondered. "I understand that films and plays involving nakedness and lovemaking have been a part of the World Council meeting in Sweden and the United Church of Christ conference at Notre Dame." The pastor-cum-answer-man, Reverend Robert Eugene Crawford from Detroit's Bushnell Church, answered each one courteously but firmly. To the last question, he simply replied that "Polite, well-scrubbed approaches to stately religion are out," and "experimental attempts to evoke perceptive insights about reality are in. This is not easy for us to get used to," he admitted, concluding that "it makes a lot more sense to our children than it does to us."[31]

After the Seventh General Synod, held in Boston in 1969, even these small certainties dwindled. That year, the opening session was disrupted by a protest by black clergy from the United Church Ministers for Racial and Social Justice, led by James Forman, a veteran of the black power movement. When Forman came forward to speak, the synod erupted into an uproar. Just weeks before, in the early morning of 11 June, Forman and the National Black Economic Development Conference occupied 475 Riverside Drive, the "nerve center" of mainline Protestant social outreach. Previously the group had attempted to occupy the headquarters of the United Presbyterian Church and the United Methodist offices and had called all black and Puerto Rican employees to go on strike. On 11 June, the group had marched to the headquarters of the UCC's Board for World Ministries (BWM) and occupied it for the next six days. As the situation dragged on, it disrupted the flow of BWM donations overseas, and tempers rose. The impasse ended temporarily when, with the help of the court system, the UCC agreed to conduct a national meeting of black leaders, focusing especially on churches. As of 18 June, the crisis looked to be over.[32]

Then came the demonstration at the synod, just a week later. The demands from Forman and the black clergy took center stage in the proceedings, "against a backdrop of tension and anxiety," as one eyewitness put it. The spokesmen of the group, Reverend Edwin Edmonds from New Haven, Connecticut, reassured the delegates that "we do not advocate overthrow of the nation"—a phrase from Forman's manifesto of the previous week. But the black pastors did raise formidable demands, many of which were then taken up at the Boston synod, including instituting a Commission for Racial Justice with a guaranteed budget, giving over to African Americans leadership of the southern black colleges under the American Missionary Association, divesting from South African financial institutions, and directing denominational business toward black-owned publishing and printing industries. The demands may seem fully justified in retrospect, but in 1969 they were to many frighteningly uncharted territory. Reverend Albert Cleage, of the Shrine of the Black Madonna in Detroit, emphasized that change was in the "self-interest" of the predominantly white denomination. Powerless people, he warned, "are a dangerous people."[33]

Though many laypeople were confused and angry, the shock of confrontation brought a permanent change of direction. No longer just a liberal, ecumenically minded group, the United Church of Christ would become a leading voice for radical social causes. In 1971, the Commission on Racial Justice sent Reverend Ben Chavis to support the "Wilmington Ten," nine young black men and one white woman arrested during a protest over discrimination in the city's public schools. Arrested and convicted of arson and conspiracy (in the course of the demonstration, a grocery store caught fire), the protesters were sentenced to long prison terms. The continued agitation among local UCC churches finally led to a successful appeal of the original conviction in 1980. The UCC also aided Cesar Chavez and the United Farm Workers in their boycott against the Nestlé Corporation and supported the campaign against South African apartheid. In 1970, the denomination called for the repeal of laws against abortion and in the following year established a Task Force on Women in Church and Society, later a permanent Coordinating Center for Women. The UCC became the first, and for a long time the only, denomination to support gay rights, with the ordination of William Johnson in 1971.[34]

HISTORY AS PROBLEM

If the 1960s and 1970s were bewildering and challenging years for the mainline churches, the 1980s and 1990s bordered on disastrous. As new evangelical churches swelled with members, money, and political influence, the old-line Protestant denominations diminished, losing numbers by the hundreds of thousands, closing down denominational offices, and all too often finding themselves on the losing end of battles in Washington.

In one sense, the mainline churches were the victims of their own success: by the late twentieth century, their values were so closely aligned with American culture—and vice versa, of course—that church membership seemed in many respects almost unnecessary. One could be an ethical, conscientious citizen without taking on the ideological baggage of institutional religion, and in a society increasingly averse to membership in any kind of social groups—whether Rotary Clubs, political parties, or bowling leagues—it is not surprising that mainline Protestant churches were some of the first to feel the loss.[35]

Yet even as boundaries blurred, in many mainline Protestant denominations they became more contentious. By the time Methodists celebrated the 250th anniversary of founder John Wesley's conversion in 1988—often referred to as "the Aldersgate" experience—even the basic facts about the story were under dispute. To some, it was Wesley's defining moment, marking the birth of Methodism; others saw it as one in a series of personal crises or "reconversions" that began with a powerful spiritual encounter three years earlier. Some found the story genuinely inspirational, while others warned that it dangerously oversimplified a complex human experience, imposing "impossible expectations about the Christian life." Indifference was hardly a problem: as Wesley scholar Randy Maddox noted wryly, the 1988 commemoration "may well be remembered more for the renewed vigor it brought to debate about the meaning of this event than for any of its celebrations."[36]

Similar disagreements faced Presbyterians when they adopted a new statement of faith in 1967. The new version was brief and clear, and as one supporter enthused, it was written in "simple idiomatic English" in a form that "the entire church can understand and enjoy." The Westminster Confession, with its archaic, seventeenth-century language, was no longer "a fully authoritative expression of the faith of our church."[37] Conservatives vehemently disagreed. Though the new confession was published as part of a collection of historic Christian creeds, they saw their denomination as deserting its ancient faith. "Many in this decade of violent change," said a California pastor, "feel that our Church is in danger of breaking continuity with its Biblical heritage." As the "highwater mark" of Presbyterian orthodoxy, Westminster's authority was undiminished across the ages.[38]

The United Church of Christ was in many ways no different, though its battle over tradition unfolded, rather typically, in the form of a long dispute among bureaucratic insiders. The basic issue was much the same as in the 1950s: the relationship of the UCC to its predecessor bodies, the Congregational Christians and the Evangelical and Reformed churches. Behind this, however, was the more fundamental question of the denomination's identity and purpose: What would distinguish the UCC from all other denominations?

INSTITUTIONAL HISTORY

The conversation started in earnest in 1963, when denominational leaders announced plans to form a new group dedicated to preserving the history of the United Church of Christ. Both of the existing historical societies from the Evangelical and Reformed and the Congregational Christian churches had continued on after the merger, with no apparent intention of disbanding. By the early 1960s, however, this was a holdover that could no longer be tolerated. As Ben Herbster reminded the leaders of both organizations, separate historical societies no longer served the interests of the UCC, "since we conceive of ourselves, irrespective of background, as one church." The denomination would "not look favorably upon allocating funds for the operations of the two societies," he warned, urging them to consider a new structure to "symbolize the unity of our overall work" and our "total historical interests."[39]

Problems began almost immediately. At the first meeting of the new Historical Commission, as it was called, the members found that though they had been budgeted $15,000 for their work, they were unlikely to receive it. The denomination was already low on funds.[40] The commission itself was equally low on energy and morale. They had been given the task of planning for the 450th anniversary of the Protestant Reformation in 1967, an event coinciding with the tenth anniversary of the UCC, but the Commission members simply could not muster common enthusiasm for the program.[41]

The possibility of a vigorous historical society dedicated to the story of the United Church of Christ grew dimmer as years passed. The first newsletter issued by the Historical Commission began with a solidly conservative "Word from the Chairman," declaring that the "separate but united task" of the historical societies was to "make certain that under the excitement of a new venture, a venture of faith, the great contributions of the Fathers are not lost or forgotten."[42] By the time of the Pilgrim anniversary in 1970, the disconnect between the goals of UCC leadership and those of the Historical Commission was obvious and painful. When the commission planned a celebration in Plymouth that promised only to unearth the old Congregational tradition of Forefathers' Day, UCC president Robert Moss urged them to find a way to contribute to the whole, to "provide historical background for the priorities which the General Synod sets for the Church." He encouraged them to address contemporary issues like "peace, amnesty, youth and racial justice." Given the possibility that the General Synod would be addressing the status of women at its upcoming meeting, why not provide some research about the role of Congregationalists in the suffrage movement? Or for that matter about the role of the Evangelical and Reformed Church in it?[43]

In 1975, the Historical Commission became the Historical Council, a step forward but not all that far. The council now answered directly to the Executive Council and the president and had no power to nominate its members or determine its budget. The original members of the commission interpreted the move as a lack of confidence in their work, as one of the members wrote to Robert Moss. Already suffering from "low morale," they were not optimistic about the priorities of the "organizational hierarchy." Clearly, history was a subject in which the UCC chose to "invest little . . . money or interest."[44] In response, Moss's spokesman admitted that it was "in the backwaters of denominational concern" but promised "more denominational attention and involvement with the preservation of our history and with a respect for our tradition. Although this may seem farfetched," he urged, the new bureaucratic arrangement could finally "crystallize our identity as a United Church of Christ."[45]

To Moss and other denominational leaders, the time was right for a new emphasis on history—as long as it took place after 1957. In his marching orders to the council, he emphasized the need to look forward rather than behind. The last General Synod, he observed in 1976, was the first in which "delegates did not appeal to the C.C. past or the E. and R. past as arguments on the issues we faced." To Moss, this suggested that "we have reached the stage where we have a new identity, and sense of unity informed by the traditions which have shaped us as well as the experience and struggle of these last nine to ten years of life together."[46]

Members of the commission continued to resist. Their mission, they believed, was "to make an essential contribution to the denomination's understanding of its identity through the cultivation of the various heritages represented throughout the church."[47] In a position paper issued in 1976, the Historical Council announced its intention to "insure continued fidelity to the guiding principles and abiding traditions of the UCC and its predecessors." History offered "reason to confess their sins and inadequacies as well as grounds for celebration and thanksgiving." The penciled-in comments by one of the council members on a preliminary draft were less nuanced: "For the denomination to forget its multiple heritage roots in its enthusiasm for unity and new directions," he said, "will be comparable to the second generation American of a newer ethnic background who wishes to forget and obliterate his past. . . . This will inevitably happen in the UCC unless it is wise enough to highly value what it already possesses."[48]

The doggedness of Historical Council members did pay off in some respects, especially with the infusion of new leadership and energy in the 1980s. As the decade began, the council began publishing its own periodical, the *Historical Intelligencer*, an effort to "remind" the churches of their denominational roots. Enthusiastically endorsed by President Avery Post in its inaugural issue, the *Intelligencer* was an interesting mix of practical advice to local church record keepers and historical articles about the denominational traditions predating the formation of the UCC. Much of the impetus came from Barbara Brown Zikmund, an accomplished church historian and later president of the Pacific School of Religion in Berkeley, California. She also wrote a two-volume series on the denomination's "hidden histories," a collection of scholarly essays presenting a racially and ethnically diverse array of stories about deaconesses, missionaries, evangelists, and social reformers in all four of the UCC's preceding denominations. This new approach honored both the past and the present, the need for knowledge of the past and the need for historical relevance. "Without diminishing the unity of our church," she told a public gathering at the 1981 synod (cosponsored by the Historical Council and the Coordinating Center for Women), "we will benefit through these encounters with our diversity."[49]

Not everyone agreed, however. In the denomination's most socially progressive circles, history was more enemy than ally, and all those statements about tradition and theology were thinly veiled attempts to slow down social progress. "Frequently, groups within the UCC use words like 'erosion,' 'pragmatism,' 'cultural captivity,' and even 'apostasy' and 'heresy' to express negative feelings about programs or leadership in our church," James Smucker, an advocate of Christians for Justice Action, wrote in 1985. "There follows an appeal to history and past creeds and confessions as the basis and norm for action today. We wonder how much listening is being done," he said. "Are the new voices of our day being heard? Or is the tendency to write new statements that defend the past an effort to ignore the possibility of the Spirit leading in strange new ways and places?" "The point is not to ignore history," he said, but to be "freed from it." "There are many who experience the truth in different ways and they should not be judged by adherence to past expressions of faith."[50]

By that time, however, the debate had broadened far beyond two sides, one in favor of history and the other not. A denominational task force, reporting in 1977, admitted that though the denomination was "known (and respected or vilified) for its courageous and controversial stands on ecumenism, racial justice, war, women's rights, labor rights, broadcasting licenses, multi-national corporations, and gay rights," the UCC was losing its way. Despite the good intentions behind the denomination's "vigorous social witness," the report continued, "the United Church of Christ also seems to have scattered its energies so frenetically in pursuing many new causes than an enervation of spirit and aimlessness have set in." The task force called for serious examination of the "implications for the tradition as a useful past," urging a new and more serious attention to the UCC Statement of Faith and constitution as well as the creeds and confessions of the Protestant Reformation and early church.[51] Another set of statements and declarations came in the early 1980s, from a range of different groups within the denomination, urging "sustained rethinking of our theological traditions (as reflected in the various traditions behind the United Church) to see how that tradition can be reappropriated in faithful and fresh ways as a discipline and resource for our life and faith." Too often, declared the thirty-nine seminary professors and theologians, all cosigners of a document addressed to the UCC Executive Council, theology was driven by "happenstance without the discipline and guidance offered to us in our theological tradition. We believe that a reconsideration of the historic and confessional roots of our church would greatly serve the mind of the church in these confused and conflicted areas." The group urged a "critical refocus on the gifts and claims of the gospel as mediated through our history of confessions, creeds, and platforms."[52]

A NEW, STRANGE SONG

All of the ambivalence, confusion, and worry about history within the UCC came to a head in 1995 with the publication of *The New Century Hymnal* (*NCH*). Here was a project, says historian Steven Marini, "designed to test the limits of a denomination's liturgical practice and indeed its own self-understanding."[53] The goal was simple, to produce an up-to-date hymnal specifically designed for use by UCC congregations, and it was well warranted. Until 1995, most churches had to juggle a mixture of old and relatively new: the old *Pilgrim Hymnal* of the Congregationalists, last published in 1958; the *Hymnal* of the Evangelical and Reformed Church, published in 1940; or the *Hymnal of the United Church of Christ*, published in 1974. But the larger purpose, and the one that quickly mired the *New Century Hymnal* in bitter controversy, was to provide hymnody in line with the General Synod's directive of 1973, requiring nonsexist, inclusive language in all the denomination's published material. This meant, at a bare minimum, removing specifically masculine language—the "men of God" would become "the people of God," for example. But as the *NCH* went through various iterations in the hands of various committees, it took a far broader view of its original marching orders.

Many of the changes involved simply updating old words and old metaphors. The *NCH* committee removed all of the "thees" and "thous" from hymn texts and reworded obscure references—"Here I raise mine Ebenezer, Hither by thy help I'm come" in one familiar nineteenth-century tune became "Here I pause in my sojourning, Giving thanks for having come."[54] Changes like these, the committee members reasoned, would make old songs more understandable and, in the end, more spiritually meaning-ful.[55] The *NCH*'s editors argued that rewording old hymns would reinvigor-ate them and ensure their continued popularity. And, after all, hadn't earlier generations rewritten their hymnody many times over?

But—and here was where critics protested—the committee also updated the wording of hymns to fit contemporary sensibilities. Not only did this involve rewording references to the old theory of the substitu-tionary atonement, that Christ's blood paid the price for sinners' salva-tion, it also meant omitting hierarchical language of any kind, including the word "Lord" to refer to the deity. Heaven was no longer "above" and the earth "beneath," and God was neither he nor she. As one critic com-plained, "someone totally unfamiliar with Jesus Christ would need to look very hard at many texts before being able to determine his gender."[56]

No arcane theological disagreement, the hymnal controversy became a powerful symbolic dispute. Much of the response was viscerally emotional, echoing laments from the now-forgotten disputes about the merger in the 1950s. "While there is much good in this new collection," an observer at the 1993 synod wrote, "what has been done to the traditional concepts creates a painful loss." These feelings often came to a peak at Christmas and Easter, when congregations suddenly discovered alternate wording to familiar and beloved old hymns.[57] After protracted struggle and by a ruling of the General Synod, the final version of the *NCH* restored the traditional language for God; but that change did relatively little to stave off a wave of controversy when the hymnal was introduced to the UCC pastors and laity.

Very quickly the *New Century Hymnal* became a defining issue both within and outside the denomination. In 1996, it hit the pages of *Newsweek* when religion editor Kenneth Woodward (a practicing Roman Catholic) publically took the *NCH* and its "hymn doctors" to task, not only for their awkwardly bowdlerized hymn texts, but for promoting an entirely "new religion," one without the fundamental Christian affirmation that "Jesus is Lord." Others joined his critique. Woodward contributed an essay to the book *How Shall We Sing the Lord's Song*, a full-out protest against the hymnal's theological agenda. Citing the overwhelmingly positive response of *Newsweek* readers to his critique, Woodward wondered why UCC offi-cials would "violate the integrity of the old hymns." Did they really feel that "they have arrived at an advanced state of linguistic purity denied benighted believers of earlier generations? If so," said Woodward, "then say it plain: we are better than they were. If you wish to honor those who, creating out of their own time and experience, wrote hymns found worthy to be sung at worship, do you honor them by retroactively cleaning up their acts? Does their faith witness make no claims on those who come after? Have UCC officials no fear at all that someday someone will clean up their act?"[58]

Fair or not, the criticisms of the *New Century Hymnal* tapped into a larger sense of uncertainty within the United Church of Christ, coming into sharp focus during the 1980s and 1990s as the denomination's membership and financial resources declined drastically. Certainly, in many respects, history was alive and well: the *Living Theological Heritage of the United Church of Christ* came out in installments during the 1990s and early 2000s, as a set of seven hefty volumes of primary source material documenting the tradition back to the early Christian church and up through the first four decades of the UCC. But most of the editors worked with the conviction that they were swimming against a heavy tide. The real danger to the UCC, said Reinhard Ulrich, editor of volume one, was not "theological intransigence" but "losing [its] identity as a distinctly Christian community." The UCC as a denomination was in "grave danger," historian Charles Hambrick-Stowe agreed, of "unrooted ahistorical idiosyncrasy" and "sect-like isolation" from the rest of the Christian world.[59]

CONCLUSION

The United Church of Christ had come a long way in a surprisingly short span of time, from the grand ecumenical vision of the late 1950s and early 1960s to the specter of sectarianism in the 1990s. In many ways, the denomination's identity problem was unique, reflecting its unusual beginning as a merger between two Protestant traditions with substantial differences in style and structure. And no doubt the vexed relationship with the past was also an emotional consequence of the merger years, an angry and painful episode that did little to inspire nostalgia among those who had lived through it.

In other ways, however, the UCC's relationship with its past is broadly universal. Few mainline Protestants today, one would hazard a guess, could say much about their denomination's history or any of its doctrinal or organizational distinctions. Certainly, some of this reflects the general dearth of history in American society, our emphatic orientation to the new and improved, and it also reflects the lack of religious "literacy" in the population at large. Survey after survey has shown that few Americans— even regular churchgoers—have much basic knowledge about the Bible, let alone could explain the theological differences between a Calvinist and an Arminian, or even a Catholic or a Protestant. If the voluminous output of nineteenth-century religious publishing houses is any indication, Protestants a century ago genuinely enjoyed parsing denominational distinctions, perhaps even more than arguing points of doctrine. Fortunately or unfortunately, this is not so today. The historical profession, now broken down into a myriad of specialties and subspecialties, has not helped much either. Sweeping epics, or for that matter up-to-date and readable histories of particular denominations, are few and far between.

The historylessness also reflects the increasingly transient nature of American religion itself. Few churches are composed of lifetime Presbyterians or Methodists or Baptists or Congregationalists; denominational switching is now the rule rather than the exception. The United Church of Christ may be one of the most eclectic, in fact, with some 40 percent of its new members coming from Roman Catholic backgrounds.[60]

All this does not mean that history has disappeared from mainline churches, however. If anything, it has endured with surprising persistence, surfacing everywhere, from debates over the meaning of Wesley's Aldersgate experience to updating the Westminster Confession to the gender-neutral language of the *New Century Hymnal*. There is no doubt that past legacies are a powerful, though often unarticulated, presence in denominational and congregational life today. Indeed, in these days of religious roaming, yearning for connection with the past seems to be growing stronger. "Retraditioning" has become a familiar word in mainline churches, though it comes with a variety of meanings. Some popular authors like Marcus Borg and John Shelby Spong have urged Christians to break free from the orthodoxies of the past and create a new faith for the modern age; others have called for a return to the purity of the early church, turning from the "empty larders of secularism," as Thomas Oden writes, to "an inexhaustible store of nourishment in ancient Jewish and Christian wisdom."[61] Between those two extremes is a rich and thoughtful conversation about the meaning and purpose of tradition and its continued relevance. A host of writers and scholars associated with "emergent" Christianity—Phyllis Tickle, Diana Butler Bass, and Brian McLaren—have found a willing and enthusiastic audience in mainline churches across the United States.[62] In many ways, in fact, the conversation about the past has become richest and most thoughtful among Protestants considered the least "traditional," the centuries-old Presbyterian and Methodist, Baptist, Episcopal, Lutheran, and Congregational churches.

Yet what is missing from this conversation is awareness within those mainline denominations of their own stories. They do not have a sense of place drawn from their own origins, not just those of early Christianity. This is a kind of history different from the "famous firsts" and lists of accomplishments on denominational Web sites; a usable past for mainline Protestants would need to be as compelling and as morally complex as the people who once lived it.

The possibilities are vast. As this book has shown, American Congregationalists have used their past in many different ways over the last two centuries: The Pilgrim story has been a source of unity, a reason for debate, and an occasion for moral instruction and corporate pride. It has inspired serious thought and study, and it has created a yearning for common rituals and greater organizational sophistication. History has served as entertainment and reason for travel, the subject of imaginative plays and tableaux and pageants. To be sure, Congregationalists regularly misinterpreted and often trivialized their Pilgrim ancestors or at times used them to belittle their Baptist, Presbyterian, and Unitarian cousins. More important in the long run, however, is what history helped Congregationalists to avoid. At key points, as we have seen, it allowed them to stand aside from the competition to be the most "biblical" of all Protestants; it directed their passions toward tolerance and larger Christian unity rather than maintaining the purity of their theological system. These choices brought their own set of problems, of course, and in the end contributed to the denomination's ongoing debate about its core identity. But all told, the Congregationalists' story suggests that twentieth-century Protestant liberalism is much more than a one-dimensional tale of religious indifference or feckless decision making—though those elements are certainly present, as, of course, they are for everyone. It is also, in the end, about paths not taken. It is about people who learned to live with ambiguities, who chose to believe without demanding certainties.

Indeed, if any one trait defines the cultural ethos of mainline Protestantism, it is the role of history. For all the legendary differences separating mainliners from their evangelical cousins—in worship styles, politics, and piety—the two are still close relatives, sharing a common American Protestant tradition. What separates them, as this book suggests, is their understanding of history, particularly the idea of historical change as a process, one that can be messy and complicated and, in the end, ambiguous. Evangelicals read the Bible with an immediacy born of the conviction that it is essentially timeless—not shrouded in some distant unknowable past or written for people in another time and place. As anthropologist Tanya Luhrman observes, evangelicals "read the most obscure and historical texts—Judges, for example—as if they were written for *us*, to help us understand how God wanted us to be with him." God is intensely personal, not the distant deity of the Israelites but one who "worries with you about whether to paint the kitchen table." Time and historical process do not pose an obstacle to the evangelical social vision either. Sociologist James Davison Hunter explains that evangelicals imagine change as a relatively straightforward shift in worldviews: if Christians were "more Christian," so the thinking goes, and if the truth were more widely believed, then the world would become a better place. Modern culture is not some end result of an endlessly complicated and sometimes arbitrary historical process; it can be moved and shaped by the power of ideas—the right ideas.[63]

The strength of mainline Protestantism—its long history—is also its weakness. On the one hand, as the Congregationalists' story demonstrates, an awareness of the past can fuel a progressive impulse: as the heirs of the Pilgrims came to terms with their much revered historic tradition, they were able to move beyond their founding story and to keep current with the times. This is perhaps the spirit behind the UCC's current tagline, "Our faith is two thousand years old, but our thinking is not." Making peace with one's ancestors, however, does not mean forever relegating them to the rearview mirror. The past is as real and as consistently challenging as the people who created it, and its demands are not easily satisfied. The most important work of any religious tradition is to recognize—sometimes to celebrate and other times to fiercely mourn—its enduring power.

Notes

INTRODUCTION

1. The term "mainline" is tricky, often contested because it is no longer accurate numerically but still useful to indicate the long-term insider status of white northern Protestants. I will use it interchangeably with "old-line" Protestants but not with "liberal." Most mainliners are less adamant about biblical inerrancy and social mores like homosexuality and abortion than most evangelicals but still agree that the Bible is authoritative and that moral standards are worth defending. See, for example, the summary in Wuthnow and Evans, *Quiet Hand of God*, 1–24.

2. Ellingson, *Megachurch and the Mainline*, 24.

3. This criticism goes back a long way, from the novels of John Updike and Peter DeVries to Kelley, *Why Conservative Churches Are Growing*.

4. Balmer, *Grant Us Courage*, 148.

5. Putnam and Campbell, *American Grace*, 104–5, 122–23; Wuthnow and Evans, *Quiet Hand of God*, 5–6. The problem of mainline decline is multifaceted. Sociologists point out that falling church membership mirrored birthrate figures. See Michael A. Hout, Andrew Greeley, and Melissa J. Wilde, "The Demographic Imperative in Religious Change in the United States," *American Journal of Sociology* 107 (September 2001): 468–500. Mainline churches have also been hurt by changes in "upward switching"—that is, they are no longer the destination for the upwardly mobile, who are now also joining evangelical churches.

6. This argument comes from David Hollinger, "After Cloven Tongues of Fire: Ecumenical Protestantism and the Modern American Encounter with Diversity," in Hollinger, *After Cloven Tongues of Fire*, 18–55. See also Demerath, "Cultural Victory and Organizational Defeat."

7. Putnam and Campbell, *American Grace*, 6, 542–50. See also *Pew Forum on Religion and Public Life Religious Landscape Survey, Report 2, Religious Beliefs and Practices, Social and Political Views, Key Findings* (religions.pewforum.org).

8. The "self-interrogating" phrase is from Hollinger, "After Cloven Tongues of Fire," 23. The literature on twentieth-century mainline Protestantism has been growing rapidly in recent years, with several well-received publications. See, for example, Coffman, *Christian Century and the Rise of the Protestant Mainline*; Hedstrom, *Rise of Liberal Religion*; Schmidt and Promey, *American Religious Liberalism*.

9. Lofton, "The Methodology of the Modernists," 376–77. Sociologist Christian Smith attributes evangelical success to their ability to stay "embattled," rallying around important symbolic boundaries—biblical inerrancy, women's

ordination—to create a working subculture. Other Protestants did this, too, I would argue, though less effectively, to a large degree because of their prior commitment to ecumenism and because, as this book shows, they did not succumb to Biblicism. See Smith, *American Evangelicals*, 89–119.

10. Pelikan, *Vindication of Tradition*, 78.

11. Wuthnow, *Restructuring of American Religion*, 298.

12. Smith, *American Evangelicals*, 92.

13. Not all Congregationalists are part of the UCC. The National Association of Congregational Christian Churches consists of those who did not participate in the merger of 1957; the Conservative Congregational Christian Conference began in 1948 and is composed of churches with a more conservative evangelical theology.

14. Though historians today make careful distinctions between Pilgrims and Puritans, Congregationalists did not until well into the twentieth century. Against all the rules of historiography, I will follow their usage.

15. Stephens and Giberson, *Anointed*; Berman, *All That Is Solid Melts into Air*.

16. The theoretical literature on memory and time is vast and growing. See, for example, LeGoff, *History and Memory*; Schiffman, *Birth of the Past*; and Fritzsche, *Stranded in the Present*.

CHAPTER 1

1. Kirbye, *History of the First Congregational Church, Medina, Ohio*, 79.

2. Stowe, *Minister's Wooing*, 64.

3. On the foundational importance of congregation in American religious history, see Timothy L. Smith, "Congregation, State, and Denomination"; and Holifield, "Toward a History of American Congregations." Denominations, such as they were in the early nineteenth century, existed mostly for ordaining clergy and negotiating grievances. Wright, "Growth of Denominational Bureaucracies."

4. The earliest church census (1854) found 1,270 churches in New England (about half of which were in Massachusetts) and 325 in the Midwest and West. See *Yearbook of the American Congregational Union for the Year 1854*, 309–11.

5. Conforti, *Imagining New England*, 123–50; Wood, *New England Village*, 119–34; Hansen, *Very Social Time*, 106–9. A stranger visiting one rural Massachusetts town was so appalled by the local cemetery that he resolved "never to die [there]." See Howes, *History of the Town of Ashfield*, 244.

6. On local independence, see Cooper, *Tenacious of Their Liberties*; and Hall, *Reforming People*.

7. Upham, *Ratio Disciplinae*, 57. On the role of covenants, see Weir, *Early New England*, 136–71; and Burrage, *Church Covenant Idea*.

8. For commentary and text, see Walker, "The Cambridge Synod and Platform," in *Creeds and Platforms*, 157–237. Walker points out that the Platform also reflected a movement toward Presbyterianism in the years after Oliver Cromwell, not just in the use of terms like "presbytery" and "synod," but in the Platform's

emphasis on the larger church and its role in adjudicating differences between congregations.

9. Mitchell, *Guide to the Principles and Practices*, 214.

10. Finke and Stark, *Churching of America*, 76, 78, 103–4.

11. Conforti, *Imagining New England*, 81.

12. Silverman, *Life and Times of Cotton Mather*, 158–59. See also Gay, *Loss of Mastery*; Arch, *Authorizing the Past*; and Bruce Tucker, "Reinterpretation of Puritan History in Provincial New England."

13. William Bradford, *Bradford's "History of Plimouth Plantation,"* 7.

14. Bulkeley, *Gospel Covenant*, cited in Zakai, *Exile and Kingdom*, 6, also 56–93.

15. Murphy, *Prodigal Nation*, 39; Stout, *New England Soul*, 62–63.

16. Bozeman, *To Live Ancient Lives*, 14. See also Thuesen, *In Discordance with the Scriptures*, 6–11; Bercovitch, *Puritan Origins of the American Self*, 35–71; and Eliade, *Myth and Reality*, 21–38.

17. Zakai, *Jonathan Edwards' Philosophy of History*, 149, 251; Jonathan Edwards, *Faithful Narrative*.

18. Blake, *First Quarter Century of the Winslow Church*, 4.

19. Fiske, *Historical Discourse Commemorative of the Belleville Congregational Church*, 3.

20. Kammen, *Mystic Chords of Memory*, 52–56, 87–90.

21. Fritsche, *Stranded in the Present*, 42; Anderson, *Imagined Communities*; Bancroft, *History of the Colonization of the United States*, 2.

22. Moses Miller, *Historical Discourse*, 34, 10.

23 Durfee, *Advantages of Retrospection*, 8.

24. Rouse, *Fiftieth Anniversary*, 14–16.

25. Roe, *History of the First Ecclesiastical Society in East Windsor*, 21, 22.

26. Stebbins, *Centennial Discourse*, 44, 45.

27. Dodge, *Sermon Delivered in Haverhill*, 21.

28. Mark Tucker, *Centennial Sermon*, 52.

29. Bond, *Historical Discourse*, 44.

30. Lunt, *Two Discourses*, 57.

31. Stebbins, *Centennial Discourse*, 76.

32. Ibid., 75.

33. See, for example, Edward G. Adams, *Historical Discourse*; and Blake, *First Quarter Century of the Winslow Church*.

34. Bond, *Historical Discourse*, 50–51.

35. *Memorial of the Twenty-Fifth Anniversary of the Settlement of Rev. Joshua Emery*, 38, 55.

36. Rich, *Historical Discourse*, 85.

37. Edward G. Adams, *Historical Discourse*, 19.

38. Reverend Foster's remarks are found in Moses Miller, *Historical Discourse*, 55–56, 58.

39. *Jubilee of the South Congregational Church*, 28–29; Rouse, *Fiftieth Anniversary*, 56.

40. Blake, *First Quarter Century of the Winslow Church*, 50–51, 53, 55, 57–61, 66–67.

41. Eire, *Very Brief History of Eternity*, 123, 109.

42. Storrs, *Discourse Delivered at Stoughton, Mass*, 10; Thompson, *Better Land*, 205; Woods, *Heaven of Christians*, 16–17.

43. Brown, *Cult of the Saints*, 63. On "Protestant saints," see also Brekus, *Sarah Osborn's World*, 329–33.

44. Larkin, *Reshaping of Everyday Life*, 62–104.

45. Joseph Clark, *Historical Sketch of the Congregational Churches in Massachusetts*, iii–vi.

46. Ibid., 282.

47. Langworthy, "Lessons from Statistics," 293–96.

CHAPTER 2

1. Seelye, *Memory's Nation*, 23–40.

2. Howe, *What God Hath Wrought*, 91–124; Conforti, *Imagining New England*, 115–22; Guyatt, *Providence and the Invention of the United States*, 137–72.

3. Seelye, *Memory's Nation*, 74, 75. See also Erickson, "Daniel Webster's Myth of the Pilgrims," 44–64.

4. Seelye, *Memory's Nation*, xv.

5. Cuckson, *First Church of Plymouth*.

6. The literature on the social construction of collective memory is vast. Some foundational texts are Halbwachs, *On Collective Memory*; and Connerton, *How Societies Remember*. On identity formation, see, for example, Somers, "Narrative Construction of Identity."

7. Mitchell, *Guide to the Principles and Practices*, 31.

8. "Correspondence," *Christian Herald*, 30 April 1853, n.p.

9. For a summary, see Holifield, *Theology in America*, 127–56.

10. Stowe, *Minister's Wooing*, 194.

11. The best source remains H. Shelton Smith, *Changing Conceptions of Original Sin*.

12. [Asa Mahan], "Ask for the Old Paths," *Oberlin Evangelist*, 3 January 1844, 4.

13. Lundy, *Review of Bishop Hopkins' Bible View of Slavery*, 9.

14. "Doctrinal," *Christian Register*, 12 May 1827, 73.

15. Bendroth, *School of the Church*, 6–11; Joseph Clark, "Progress of Congregationalism," in *Yearbook of the American Congregational Union for the Year 1854*, 307, 308. The original article was written in 1847.

16. Meehan, "Denominating a People."

17. Wright, *Congregational Polity*, 36; Wright, "The Dedham Case Revisited," in Wright, *Unitarian Controversy*, 111–35.

18. Allyn, *A Sermon, Delivered at Plimoth, December 22, 1801, Commemorative of the Pious Ancestry, Who First Imigrated [sic] to That Place, 1620* (Boston, 1801), cited in Seelye, *Memory's Nation*, 119.

19. Judson Sr., *A Sermon, Preached in the New Meeting House, Plymouth, December 22, 1802, in Memory of the Landing of Our Ancestors* (Boston, 1802), cited in Seelye, *Memory's Nation*, 120–21. John Quincy Adams was the official speaker that year, and in his address he made a famous connection between the Mayflower Compact and the Constitution, a theme that would be repeated often in years ahead. Judson was the father of the famous missionary Adoniram Judson Jr. and like his son also became a Baptist in later life.

20. Beecher, "Reasons for a Religious Magazine in Boston," *Spirit of the Pilgrims* 1 (1828): 8.

21. Hawes, *Tribute to the Memory of the Pilgrims*, 15, 163.

22. Conforti, *Imagining New England*, 191–92; Dawson, *Unusable Past*, 5–6.

23. "May's Letters to Hawes," *Christian Examiner*, n.s., 1 (1831): 302; May, *Letters to the Rev. Joel Hawes*, 4, 42.

24. Parker, *Discourse on the Transient and Permanent in Christianity*, 11, 18, 23.

25. Bellows, *Some of the Points of Difference*, 4, 5; "Old and New," *Monthly Religious Magazine* 10 (June 1853): 243, 244.

26. Cobb, *God's Culture of His Vineyard*, 21; Braman, *Centennial Discourse*, 6.

27. Mitchell, *Guide to the Principles and Practices*, 29, 30.

28. Hawes, *Tribute to the Memory of the Pilgrims*, 186; Punchard, *View of Congregationalism*, 8.

29. Wigger, *Taking Heaven by Storm*, 3, 46.

30. Rohrer, *Keepers of the Covenant*, 147.

31. This was true of Massachusetts especially. In Connecticut, the Saybrook Platform of 1708 laid out a system of consociations, or ministers' groups, with powers to oversee the ordination of local pastors. Geographically closer to the Presbyterians in New York, Connecticut Congregationalists played a primary role in creating the Plan of Union.

32. General Association of Illinois, *Historical Papers*, 22.

33. Kennedy, *Plan of Union*, 218. See also Richard Taylor, "Contributions toward an Ecclesiastical History of the Great Lake States," 4–31; "Lax Doctrines at the West," *Oberlin Evangelist*, 4 August 1852, 126; and Marsden, *Evangelical Mind*.

34. The best account remains Timothy Smith, *Revivalism and Social Reform*, 103–14.

35. *Minutes of the Western Congregational Convention*, 4–5.

36. Ibid., 10.

37. "Congregationalism in Ohio," *Oberlin Evangelist*, 7 July 1852, 109.

38. "The Convention at Albany," *Congregationalist*, 10 October 1852, 158; "General Association of Massachusetts," *Congregationalist*, 2 July 1852, 105.

39. *Proceedings of the General Convention of Congregational Ministers and Delegates in the United States*, 71.

40. "General Convention of Congregationalists at Albany," *Oberlin Evangelist*, 27 October 1852, 174–75, 185.

41. *Proceedings of the General Convention of Congregational Ministers and Delegates in the United States*, 45.

42. Wellman, *Church Polity of the Pilgrims*, 7, 100.

43. Baker, *Thanksgiving*, 62–77.

44. "Fore-Fathers Day," *Congregationalist*, 18 December 1857, 201; "Don't Forget the Fathers," *Congregationalist*, 12 December 1856, 198.

45. "Christian Union at the West," *Congregational Herald*, 16 December 1853; "Address to the General Association of New York," in General Association of New York, *Minutes of the General Association of New York*, 16.

46. "Church Extension and 'The Esprit du Corps,'" *Congregationalist*, 16 July 1852, 113.

47. "Congregational Church Polity, An Essay Read by Rev. J. M. Williams, before the Congregational Association of Chicago, at Its Last Meeting," *Congregational Herald*, 4 June 1853, n.p.

48. General Association of Illinois, *Minutes of the General Association of Illinois*, 9–12.

49. Rouse, *Fiftieth Anniversary*, 40.

50. "Congregationalism in New England," *New Englander* 1 (October 1843): 571.

51. Woods, *Unfinished Report of the Committee on Congregationalism in Massachusetts*, 8.

52. *Reasons Why I Am a Congregationalist*, 6.

53. Mather, *Ratio Disciplinae*, 6; "An Attestation, from the Very Reverend Dr. Increase Mather," in ibid., i.

54. *Statement of Facts in Relation to the Evangelical Church of Seabrook and Hampton Falls, and the Rev. S. T. Abbott*, Dexter collection of ecclesiastical councils, box 12, Congregational Library, Boston, Mass.; *Statement of Facts, Pertaining to the Recent Division of the Congregational Church in Ashfield, Mass* (Printed for the publishers, 1855); *The Result of an Ecclesiastical Council, Convened at Detroit, May 29, 1854, by the First Congregational Church of Grand Rapids, Michigan* (Grand Rapids, Mich., 1854); *A Narrative of Late Difficulties in the South Church in Reading Mass* (North Wrentham, Mass., 1835), 12. Historian and journalist Henry Martyn Dexter compiled years' worth of ecclesiastical councils, from 1629 to 1889 (and records of ministerial misdoings), apparently because there was no other Congregational body keeping official track.

55. Some lists also include Hawes, *Tribute to the Memory of the Pilgrims*. For a complete list, see Fagley, "Brief Annotated Bibliography."

56. General Association of Connecticut, *Congregational Order*, 9–19. The manual included a lengthy and detailed set of grievance procedures, 37–42.

57. Storrs, introduction to Punchard, *View of Congregationalism*, xvi.

58. Hawley, *Congregational Tracts*, n.p.

59. Bela Edwards, "A Puritan Library in New England," 590–98; *Fortieth Annual Report of the Directors of the American Congregational Association* (Boston, 1893), 7–18. See also American Congregational Association, *Historical Sketch of Its Organization*, 3–11; "The New Congregational House," *Congregationalist*, 29 October 1898, 528, 529.

60. Sewall Harding, "Doctrinal Tract and Book Society," *Congregational Herald*, 24 March 1854, n.p.; "Correspondence," *Congregational Herald*, 7 May 1853, n.p.

61. General Association of Michigan, *Minutes of the General Association of Michigan*, 7; General Association of Iowa, *Minutes of the General Association of Iowa*, 8.

62. Beecher, *Sermon Preached before the Chenango Association*.

63. Mead, *Lively Experiment*, 108–13. See also Hughes and Allen, *Illusions of Innocence*.

64. Hatch, *Democratization of American Christianity*, 168. The Christians were intensely opposed to Calvinism and social privilege, and therefore most deeply to the Congregational clergy. By the twentieth century, they had moderated enough (or lost a sense of their own history) to merge with the Congregational churches, without a trace of irony.

65. *Memoir of Elder Abner Jones by His Son A. D. Jones* (Boston, 1842), 28.

66. Mitchell, *Guide to the Principles and Practices*, 72; Pond, *The Church*, 13.

67. Upham, *Ratio Disciplinae*, 15–23.

68. Hawes, *Tribute to the Memory of the Pilgrims*, 77, 78.

CHAPTER 3

1. "National Trinitarian Council," *Boston Evening Transcript*, 16 June 1865.

2. Patton, "Account of the National Council at Boston," 13–14, 15.

3. Walker, *Creeds and Platforms*, 576.

4. General Association of Illinois, *Minutes of the General Association of Illinois*, 17, 18.

5. Patton, "Account of the National Council at Boston," 5, 30.

6. W. T. Savage, "The National Council of Congregational Churches," *Boston Review* 5 (May 1865): 286; John Pike, "Sliding Scale of Faith," *Boston Review* 5 (May 1865): 235, 236.

7. "Proposed National Council of Congregational Churches," *Congregational Quarterly* (January 1865): 47–50.

8. *Debates and Proceedings*, 251. On Quint's Civil War perspective, see his article, "Hints upon the Work of Our Churches, as Affected by the Present State of the Country," *Congregational Quarterly* (January 1865): 42–47.

9. *Debates and Proceedings*, 326.

10. Ibid., 244–45. Pomeroy was part of the radical wing of the Republican Party and supported Salmon P. Chase for the nomination in 1864. In 1873, he was implicated in a bribery scandal that would dog him for the rest of his career.

11. "The National Congregational Convention," *Zion's Herald*, 28 June 1865, 102.

12. Patton, "Account of the National Council at Boston," 4–5; "American Congregational Association," *Congregational Quarterly* (January 1865): 128.

13. *Debates and Proceedings*, 26.

14. Ibid., 54.

15. Ibid., 186, 190.

16. Ibid., 144.

17. Ibid., 171.

18. Ibid., 242.

19. Ibid., 291.

20. Ibid., 281–82.

21. Ibid., 32.

22. Ibid., 32, 47. On Sturtevant's views, see Sturtevant, *Julian M. Sturtevant*, 163–64, 273–74.

23. *Debates and Proceedings*, 97, 161.

24. Ibid., 116.

25. "Congregationalism," *Boston Daily Advertiser*, 16 June 1865. See also "A Glance at Orthodoxy," *Christian Register*, 17 June 1865, 1.

26. *Debates and Proceedings*, 246.

27. *Report of the Convention of Unitarian Churches Held in New York*, ix, 13–14.

28. "The Orthodox National Council," *Christian Register*, 1 July 1865.

29. *Debates and Proceedings*, 344–47.

30. Ibid., 345.

31. Ibid., 350, 351, 352, 353.

32. Ibid., 354–55.

33. Ibid., 356.

34. Ibid., 357.

35. Patton, "Account of the National Council at Boston," 23.

36. Ibid., 23; Amory Bradford, *Pilgrim in Old England*, 208.

37. Perkins, *Handbook of Old Burial Hill*, 5, 6.

38. Patton, "Account of the National Council at Boston," 24.

39. Gulliver, "The Excursion to Plymouth," *Independent*, 6 July 1865, 1.

40. *Debates and Proceedings*, 361; Walker, *Creeds and Platforms*, 565.

41. Alonzo Quint, "The Action of the Council of 1865," *Congregational Quarterly* 8 (1866): 12.

42. Barton, *Congregational Creeds and Covenants*, 153.

43. Amory Bradford, *Pilgrim in Old England*, 208.

44. Patton, "Account of the National Council at Boston," 24.

45. *Debates and Proceedings*, 363.

46. Ibid., 363, 364.

47. Patton, "Account of the National Council at Boston," 24, 25.

48. *Debates and Proceedings*, 366, 367.

49. Patton, "Account of the National Council at Boston," 23.

50. *Debates and Proceedings*, 434.

51. Ibid., 440.

52. Ibid., 445, 446, 447.

53. Leonard Bacon, *Christianity in History*, 16. See also Leonard Bacon, *Genesis of the New England Churches*.

54. Shedd, *Lectures upon the Philosophy of History*, 27, 28.

55. Ibid., 15–16; Shedd, *Nature and Influence of the Historic Spirit*, 44. See also Wacker, *Augustus H. Strong*, 24–31.

56. "Neander's Church History," *Christian Review*, December 1836, 565–81; Pond, *History of God's Church*, 24, 26.

57. Shedd, *Nature and Influence of the Historic Spirit*, 42.

58. Fisher, *Law of Progress*, 3.

59. J. T. T. "The Past," *Congregationalist*, 6 March 1857, 37.

60. *Debates and Proceedings*, 454.

61. Ibid., 459, 460.

62. Theodore Davenport Bacon, *Leonard Bacon*. For a text of the report, see National Council of Congregational Churches, *Ecclesiastical Polity*.

63. "The Orthodox National Council," *Christian Register*, 1 July 1865; Patton, "Account of the National Council at Boston," 30.

64. Cited in Benjamin Wisner Bacon, *Theodore Thornton Munger*, 161.

65. Conforti, *Imagining New England*, 195.

66. Baker, *Thanksgiving*, 67–77.

CHAPTER 4

1. "Jubilee Matters," *Congregationalist*, 30 June 1870, 204.

2. Von Rohr, *Shaping of American Congregationalism*, 276–77; "How Jubilee Matters Get On," *Congregationalist*, 4 August 1870, 244.

3. "The Memorial Record," *Congregationalist*, 8 September 1870, 284.

4. Conforti, *Imagining New England*, 230, 231. On memory and material objects, see Connerton, *How Modernity Forgets*.

5. Kammen, *Mystic Chords of Memory*, 100.

6. Sandhurst, *Great Centennial Exhibition*, 156; Kammen, *Mystic Chords of Memory*, 135–36.

7. Henry Martyn Dexter, "A Congregational Jubilee," *Congregationalist*, 23 December 1869, 401.

8. "How to Order Our Jubilee Year," *Congregationalist*, 13 January 1870, 12;

9. John W. Harding, "Are Our Churches Doomed?" *Congregationalist*, 31 July 1870, 226.

10. "How to Order Our Jubilee Year," *Congregationalist*, 13 January 1870, 12.

11. W. A. Stearns to Henry M. Dexter [hereafter HMD], 15 January 1870; J. W. Andrews to HMD, 31 December 1869; George F. Magoun to HMD, January 1870; Joseph Thompson to HMD, 29 December 1869, all in Charles Richardson Correspondence, RG 160, collection number 4868, Congregational Library, Boston, Mass.

12. "Letter Missive," *Pacific*, 17 February 1870, 1; "To All Congregational Churches," *Congregationalist*, 3 February 1870, 33.

13. Dexter, *Memoranda, Historical, Chronological*, 1.

14. "The Broadway Tabernacle Convention," *Congregationalist*, 10 March 1870, 76.

15. "National Pilgrim Memorial Convention," *Congregationalist*, 5 May 1870, 137.

16. "The Chicago Convention Declaration," *Pacific*, 19 May 1870, 1.

17. Dexter, *Memoranda, Historical, Chronological*, 9, 15, 38.

18. "Editorial," *Pacific*, 12 January 1871; "Pilgrim Celebration," *Congregationalist*, 29 December 1870, 410; "Editorial," *Congregationalist*, 5 January 1871, 4. See also the description in "The Pilgrim Celebrations," *Pacific*, 12 January 1871, 1.

19. "The Convention at Chicago," *Pacific*, 19 May 1870, n.p.

20. "Pilgrim Celebration," *Congregationalist*, 29 December 1870, 410.

21. "Massachusetts," *Congregationalist*, 29 December 1870, 412; "The Pilgrim Memorial Festival," *Pacific*, 26 January 1871.

22. Free Congregational Church, Providence, *Pilgrim Jubilee*, 6.

23. "Roger Williams, *Watchman and Reflector*, 29 December, 1870, n.p.; "Thanksgiving Day, 1870," *Watchman and Reflector*, 24 November 1870, n.p.

24. "Editorial," *Zion's Herald*, 29 December 1870, 1.

25. C. Thurston Chase, "Congregational Clubs," *Congregationalist*, 6 September 1902, 365.

26. "From Boston," *Advance*, 1 January 1885, 868. May was the usual time in many Protestant denominations for orchestrated meetings of all the missionary and benevolent societies.

27. "Forefathers' Day," *Congregationalist*, 30 December 1875, 410.

28. *Pilgrim Jubilee*, 5. On the "Pilgrim polity," see also Samuel Wolcott, "The Pilgrim Idea," *Congregationalist*, 19 May 1870, 153; and J. E. Rankin, "The Pilgrims and Their Polity," *Congregationalist*, 26 May 1870, 162.

29. "A National Congregational Body," *Congregationalist*, 7 July 1870, 212.

30. "A National Conference," *Congregationalist*, 22 December 1870, 404.

31. "A Word to the Dispersed," *Pacific*, 16 June 1870. For a sample sermon, see "The Civil Building of the Pilgrims," *Pacific*, 17 November 1870. In 1870, according to the United States census, which tended to be more conservative in its figures than the Congregational yearbooks, California listed 36 churches with about 12,000 members. Oregon and Washington accounted for another 8. Of the total number of Congregational churches (2,715) and "sittings" (1,117,212), almost one-quarter (502 and 269,314, respectively) were in Massachusetts alone. *Ninth Census*, vol. 1: *The Statistics of the Population of the United States* (Washington, D.C., 1872), 510.

32. "The Convention at Chicago," *Pacific*, 19 May 1870, n.p.

33. "The Jubilee and the Pacific," *Pacific*, 27 October 1870, n.p. See also "A Memorial Church," *Pacific*, 14 March 1870; "The Jubilee Year," *Pacific*, 28 April 1870.

34. J. O. Means, "Council or Conference?," *Congregationalist*, 9 November 1871, 353; A. Hastings Ross, "The National Council, Its Name," *Congregationalist*, 26 October 1871, 337.

35. "The National Council," *Congregationalist*, 23 November 1871, 369.

36. "Meeting of the Committees in the Proposed National Council," *Congregationalist*, 29 December 1870, 410.

37. According to Congregational sources, in the 1860s Massachusetts reported only about a 3 percent increase in church members, while Illinois reported 8 percent and Ohio nearly 10 percent. "Summary of Statistics," *Congregational Quarterly* 5 (Boston, 1864), 97; "Summary II," *Congregational Year-Book* (Boston: Congregational Publishing Society, 1883), 212. On individual church figures, see "Congregational Statistics," *Congregationalist*, 23 February 1871, 60. The fourth largest church was Chicago's First Church, with over 700 members.

38. *Addresses at the Laying of the Corner Stone*, 11.

39. Leonard, *Story of Oberlin*, 266–67.

40. "The National Council," *Congregationalist*, 23 November 1871, 369.

41. "Place and Meeting of the National Council," *Pacific*, 14 December 1871.

42. "Pray for the Council," *Congregationalist*, 9 November 1871, 356.

43. *Minutes of the National Council*, 11, 12.

44. "The National Council," *Congregationalist*, 23 November 1871, 369.

45. *Minutes of the National Council*, 31–32.

46. Hood, *National Council of Congregational Churches*, 81, 83.

47. "New-Fangled Congregationalism," *New Englander* (January 1878): 6.

48. A. D. Smith to HMD, 13 July 1875, Dexter Correspondence, Congregational Library, Boston, Mass. On the Beecher scandal, see Applegate, *Most Famous Man in America*.

49. Ross, *Pocket Manual of Congregationalism*. In the late nineteenth century, most Congregational churches took out incorporation papers, doing away with the old system of societies (the central issue in the Dedham case of 1820) and clearing the way for full ownership of buildings and property. On state manuals, see, for example, *Manual of the Principles, Doctrines and Usages of Congregational Churches*; *Congregational Manual for the Iowa Churches*; *Hand-Book of the Congregational Churches of California*.

50. The complete list is found in Fagley, "Brief Annotated Bibliography."

51. *Minutes of the National Council of the Congregational Churches at the Fourth Session, Held in St. Louis, Missouri, November 11–15, 1880* (Boston: Congregational Publishing Society, 1880), 133–38.

52. Walker, *Creeds and Platforms*, 582.

53. Love, "The New Congregational Creed Insufficient," *New Englander* (July 1885): 5; Cook, *Boston Monday Lectures*, 147.

54. White, *Liberty and Justice for All*, 130–47. See also, for example, Gladden's address as retiring moderator, "The Church and the Social Crisis," in *The National Council of the Congregational Churches of the United States . . . Thirteenth Triennial Session, Cleveland, Ohio, October 8–17, 1907* (Boston: Secretary of the National Council, 1907), 1–21. For a general narrative of these meetings, see Hood, *National Council of Congregational Churches*.

CHAPTER 5

1. See Taylor, "That Obnoxious Doctrine"; Thomas P. Field, "The 'Andover Theory' of Future Probation," *Andover Review* 7 (May 1887): 461–75; Thompson, *Future Probation and Foreign Missions*.

2. The difference was between a view of sin as "imputed," inherited through Adam, or as a free and therefore culpable act. For a summary, see Bendroth, *School of the Church*, 6–16; H. Shelton Smith, *Changing Conceptions of Original Sin*, 106–8.

3. *Constitution and Associate Statutes of the Theological Seminary in Andover*, 19–20.

4. Glenn Miller, *Piety and Intellect*, 65. See also *Progressive Orthodoxy*.

5. "The Andover Creed Musically Interpreted," *Christian Register*, 21 June 1883.

6. William Jewett Tucker, *My Generation:*, 196–201. See also "Argument of Henry M. Dexter," in *The Andover Case* (Boston, 1887), 104–74.

7. Edwards Park to George Leon Walker, n.d. [1891?], Walker papers, box 5, Yale Divinity School, RG 51 (hereafter YDS).

8. Some liberal critics, however, saw the conservatism in Dexter's approach and his inability to recognize "the progressive, developing changes in our system." See "Literary Notices," *Boston Recorder* 5 (September 1865): 508–10.

9. Dexter, *Street Thoughts*.

10. The full bibliography was published as an appendix to Dexter, *Congregationalism of the Last Three Hundred Years*; "December Meeting, 1890," *Proceedings of the Massachusetts Historical Society*, 2nd ser., 6 (December 1890): 180.

11. Dexter, *Congregationalism*, 297.

12. Ibid., 158 n. 2.

13. William L. Ledwith, "The Record of Fifty Years, 1852–1902. Historical Sketch of the Presbyterian Historical Society," *Journal of Presbyterian History* 1 (December 1902): 370–80; Richard Pierard, "American Baptist Historical Society," *American Baptist Quarterly* 22 (September 2003): 283–89; *Proceedings of the Board of Managers of the Western Methodist Historical Society*, 11.

14. Weston, *Baptist Movement of a Hundred Years Ago*, 4, 15; Samuel Miller, *Presbyterianism*, 7–8.

15. Elizabeth Clark, *Founding the Fathers*, 136, 142–43, 172–73.

16. Cramp, *Baptist History*, 585; "What Do We Do More Than Others?," *Zion's Herald and Wesleyan Journal*, 5 March 1845, 1. Denominational history-writing was also competitive within denominations. Princeton theologian Charles Hodge wrote the first scholarly account of American Presbyterian history (*Constitutional History of the Presbyterian Church*) in response to an account sympathetic to slavery written by Hill, *History of the Rise*.

17. Dexter, *Congregationalism*, xiii, ix.

18. Dexter, *As to Roger Williams*, v, vi, 137, 138.

19. "Personal Correspondence with Rev. I. M. Atwood, D.D., in regard to certain slanders circulated by him and which he was slow to retract, 1880–1881," Ministerial Pamphlets, Dexter Correspondence, Congregational Library, Boston, Mass.

20. Henry Martyn Dexter to I. M. Atwood, 23 January 1880; I. M. Atwood to Henry Martyn Dexter, 27 August 1880; Henry Martyn Dexter to I. M. Atwood, 19 January 1881, in ibid.

21. "December Meeting, 1890," *Proceedings of the Massachusetts Historical Society*, 2nd ser., 6 (December 1890): 176–85.

22. Alexander MacKenzie, "Remarks on the Death of Henry M. Dexter," *Proceedings of the Massachusetts Historical Society* 6 (1890, 1891): 185; John E. Sanford, "Memoir of Rev. Henry Martyn Dexter, D.D., LL.D.," *Proceedings of the Massachusetts Historical Society* 7 (November 1891): 102.

23. Davis, "A Labor of Love and Years," *Congregationalist and Christian World*, 25 November 1905, 767.

24. Williston Walker, "The Pilgrims," 7, 12, manuscript, Walker papers, box 7, YDS.

25. Leonard Bacon to George Leon Walker, 3 February 1879; George Day to George Leon Walker, 24 November 1890, both in Walker papers, box 5, YDS.

26. Elizabeth Clark, *Founding the Fathers*, 142, 143.

27. Ibid., 177. On Neander and Mosheim, see ibid., 136, 142–43, 172–73; "Neander's Church History," *Christian Review*, December 1836, 565–81; and David Hogan's introduction to *Epitome of the Ecclesiastical History of John Lawrence Mosheim*, 10.

28. Wacker, *Augustus H. Strong*, 38; Davaney, *Historicism*, 63.

29. Hart quoted in Novick, *That Noble Dream*, 38.

30. Wacker, *Augustus H. Strong*, 39–40.

31. Hall, "Calvin and Calvinism,"156–57; Pease, "On Interpreting Puritan History," 232–34.

32. Walker, "Changes in Congregationalism," 7, 18, Walker papers, box 6, YDS.

33. Walker, *History of the Congregational Churches of the United States*, 431.

34. Ibid., 426, 430–36.

35. Walker, "Eighty Years of Congregationalism," *Congregationalist*, 12 March 1896, 420.

36. George Gordon to Williston Walker, [1909], Walker papers, box 5, YDS.

37. Adams, *Massachusetts*, 12.

38. Charles Francis Adams to Williston Walker, 6 January 1894, Walker papers, box 5, YDS.

39. Charles Jefferson, "The Unpopularity of the Puritans," *Advance*, 6 February 1908, 171. See also Dawson, *Unusable Past*, 44, 77–85.

40. *Illinois Society of Church History. First Annual Meeting* (Chicago, 1892), 6, 7; *Illinois Congregational Society of Church History* (1899), n.p. For an analysis of denominational histories of Congregationalism, see Bendroth, "New Directions on the Congregational Way."

41. Foster, "The Field and Work of a Local Church History Society," in *Papers of the Ohio Church History Society* (Oberlin, Ohio, 1899), 1:1, 2, 12, 13.

42. Walker, *Ten New England Leaders*, 5, 6.

43. See Richard Pierce, "Legal Aspects of the Andover Creed," *Church History* 15 (March 1946): 28–47.

44. "The Unitarian Movement," *Advance*, 23 April 1908, 517.

45. "Let Us Understand One Another," *Advance*, 14 May 1908, 613.

46. "One Who Grieves But Who Is Not Without Hope," *Congregationalist*, 18 April 1908, 511; "Attempted Defense of the Andover Alliance," *Advance*, 16 April 1908, 491.

47. "Congregationalism's Conflict," *Advance*, 28 May 1908, 679; "Attempted Defense of the Andover Alliance," *Advance*, 16 April 1908, 492.

48. "The Theological School in Harvard," *Congregationalist*, 22 June 1922, 774.

49. See Bendroth, *School of the Church*, 117–31.

50. "The Andover-Harvard Supreme Court Decision," *Congregationalist*, 1 October 1925, 422.

51. Vaughan Dabney, "Andover Newton: Appreciation and Interpretation," *Institution Bulletin* 24 (February 1932): 13.

52. See, for example, Leach, *Land of Desire*.

1. Wacker, *Augustus H. Strong.* See also, for example, Turner, *Without God*; Marsden, *Soul of the American University.*

2. Kirbye, *History of the First Congregational Church,* 70, 72.

3. "The New Religious Experience," *Outlook,* 14 February 1903, 376, 377.

4. The best general source is Noll, *America's God.*

5. Sandeen, *Roots of Fundamentalism*; Marsden, *Fundamentalism and American Culture.*

6. Spencer quoted in Turner, *Without God,* 250–51.

7. Wacker, "Second Thoughts on the Great Commission."

8. L. A. Lippitt, "Liberal, Fundamentalist, or Faithful," *Congregationalist,* 15 January 1925, 79.

9. Machen, "History and Faith," 1. Machen's views followed that of his predecessors at Princeton. See Charles Hodge, "Inspiration," *Biblical Repertory and Princeton Review* 29 (1857): 600–698; William Henry Greene, "The Anti-Bible Higher Criticism," *Presbyterian Quarterly* 6 (1892): 341–59; A. A. Hodge and B. B. Warfield, "Inspiration," *Presbyterian Review* 6 (1881): 225–60.

10. Smith B. Goodenow, "The Inspired Truthfulness of the Original Scriptures," *Truth* 20 (1894): 50.

11. "Monumental Evidence," *Truth* 20 (1894): 122.

12. "No Stopping Place," *Truth* 20 (1894): 9.

13. Troeltsch, Franklin Baumer, and Henry Sedgwick quoted in Howard, *Religion and the Rise of Historicism,* 16.

14. "Spiritual Work," *Advance,* 16 April 1903, 509.

15. "What They Are Talking About," *Advance,* 4 June 1903, 707–8.

16. *Pilgrim Quarterly for Senior Classes* 8 (January–March 1887): n.p.

17. *Pilgrim Series Intermediate Quarterly* 18 (July–September 1901): 3.

18. *Pilgrim Series Senior Quarterly* 28 (January–March 1907): S1-3–S2-3.

19. Munger, "Where We Are," *Congregationalist and Christian World* [hereafter *CCW*], 18 October 1902, 545.

20. "Tradition, Reason and Faith," *CCW,* 9 August 1902, 192–93.

21. "Our Readers' Forum: Where Shall We Stop," *CCW,* 9 August 1902, 209; "The Professor's Chair," *CCW,* 23 September 1905, 413; "Our Readers' Forum," *CCW,* 8 August 1908, 183.

22. "The Professor's Chair," *CCW,* 3 February 1906, 149; "The Professor's Chair," *CCW,* 19 May 1906, 712; "The Professor's Chair," *CCW,* 18 November 1905, 713; Eugene W. Lyman, "Building a Faith for Today [Professor Lyman's Question Box]," *CCW,* 29 April 1915, 539. See also John W. Buckingham, "The War of Beliefs," *Advance,* 12 January 1911, 44; "Our Readers' Forum: Time to Call a Halt," *Congregationalist and Advance,* 24 January 1918, 98.

23. "The Professor's Chair," *CCW,* 3 March 1906, 322. See also "The Professor's Chair," *CCW,* 18 November 1905, 713.

24. *Silver Jubilee Celebration,* 35.

25. George Warren Stearns, "Two Centuries in God's Work," in Stearns, *Two Hundredth Anniversary*, 9, 10.

26. *Commemorative Services of the First Church in Newton Massachusetts*, 44, 53, 54–55.

27. Walker, "Changes in Theology among American Congregationalists," *American Journal of Theology* 10 (April 1906): 208; "The Theology of Congregationalists," *CCW*, 26 May 1906, 744.

28. Walker, "Changes in Theology," 205.

29. See, for example, Bushnell, *Nature and the Supernatural*.

30. Bushnell, "Living to God in Small Things"; Bushnell, *Christian Nurture*, 10.

31. Palmer, "Why I Am a Minister," *Congregationalist*, 9 April 1925, 461; Jefferson, "Why I Entered the Ministry," *Congregationalist*, 14 May 1925, 617–18; John Wells Rahill, "Why I Entered the Christian Ministry," *Congregationalist*, 18 February 1926, 200; Roy C. Helfenstein, "Home Influences and Life Work: A Spiritual Autobiography," *Advance*, 31 May 1934, 167–68.

32. H. A. Bridgman, "Four Good Things in Congregationalism," *CCW*, 9 December 1905, 853.

33. *Defense before the Council*, 63, 64, 65.

34. "Editorial," *Pacific*, 15 April 1896; "The Latest Heresy Trial," *Congregationalist*, 2 April 1896, 538–39.

35. Hawkins, "The Challenge of Fundamentalism," *Congregationalist*, 11 May 1922, 587–88.

36. "My Sympathy in the Dayton Case: A Contributed Editorial by President Irving Maurer," *Congregationalist*, 23 July 1925, 103. Readers generally agreed. See "The Modernists' Concern," *Congregationalist*, 13 August 1925, 213.

37. M. S. Freeman, "The Situation in Tennessee," *Congregationalist* 23 July 1925, 105. For a similar response, see also Fred P. Ensminger, "A Day at Dayton," *Congregationalist*, 30 July 1925, 139–40.

38. *National Council of the Congregational Churches of the United States . . . Twelfth Regular Meeting, Springfield, Massachusetts, October 16–23, 1923* (New York: Office of the National Council, 1923), 230.

39. Cavert, *American Churches in the Ecumenical Movement*, 35, 36.

40. Piper, *American Churches in World War I*.

41. "Sunday Bicycling," *Congregationalist*, 14 May 1896, 788.

42. "The 'Congregationalist's' Pilgrims," *Congregationalist*, 4 June 1896, 900.

43. "Austerfield: The Cradle of the Pilgrim Fathers: An Appeal to the American People," pamphlet, Doncaster, England, 1896.

44. Mrs. S. S. Smith to the editor of the *Congregationalist*, 18 December 1896, Small collections, RG 4938, Congregational Library, Boston, Mass. (hereafter CL). See *Book of the Pilgrimage*.

45. See, for example, *Congregationalist*, 2 April 1896, 534.

46. Taves, *Fits, Trances, and Visions*, 254–55.

47. Morton Dexter to the Party, 4 July 1896, Small collections, RG 4938, CL.

48. Advertisements, *The Congregationalist*, 7 January 1897; review in *The Interior*, 24 December 1896.

49. "Editorial," *Congregationalist*, 25 December 1890, 462. During this time, the *Congregationalist* began printing elaborate orders of worship, complete with lengthy liturgies and printed prayers—all, of course, anathema to the group fleeing high-church Anglicanism in 1620. The service of 1897, the work of a Connecticut churchwoman, Mrs. May Churchill Talcott, introduced a new repertoire of sacred texts, including readings from William Bradford's "Journal," John Robinson's "Charge to the People," and the Pilgrims' "Decision to Emigrate to America." Her service finished with an "Ode to the 22nd of December" previously composed for an anniversary ceremony at Plymouth. "Editorial," *Congregationalist*, 4 November 1897, 641; "The Congregationalist Services, No. 34," *Congregationalist*, 4 November 1897, 664–65.

50. *Congregational Club of Chicago*.

51. Landsberg, *Prosthetic Memory*, 2.

52. "The Knights of King Arthur," *Congregationalist and Advance*, 28 February 1918, 266.

53. Snow, *Performing the Pilgrims*, 16.

54. "A Notable Pilgrim Parade in Omaha," *Congregationalist and Advance*, 9 December 1920, 738.

55. Frederick Brooks Noyes, "The Call of the Cape," *Congregationalist and Advance*, 16 September 1920, 342–43.

56. *The National Council of the Congregational Churches of the United States* (Boston, 1917), 48, 146.

57. Henry Atkinson, *The Tercentenary Program of Social Service for the Churches*.

58. See, for example, the advertisement in the *Congregationalist* 30 September 1920, 416; National Council of Congregational Churches, *Pilgrim Deeds and Duties*; Marble, *Women Who Came in the Mayflower*.

59. Bates, *Pageant of Pilgrims*, v, vi.

60. "The Passing of Dr. William E. Barton," *Congregationalist*, 18 December 1930, 817; William E. Barton, *Safed and Keturah* (Boston: Pilgrim Press, 1921), vii–viii; Barton, *The Wit and Wisdom of Safed the Sage* (Boston: Pilgrim Press, 1919), vi–vii.

61. See, for example, Eaton, *Dramatic Studies from the Bible*.

62. "The Scriptural Play," *Pacific* 71 (November 1921): 1.

63. "Our 'Camino Real': The Drama Made to Serve the Pulpit," *Congregationalist*, 19 February 1925, 238.

64. Chester Ferris, "The Reviving of Religious Drama," *Congregationalist*, 11 March 1926, 305.

65. Ibid., 305.

66. Allan Knight Chalmers, "Who Was Abraham? Learning Bible Stories through Impromptu Dramatization," *Congregationalist*, 11 September 1924, 336–37.

67. Dickinson, *A Century of Church Life*, 7; *Jubilee of the South Congregational Church*, 27.

68. Stearns, *Two Hundredth Anniversary*, 12.

69. Second Church in Newton, *Our Church*, 7; *A Silver Jubilee Celebration*, 36, 37; Henry Stimson, "Religious Progress of Fifty Years," in *Fiftieth Anniversary of the Founding of Pilgrim Congregational Church*, 17, 21.

70. Charles H. Richards, *Improvement of Worship*, 3.

71. Second Church in Newton, *Our Church*, 81.

72. First Congregational Church, Kalamazoo, *Our Church*, 11, 23.

73. *Jubilee Year: Fiftieth Anniversary of the Organization of the First Congregational Church and Society of Detroit, Michigan* (Detroit, 1894), 84.

74. Ibid., 103, 105, 106.

75. "Outstanding Tercentenary Events: What to See and Where and When to See It," *Congregationalist and Herald of Gospel Liberty* [hereafter *CHGL*], 10 July 1930, 55.

76. "Ho for Bournemouth!," *CHGL*, 12 June 1930, 778.

77. "With the Goodwill Pilgrimage," *CHGL*, 17 July 1930, 74.

78. "The Seminary in Theology: Interesting Discussions on Shipboard," *CHGL*, 17 July 1930, 71.

79. "With the Goodwill Pilgrimage," *CHGL*, 24 July 1930, 105–6.

CHAPTER 7

1. Justus Buchler, "George Santayana's 'The Last Puritan,'" *New England Quarterly* 9 (June 1936): 282; George W. Howgate, *George Santayana* (Philadelphia: University of Pennsylvania Press, 1938), 264, 265.

2. "We See Ourselves in the Mirror: Some Observations on the Coming Council at Oberlin," *Advance*, 7 June 1934, 179.

3. Robert Moats Miller, *American Protestantism and Social Issues*, 81.

4. Theodore C. Hume, "Congregationalism Today . . . and Tomorrow," *Advance*, 1 April 1938, 160.

5. Conforti, *Imagining New England*, 263–309.

6. Kammen, *Mystic Chords of Memory*, 444–80.

7. Townsend, *History's Babel*, 136.

8. Piper, *American Churches in World War I*. One of the main offenders in *Preachers Present Arms* was Congregationalist Newell Dwight Hillis of the Plymouth Church in Brooklyn, where Henry Ward Beecher once served.

9. Robert A. Schneider, "Voice of Many Waters," 95. See also Carter, *Decline and Rise of the Social Gospel*.

10. United States Department of Commerce, Bureau of the Census, *Religious Bodies: 1926 v. 2 Separate Denominations* (Washington, D.C.: U.S. Government Printing Office, 1929), 446. Although membership was predominantly urban, the majority of Congregational churches were rural. By way of comparison, Baptists gave about $34 million but reported far more churches, 7,611. See also "What Sort of People Are We?," *Advance*, July 1948, 34–35. The sample included Catholics, Methodists, Baptists, Presbyterians, Lutherans, Episcopalians, Disciples of Christ, Latter Day Saints, Christian Scientists, Reformed churches, and Jews.

11. Fitch, "The Future of the Congregationalists," *Christian Century*, 22 June 1922, 779. See also the reply by Methodist author Lynn Harold Hough, "The Future of the Congregationalists," *Christian Century*, 29 June 1922, 809–11.

12. Marshall Dawson, "Dr. Cadman's Radio Service: Personal Impressions of a Great Ministry," *Congregationalist*, 8 January 1925, 43; "Dr. Cadman in Boston,"

Congregationalist, 26 February 1925, 262–63; G. Leland Green, "Cadman," *Advance*, 1 September 1936, 554.

13. Roger W. Babson, "A Message to Laymen," *Congregationalist*, 8 February 1934, 95.

14. Babson, "Capitalism Is Not Dead," *Advance*, 30 August 1934, 440. See also Babson, *Actions and Reactions*.

15. Fifield, *Tall Preacher*, 121–22.

16. Ibid., 123–24, 128.

17. Ibid., 124–25. The advisory board of Spiritual Mobilization boasted an array of prominent names in academia as well: Gordon Sproul, president of the University of California, Berkeley; Roscoe Pond, of the Harvard Law School, and Rufus von KleinSmid, chancellor of the University of Southern California.

18. Robert Moats Miller, *American Protestantism and Social Issues*, 37. Like the other northern Protestant denominations—and many Americans at the time—Congregationalists also supported the Volstead Act of 1919, prohibiting the sale of alcohol. In fact, in 1928, the leading denominational journals broke an old rule against partisanship and openly campaigned for Republican presidential candidate Herbert Hoover over Democrat Al Smith—Hoover had pledged to support prohibition, and Smith was a notorious "wet." But a flurry of dispute in the pages of the *Congregationalist* in early 1926 ended with the editor's plea for tolerance and civility. "Decent men and women," he insisted, "no matter how deep their differences of opinion, even upon so vexed a subject as prohibition, ought to be able to treat one another with courtesy and magnanimity." "Are Congregationalists 'Wet' or 'Dry'?" *Congregationalist*, 22 April 1926, 486. See previous "Congregational Churches and the Volstead Act," *Congregationalist*, 22 April 1896, 497.

19. "Money Changers in the Temple," *Advance*, 19 April 1934, 52; "Dr. Magill Must Choose," *Advance*, 10 May 1934, 116–17.

20. "Dr. Magill and the Utilities: Our Readers Discuss the Question," *Advance*, 3 May 1934, 102–4. An "economic plebiscite," conducted by the CSA in 1938, did not garner enough responses to paint an adequate picture of laypeople's attitudes. See Elizabeth Whiting, "The Economic Plebiscite," *Advance* 1 October 1938, 449.

21. "Opening a New Frontier," *Christian Century*, 12 September 1934, 1133–35; Arthur E. Holt, "A Proposal for the General Council," *Advance*, 10 May 1934, 119–20.

22. A. Burns Chalmers, "The Need of New Action," *Advance*, 31 May 1934, 170.

23. "Social Relations: A Symposium," *Advance*, 7 June 1934, 191.

24. George L. Cady, "All Things New," *Advance*, 31 May 1934, 170.

25. *General Council of the Congregational and Christian Churches of the United States, Minutes of the Second Regular Meeting, Oberlin, Ohio, June 21–27, 1934* (New York and Dayton, Ohio, 1934), 88–90, 101. The Oberlin Council left the question of funding open, initially re-allocating funds from the Commission on Missions for an initial budget of $60,000.

26. Ibid., 107–8. The second part of this resolution called for total abstinence and the "elimination of private profit" from the liquor industry.

27. McElvaine, *Great Depression*, 205, 224–49.

28. Carter, *Decline and Rise of the Social Gospel*, 151.

29. Robert Moats Miller, *American Protestantism and Social Issues*, 77.

30. Miron Morrill, ed., *Methodist Youth Council* (Chicago, 1934), 1, 178, quoted in ibid., 68.

31. There is little actual evidence of conspiracy. The resolution originated in one of the study groups, organized in advance of the General Council meeting in 1934 to discuss various issues in a seminar format. Advance material noted that the Seminar on the Social Gospel and Economic Problems would discuss the "implications of the Social Gospel . . . for industrial and urban life" and the "design for a socialized economy." The agenda included an analysis of capitalism and its defects, "social experiments" in Russia, Italy, Germany, and Great Britain, and an appraisal of the New Deal and the characteristics of a planned economy, led by Harry F. Ward. The leaders and personnel certainly overlapped with the CSA but never explicitly or directly. See *Outline of Seminar Programs, General Council Meeting, Oberlin, Ohio, June 21–27, 1934* (New York and Dayton, Ohio: General Council of the Congregational and Christian Churches, 1934), 18–19; "Resolutions Originating with the Seminar on the Social Gospel and Economic Problems," CSA collection, box 2, FC-1, Congregational Library, Boston, Mass. (hereafter CL). For an overview, see Frank E. Barrows, "A Layman's Concern at the Council for Social Action," CSA collection, box 2, FC-3, CL.

32. Ethelbert V. Grabill, "Laymen and the General Council," *Advance*, 15 November 1934, 657.

33. *General Council of the Congregational and Christian Churches of the United States, Minutes of the Second Regular Meeting, Oberlin, Ohio, June 21–27, 1934* (New York and Dayton, Ohio, 1934), 95. Laywomen's representation at national meetings was a complicated issue also. Some worried about the low representation of laymen at the meeting and even volunteered to stay home the next time. See Margaret K. Howard, "Women's Interests at the Council," *Advance*, 5 July 1934, 275–76. When the denomination dissolved the Women's Foreign Missionary Society in 1926 (formed in 1869), women received a set proportion of votes in the reorganized missionary council but had no more official say at national meetings. See "What Is Doing about the Merger?," *Congregational News Letter* 11 (November 1926): 2; American Board of Commissioners for Foreign Missions, Prudential Committee, Story of the Unification of the Boards: Adopted by the Prudential Committee on October 22nd 1926 for the Annual Meeting of the American Board at Akron, pamphlet, 1926, CL; Mrs. Franklin Warner, "About Face, Women!" (Boston: Women's Board of Missions [1926]); Mrs. Franklin Warner, "The Future of Woman's Work," *Congregational News Letter* 11 (March 1926): 4; "Report of the Meeting of State Presidents and Representatives," Congregational Christian Churches Commission on Missions, box 4-13, Commission on Missions collection, CL; Committee of Nine for the Study of Women's Work, March 16, 1933, Pamphlet collection, CL. The Committee of Nine recommended creating the position of secretary for women's work within the existing structure, recognizing as they did that this was likely an ineffective step backward into the old arrangement.

34. Reverend Sarah A. Dixon, "Women in the Congregational Ministry," *Congregationalist*, 1 May 1924, 566–67. A report to the National Council in 1921 concluded that "there is no occasion for a ruling . . . beyond the mere recognition of the existing status" of ordained women. See "Report of the Commission on Ordained Women, Church Assistants, and Lay Workers," in *The National Council of the Congregational Churches of the United States . . . 19th Regular Meeting, Los Angeles, California, July 1–8, 1921* (New York: Office of the General Council, 1921), 39, 40.

35. Dunning, *Congregationalists in America*, 526; Walker, *History of the Congregational Churches in the United States*, 433.

36. William W. Patton, "The CSA and the Profit Motive," *Advance*, 25 October 1934, 594. Ultimately this church, and others, refused to provide financial support to the CSA.

37. "Letters to the Editor," *Advance*, 2 August 1934, 349.

38. Roy Campbell, "Let's Not Be Tagged!" *Advance*, 20 September 1934, 498.

39. "From Our Readers: The Oberlin Platform," *Advance*, 26 July 1934, 340.

40. "What Our Readers Are Thinking: Is This Fair Comment?," *Advance*, 2 August 1934, 369.

41. "How the Brethren Feel," *Congregationalist and Advance* [hereafter *CA*], 1 May 1919, 552; "The Episcopal-Congregational Proposals: Still Further Reaction from Our Readers," *CA*, 8 May 1919, 597; "Episcopal-Congregational Unity: Trends of Sentiment in Both Communions," *CA*, 1 May 1919, 559. The agreement would have allowed Congregational ministers to receive ordination by an Episcopal bishop and official status within the local diocese. In June 1920, the two denominations issued a joint "Concordat" outlining the shape of further negotiations and the scope of the theological issues before them ("An Approach toward Unity: Episcopalians and Congregationalists Unite in a Proposal," *CA*, 3 April 1919, 436, 446; "A Tentative Basis for Church Union," *CA*, 1 July 1920, 14). In this case, however, history won over ecumenical unity. When Will Barton stood up in the General Council meeting of 1923 and pronounced the Episcopal proposal "completely fatuous," those present stood up and cheered ("National Council Notes," *Pacific* 73 [November 1923]: 2). Congregationalists also participated in a proposal, first floated in 1918, for a general union of American Protestant churches. A referendum conducted by the National Council in 1925 found broad support, with forty-four of fifty-one state conferences approving the move and the remainder more silent than actively opposed. Though this plan also fell through, Congregationalists were the last of the participating denominations to give up on the idea.

42. "Our Denominational Paradox," *Congregationalist*, 31 January 1924, 133.

43. Herring, *Place of Congregationalism in Recent History*, 10.

44. "Making Congregationalism Christian," *Congregationalist*, 17 April 1924, 486; George Richards, *Nature of the Church according to the Teaching of Congregationalists*, 16.

45. Edward S. Steele, "Letters to the Editor: A Thoroughbred Congregationalist," *Advance*, 1 June 1938, 241.

46. Charles C. Merrill, "Our Developing Congregationalism," *Congregationalist*, 22 October 1923, 556; Humphrey, "The Union of the Congregational and the Christian Churches," 293.

47. Hermon Eldredge, "Our Wider Fellowship," *Herald of Gospel Liberty*, March 1930, 150.

48. The "and" was later dropped because of the implication that "Congregationalists" were not "Christian." The only real issue in 1931 was financial: given that the Christians were struggling financially, some Congregationalists feared that the merger would drain pension funds and other denominational resources. See William P. Minton, "Some Little-Known Aspects of the Congregational Christian Church Merger," General Council of the Congregational Christian Churches Records, box 2, CL.

49. *General Council of the Congregational and Christian Churches of the United States, Minutes of the Second Regular Meeting, Oberlin, Ohio, June 21–27, 1934* (New York, 1934), 112; John R. Scotford, "Let's Not Be an 'Ism,'" *Advance*, 14 June 1934, 215.

50. "What Our Readers Are Thinking: Fellowship Church," *Advance*, 13 September 1934, 484.

51. "The Denominational Name," *Advance*, 1 January 1943, 39; "What Our Readers Are Thinking: A Proposed Name," *Advance*, 2 August 1934, 369; "Other Pilgrims," *Advance*, 1 February 1943, 51.

52. Peel, *Inevitable Congregationalism*; Micklem, *Congregationalism To-Day*.

53. Theodore Hume, "Congregationalism Today . . . and Tomorrow," *Advance*, 1 April 1938, 159–61.

54. See Ernest Graham Guthrie, "The Church and Church Order in the Congregational Conception," *Advance*, 1 September 1938, 406–7; A. C. McGiffert, "The Continuities of Congregationalism," *Advance*, 1 May 1938, 211–12; Douglas Horton, "Trinitarian Aspect of Congregationalism," *Advance*, 1 June 1938, 245–46; "Re-Thinking Congregationalism," *Advance*, 1 April 1938, 154.

55. Robert Moats Miller, *American Protestantism and Social Issues*, 278–79.

56. In fact, the CSA ran afoul of the House Committee on Un-American Activities. See "Information from the Files of the Committee on Un-American Activities," General Council of the Congregational Christian Churches Records, box 109, CL. The date is blacked out, but the report appears to be from the late 1940s.

57. Kenneth Stokes, "C.S.A. under Fire: A Study of the CSA and It's [*sic*] Critics," social ethics paper, Yale University, 10 October 1952, CSA collection, box 1, BR-2, CL.

58. Rhinesmith, "League to Uphold Congregational Principles," 40–41.

59. Dana, "Statement on Behalf of the Congregational Lay Group of Minnesota to the Executive Committee of the General Council of Congregational Christian Churches," 4 March 1952, General Council of the Congregational Christian Churches Records, box 109, CL.

60. Ibid.

61. Conn, "Memorandum to the Board of Review," General Council of the Congregational Christian Churches Records, box 109, CL.

62. "The Congregational Christian Churches and Politics," General Council of the Congregational Christian Churches Records, box 109, CL.

63. "Congregationalist Action Protested," *New York Herald Tribune*, 3 March 1952, quoted in Rhinesmith, "League to Uphold Congregational Principles."

64. *They're Using Our Church* (Minneapolis, Minn.: Committee Opposing Congregational Political Action, 1952), n.p. The booklet was filled with errors of fact, repeating the claim that the CSA was behind the antiprofit motive resolution in 1934 and accusing a CSA member of being a documented communist "fellow traveler." Yale historian Roland Bainton (a leading Congregational layman) found the league's position "sufficiently curious to provoke a comment" and pointed out one of the fundamental inconsistencies in the rhetoric against the CSA. On the one hand, the league declared that Congregationalists had no business participating in politics; and on the other, said Bainton, they celebrated the denomination's historic role in creating American political institutions. In fact, said Bainton, neither claim was accurate. "Letter to the Editor," *Advance*, 5 April 1954, 26.

65. "The Report of the Board of Review of the General Council of the Activities of the Council for Social Action," September 1953, General Council of the Congregational Christian Churches Records, box 109, CL. In 1952, the General Council also formally rescinded the profit motive resolution of 1934. "Congregational Unity Is Kept," *Christian Century*, 16 July 1952, 831.

66. Herman F. Reissig to Russell Clinchy, 4 April 1952, CSA collection, box 1, BR-17, CL.

67. "U.S. at War: Song of Happiness," *Time*, 10 August 1942.

68. Clinchy, *Faith and Freedom*.

69. "An Address by the Rev. Russell J. Clinchy, Assistant to the Chairman, League to Uphold Congregational Principles, . . . Given at the General Council of the Congregational Christian Churches, New Haven, Conn., 24 July 1954," CSA collection, box 1, BR-17, CL. A description and summary of Clinchy's talk, given at the Park Church in Grand Rapids, Michigan, is also available. See Ray Gibbons to Reverend Albert Buttrey, 28 November 1953, CSA collection, BR-17, CL.

70. Stafford, "Social Action and the General Council," CSA collection, BR-4, CL.

71. "Intra-Church Dispute: Congregational Assails Civil Rights Study," *New York Herald Tribune*, 2 February 1956, 10. The league was objecting to a CSA inquiry into threats to the civil liberties of Congregational Christian clergymen—in the league's view, the fundamental threat was communism. Albert Palmer to John Payne, 6 February 1952, CSA collection, BR-5, CL.

CHAPTER 8

1. "Congregational Inclusiveness," *Congregationalist*, 30 March 1922, 390–91.

2. Finke and Stark, *Churching of America*, 234–36.

3. Palmer D. Edmunds to John R. Scotford, 20 December 1947, Youngs papers, Merger correspondence, B14/F1, Congregational Library, Boston, Mass. (hereafter CL).

4. Henry F. May, "The Recovery of American Religious History," *American Historical Review* 70 (1965): 81.

5. Ibid., 90.

6. Edward D. Younger, "Those Things Which Cannot Be Shaken," *Foundations* 1 (January 1958): 3.

7. "The New Church: A Summons to Action," *Presbyterian Life*, 15 July 1958, 16.

8. "Information Sheet: A Brief Narrative of the Beginnings of the Congregational Christian Historical Society," Congregational Christian Historical Society collection, RG 1187 (hereafter CCHS collection), CL.

9. "Report of the Joint Committee on Proposals for Formation of a Congregational Christian Historical Society," 9 July 1951, 2, CCHS collection, CL. See also Vaughan Dabney, "Retrospect and Prospect," 14 April 1964, CCHS collection, CL. Despite its inherent pessimism, during its first ten years the society had some success, especially recruiting laypeople to serve as "local church historians." In a decade, the number of volunteers had grown from just 30 to 1,220 in thirty-eight states and the District of Columbia.

10. Fagley, "Concerning the History of Our Churches," *Congregational Bulletin* 4 (January 1953): 6. See also Frederick Fagley, "To Preserve Our Heritage," *Advance*, 24 November 1952, 10. The predecessor organization was the Committee on Denominational History, created to help facilitate the merger with the Christian Connection in 1931 but mainly charged with monitoring statistics and reporting to the General Council. CCHS was never directly incorporated into the denominational budget of the General Council of the Congregational Christian Churches, the UCC, or the National Association, and it remained a relatively weak organization until it was terminated in 2009.

11. Fagley, "Historical Society Report," *Advance*, 28 December 1953; "Biennial Report—Congregational Christian Historical Society," [1953], 3, CCHS collection, CL.

12. "Biennial Report," 10 January 1956, 3, CCHS collection, CL.

13. "Minutes of the Annual Meeting, 29 April 1960, 3, CCHS collection, CL; see also Fagley to Helen Kenyon, 21 September 1956, Fagley papers, CL.

14. "High Denominational Morale and Accelerated Drive toward Church Union Noted All across the World," *Presbyterian Observer*, 5 January 1948, 3. Survey cited in Wuthnow, *Restructuring of American Religion*, 81.

15. The International Congregational Council also surveyed all of its members and put together a compendium of Congregational practice. See Goodall, *Congregationalism—Plus*.

16. Ned B. Stonehouse, "A Refreshing Approach to Church Union," *Presbyterian Guardian*, 10 March 1948, 68.

17. "An Amazing Invitation," *Presbyterian Observer*, 28 June 1948, 8.

18. D. P. McGeachy, "The Westminster Assembly: IV. The Westminster Assembly and Its Fruit," *Presbyterian Survey*, October 1943, 477; D. P. McGeachy, "The Westminster Assembly, V. Three Centuries and Now," *Presbyterian Survey*, November 1943, 524, 525.

19. John Murray, "A Notable Tercentenary," *Presbyterian Guardian*, 10 June 1943, 161; "Editorial: Reformation Day," *Presbyterian Guardian*, 25 October 1944, 301.

20. Wuthnow, *Restructuring of American Religion*, 87.

21. Two dissertations, both written in the 1960s, provide an in-depth analysis of the merger. See Peabody, "Study of the Controversy in Congregationalism"; and Harvey, "Individualism and Ecumenical Thought." See also Nathanael Guptill, "The Rocky Road to Union," *Historical Intelligencer* 4 (1986): 4–9. Throughout I use the word "merger" to describe the ecumenical process, though it was not the preferred term by either the E&R or Congregational Christian sides. They advocated for the term "union." My use follows its prominence in all manuscripts and published material for the period. See Douglas Horton to Perry D. Avery, 8 November 1954, General Council of the Congregational Christian Churches Records, box 33, CL. On Horton's life and career, see Trost, *Douglas Horton and the Ecumenical Impulse*.

22. Carl E. Schneider, "Journey into Union," in *A History of the Evangelical and Reformed Church*, 290–95.

23. "High Denominational Morale and Accelerated Drive toward Church Union Noted across the World," *Presbyterian Outlook*, 5 January 1948, 3.

24. Wilbur La Roe Jr., "The Rock whence We Were Hewn," *Presbyterian Outlook*, 7 June 1948, 7.

25. Schneider, "Journey into Union," 291.

26. Von Rohr, *Shaping of American Congregationalism*, 425–32.

27. "Comments on Christian Century Editorial," pamphlet published by Committee for the Continuation of the Congregational Christian Churches of the United States," 5; "What Is This 'Merger' of the Congregational Christian Churches with the E. and R.?," pamphlet issued by Malcolm K. Burton, New London, Conn., both in Merger Pamphlet collection, CL.

28. "Theodore R. Faville, "With Mine Own Hand," *Wisconsin Congregational Church Life*, April 1947, 3–4.

29. "To The Congregational Ministers of Minnesota," General Council of the Congregational Christian Churches Records, box 34, CL.

30. "What Is This 'Merger' of the Congregational Christian Churches with the E. and R.?," 1, pamphlet issued by Malcolm K. Burton, New London, Conn., Merger Pamphlet collection, CL

31. "The Real Issue of the Merger Controversy," Peabody papers, MS 0140, folder I.E.2.b., CL.

32. On Ockenga, see Marsden, *Reforming Fundamentalism*.

33. Gilbert M. Savery, "Do We Want a Giant Church?," *Christianity Today*, 29 April 1957, 8–9.

34. Harold John Ockenga, "Park Street Church Again Votes No," Park Street Church collection, RG 1284 B61/F8, CL.

35. "What Our Church and Members Would Lose if We Changed from our Present Form of Church Organization," n.d., 3, Merger Pamphlet collection, CL.

36. Alexander Abbott, "Is the Name 'Congregational' Important to Us?," Malcolm Burton Pamphlet collection, CL.

37. Albert Grant Walton, "Some Objections and a Proposal," *Advance*, January 1948, 10.

38. Horton to Howard Conn, 3 January 1947, General Council of the Congregational Christian Churches Records, box 34, CL. At the time, Conn was antimerger; he would change his mind before 1957.

39. Douglas Horton to Reverend Ross Cannon, 30 April 1952, General Council of the Congregational Christian Churches Records, box 34, CL.

40. "Crisis in Congregationalism" [letter to the editor from Paul W. Yinger, Riverside, Calif.], *Advance*, November 1948, 32; Albert Buckner Coe, Press Release from Congregational Christian Office of Communication, General Council of the Congregational Christian Churches Records, box 34, CL.

41. "United in Christ," brochure published by the Executive Committee of the General Council of the Congregational Christian Churches and General Council of the Evangelical and Reformed Churches, May 15, 1955.

42. For a full text of the Basis of Union, see Hilke, *Growing toward Unity*, 578–602.

43. "The Interpretations of the Basis of Union," in Hilke, *Growing toward Unity*, 662.

44. For an analysis of the vote and the complications involved, see Peabody, "Study of the Controversy in Congregationalism," 250–55. The long delay also required the Evangelical and Reformed Churches to resubmit the Basis of Union (with its "Interpretations") to the denomination.

45. *Decision of the Courts in Regard to the Proposed Union*, 7, 8.

46. Ibid., 388–89.

47. *Cadman Memorial Congregational Society*, 828, 839.

48. Ibid., 271, 282, 360.

49. Ibid., 1616, 1629, 1648, 1661.

50. Ibid., 2255–74, 2282, 2303.

51. Horton, "Of Equability and Perseverance in Well Doing," *Minutes of the General Council, Cleveland, Ohio, June 22–26, 1950*. Beyond legitimating a connectional form of Congregationalism, Horton's purpose in the speech was to argue that the General Council itself was a church body with its own rights and freedom—he changed his own title to "minister." By implication, then, the General Council was free to carry out a merger with the Evangelical and Reformed Churches.

52. Horton's *Let Us Not Forget the Mighty William Ames* is the text from a follow-up lecture to the Congregational Union of England and Wales. Horton gave a similar talk before the Congregational Christian Historical Society in 1959. Other parallel efforts include Charles Merrill's Southworth Lecture of 1951, "The Fulfillment of Congregationalism," which traced the ecumenical thread from Puritan days to the present. It is worth noting that Horton's argument reflected two schools of thought among Congregationalists about their origins and a long-standing practice of conflating Pilgrims with Puritans. In the late nineteenth century, Henry Martyn Dexter began to argue that the decentralized polity of the Plymouth Pilgrims should be standard (Dexter, *Church Polity of the Pilgrims*), and subsequent Congregational histories generally followed his

lead. Privileging the Pilgrims hinged on a much-debated story about Plymouth doctor Daniel Fuller, who was said to have convinced the Salem church that local churches should be independent. See, for example, Walker, *History of the Congregational Churches in the United States*, 100–112; and Dunning, *Congregationalists in America*, 105–9. In the twentieth century, Harvard historian Perry Miller set the tone for most historians of New England Puritanism, arguing that the true originators of the Congregational Way were the Massachusetts Bay Puritans, and that the Pilgrims represented a small and inconsequential cul-de-sac. See Miller, *Orthodoxy in Massachusetts*, 105, 128. Interestingly, however, recent scholarship has reemphasized the Pilgrim legacy and the basic commonality between Plymouth and Massachusetts Bay. See Winship, *Godly Republicanism*, 134–58, 288–89 n. 2.

53. "'Congregationalism B': Replies to the Address 'Of Equability and Perseverance in Well Doing,'" Committee for the Continuation of Congregational Christian Churches, pamphlet, 1950, 7, CL.

54. Bainton to Wendell Fifield, 27 May 1952, Merger Pamphlet collection, CL. In 1950, David Nelson Beach, pastor of the Center Church in New Haven, proposed the idea of a "conciliar Congregationalism," "which he argued was the real, time-tested core of the tradition." Congregationalists possessed a "double heritage," he said, of both freedom and corporate order. The "simple and single Separatism" of the Pilgrims and their antimerger descendants was only half of the picture. In the long run, he said, the entire history of Congregationalism from the seventeenth century onward was a continual movement toward greater unity and institutional structure. The actions of the National Council from 1871 through 1934 provided clear precedent for the formation of the United Church of Christ. The real revisionists, Beach insisted, were Malcolm Burton and his obstructionist allies, blinded by their strict allegiance to a seventeenth-century church polity. Beach to Douglas Horton and Phil Scott, 8 February 1950, General Council of the Congregational Christian Churches Records, box 33, CL; Beach to Horton, 4 March 1954, General Council of the Congregational Christian Churches Records, box 33, CL.

55. Gunnemann, *Shaping of the United Church of Christ*, 52.

56. Coe, "The Treasures of Wisdom and Knowledge," *General Council of the Congregational Christian Churches of the United States: Minutes of the Thirteenth Regular Meeting, Omaha, Nebraska, June 20–27, 1956* (New York, 1956), 94–99.

57. Quoted in Gunneman, *Shaping of the United Church of Christ*, 13.

58. Henry Van Dusen, "The Great Neglect of Our Era," *United Church Herald* 1 (October 1958): 4–5.

59. Carl E. Schneider, "The Crisis of Faith and History," *United Church Herald*, 3 (June 1960): 18–19, 34.

60. Cover letter and litany in Peabody papers, folder 1.E.2.c, CL.

61. "Message to the Churches from the Uniting General Synod," in Hilke, *Growing toward Unity*, 750–53.

62. Burton, *Disorders in the Kingdom, Part I*, 71–73.

1. Thomas Orrin Bentz, "Plymouth Revisited: A Story of Steppingstones," *United Church Herald* [hereafter *UCH*], November 1970, 8–11, 43.

2. "Pilgrims' Progress," *Congregationalist*, April 1970, 23; Robert M. Thornton, "A Step Toward Liberty: Reflections on the Mayflower Compact," *Congregationalist*, April 1970, 7; Esther C. Quaintance, "Our 350th Anniversary: What Does It Mean?" *Congregationalist*, February 1970, 10–12; Arvel M. Steece, "More Light Shall Break Forth from Thy Word," *Congregationalist*, November 1970, 11; Clyde M, Manschreck, "Puritan Upheaval: Reform, Repression, Revolution," *Congregationalist*, November 1970, 6–8.

3. Martin Bailey, "The UCC at Twenty Five," *a.d.*, June 1982, 4.

4. "Opinion Matters," *United Church News*, October/November 2007, A5.

5. "Report of Co-President Hoskins," *Minutes of the Third General Synod of the United Church of Christ, Philadelphia, PA, July 3–7, 1961* (New York: United Church of Christ, 1961), 123, 124.

6. The Commission to Prepare a Statement of Faith, First Meeting October 24 and 25, 1957, p. 2, Executive Council Records, RG 95-1, United Church of Christ Archives (hereafter UCCA).

7. Mary Ellen Lyman to Robert V. Moss, 3 October 1972, Moss Correspondence, UCCA.

8. Loring Chase, "Toward a New Statement of Faith," *UCH*, 26 March 1959, 13, 14.

9. Ibid., 47–64. James E. Wagner and Fred Hoskins to Everett C. Parker, 7 January 1960, Executive Council Records, Wagner correspondence, RG 90-1, UCCA.

10. Outler, *The Christian Tradition and the Unity We Seek*, 6.

11. See overview in John Payne, "Tradition in Ecumenical Perspective," *Prism* 4 (Spring 1989): 4–24; "Renewal of the Christian Tradition." The historians included Outler, Yale's Sydney Ahlstrom and Jaroslav Pelikan, as well as R. Pierce Beaver, William Clebsch, and H. H. Walsh. See also Minear, *The Old and New in the Church*.

12. "Proposed Statement of Faith for Church," *Lancaster Intelligencer*, 26 March 1959. Bennett quoted in "Merged Church Frames Credo in Modern Terms," *Baltimore Sun*, 25 March 1959. All press reports are included in clipping folder in the Committee on Statement of Faith collection.

13. "Statement of Faith Drafted by Merged United Church," Associated Press, 25 March 1959; "Merged Church Frames Credo in Modern Terms." See also George Cornell, "New Church Creed Born in Hotel Room," *Seattle Times*, 26 March 1959.

14. "A Decisive Chapter in Church History Will Be Written at Oberlin, Ohio, in July," *UCH*, 4 June 1959, 4–5; "Statement of Faith Adopted by Unanimous Vote," *UCH* 2 (August 1959): 6.

15. "Letters," *UCH*, 2 (June 1959): 33; "Letters," *UCH* 2 (May 1959): 31.

16. In the last years of the process, after the *Cadman v. Kenyon* court battle was over, some spokesmen, including Douglas Horton, flew the idea of a preliminary

constitution, a first draft that would make clear the direction of the new denomination. The suggestion, like everything else connected with the merger, was intensely political as the Congregational Christian Churches had never had a formal constitution. Their Evangelical and Reformed partners had no problem with the idea, reasoning that knowing what they were agreeing to before signing the bottom line seemed prudent good sense. But rather than face another round of argument, Horton quietly dropped the proposal, which looked to some like a betrayal of trust.

17. "A Memorandum Respectfully Submitted for the Consideration of the Commission Elected by the Uniting General Synod to Draft a Constitution for the UCC," October 1957, RG 94-4, UCCA.

18. Gunnemann, *Shaping of the United Church of Christ*, 65–68; Zikmund, "The Past," pamphlet issued by Office for Church Life and Leadership, 1981.

19. Fred Hoskins and James Wagner to E and R Synod Presidents and Congregational Christian Conference Executives, 27 April 1960, Executive Council Records, RG 90-1, UCCA.

20. Everett C. Parker, "Decisions That Changed Our Church," *A.D.*, 11 (June 1982): 13.

21. The description comes from Nancy Ammerman, "Golden Rule Christianity: Lived Religion in the American Mainstream," in Hall, *Lived Religion in America*, 196–216.

22. "Laymen Ask Searching Questions," *UCH*, 20 November 1958, 21.

23. *Minutes of the Eighth General Synod, Grand Rapids, MI, June 25–29, 1971* (New York: United Church of Christ, 1971), 149–51.

24. McLeod, *Religious Crisis of the 1960s*, 16.

25. Jones, *Great Expectations*, 98, 103–5.

26. Putnam and Campbell, *American Grace*, 93.

27. Ibid., 97–98.

28. Ibid., 98.

29. McLeod, *Religious Crisis of the 1960s*, 123; Brown, *Death of Christian Britain*, 2.

30. "How to Celebrate a Church Anniversary," *UCH* 12 (January 1971): 48.

31. "Ask the Pastor," *UCH* 10 (August 1969): 45; "Ask the Pastor," *UCH* 10 (February 1969), 63.

32. Telfer Mook, "Forman at 475: What Happened and What's Ahead," *UCH*, 10 (September 1969): 34, 35.

33. "Black Churchmen Achieve Recognition," *UCH* 10 (August 1969): 12–13; "Confrontation in Boston," *UCH* 10 (August 1969):, 8–11; Robert L. Haertig, "Shouts of the Spirit: Reflections on the Seventh Synod," *UCH* 10 (October 1969): 8m–9m.

34. For a summary, see Donald Freeman, "Fifty Years of Social and Ethical Perspectives and Teachings," *Prism* 21 (Fall 2007): 46–73.

35. This is the argument of David Hollinger in "After Cloven Tongues of Fire: Ecumenical Protestantism and the Modern American Encounter with Diversity," *Journal of American History* 98 (June 2011): 21–48.

36. Maddox, *Aldersgate Reconsidered*, 32, 133.

37. Arthur S. Link, "The Proposed Confession of 1967: Another View," *Presbyterian Life*, 15 March 1966, 17. Link was professor of history at Princeton University and an elder in a Presbyterian church.

38. Charles MacKenzie, "Morality of Dissent," *Presbyterian Layman*, January 1968, 2. See also "Editorial: The Lessons of History," *Presbyterian Layman*, January 1968, 2.

39. Minutes of Executive Council of the Evangelical and Reformed Historical Society, 12 March 1964; "Fact Sheet: General Principles upon Which an Historical Commission of the United Church Might Be Developed," Historical Commission, RG 90-10, UCCA.

40. The commission also received word from the Stewardship Council that it could not raise funds directly from local churches and individual members, as was the practice with other commissions. Minutes of the Historical Commission of the UCC, October 25, 1966, RG 90-10, UCCA.

41. The "membership drive" held in the fall of 1966 had brought in only $1,717.00, which barely offset the cost of the mailing itself, at $840. "To Members of the Historical Commission from Rudolph Schade," 10 March 1967, RG 90-10, UCCA. The Historical Commission received little or no funding from the denomination at this time.

42. "A Word from the Chairman," *Newsletter of the Historical Commission of the UCC* 1 (January 1966): 1. Another indication of the problems in relating to the UCC is buried in the minutes for April 1969: "After 9:00 P.M. the meeting was held against a background of rock and roll music in the next room, featuring steel guitars and the whole ball of wax. Ugh!!!!" (Minutes of the Historical Commission of the UCC, 14 April 1969, RG 90-10, UCCA).

43. Robert V. Moss to Mervin M. Deems, 30 July 1970, Moss Correspondence, RG 90-10, UCCA. Moss gave similar urging to the Executive Committee of the Historical Commission meeting that May in Plymouth. See Minutes of the Historical Council of the UCC, 4 May 1970, RG 90-10, UCCA. In 1974, the commission began to promote Heritage Sunday instead of Forefathers' Sunday and the Totenfest celebration from the E&R tradition, a move that was reflected in the denominational desk calendar beginning that year. See RG 90-11, UCCA.

44. Lowell Zuck, Chair, to Robert V. Moss, 27 March 1975, Moss Correspondence, RG 90-11, UCCA.

45. Merlyn Matthews to Lowell Zuck, 2 April 1975 (on behalf of Robert Moss), Moss Correspondence, RG 90-11, UCCA.

46. President Robert V. Moss's Presentation to United Church of Christ Historical Council Meeting, 9-10 April 1976, RG 90-11, UCCA.

47. Minutes of the UCC Historical Council, 9-10 April 1976, RG 90-11, UCCA.

48. "Position Paper to the Executive Council, UCC from the Historical Council, UCC Concerning Program and Financing of the Historical Council and Its Related Agencies, the Archives of the UCC, the ERHS, and the CCHS," submitted 1 August 1976, RG 90-11, UCCA.

49. Barbara Brown Zikmund, "Unity and Diversity: Insights into the Histories of the United Church of Christ," *Historical Intelligencer* (Fall 1981): 20–28. See also Zikmund, *Hidden Histories*.

50. James R. Smucker, "Response: Christians for Justice Action," *New Conversations* 8 (1985): 43.

51. "Seminar Report: Toward the Task of Sound Teaching in the United Church of Christ," in Herzog, *Justice Church*, 140–53.

52. "A Most Difficult and Urgent Time," *New Conversations* 8 (Spring 1985): 2, 3. This document was one of several published in that issue of *New Conversations*. See also "The Craigville Colloquy Letter," 7–10; and "The Dubuque Declaration," 16.

53. Marini, *Sacred Song in America*, 194.

54. Ibid., 200–202.

55. Arthur G. Clyde, "The New Century Hymnal: A Theological and Liturgical Expression," *Prism* 10 (Fall 1995): 27–35. Clyde was the *UCH* editor.

56. John Ferguson, "The New Century Hymnal: A Review," *Prism* 10 (Fall 1995): 40.

57. *Balaam's Courier*, 17 July 1993, 4, pamphlet in author's possession.

58. Richard Christensen, *How Shall We Sing the Lord's Song?*, 41, 55.

59. Richard Ulrich, "Ancient and Medieval Legacies," in *Ancient and Medieval Legacies*, vol. 1 of *The Living Theological Heritage of the UCC* (Cleveland, Ohio: Pilgrim Press, 1995), 3; Charles Hambrick-Stowe, "The Rock from Which We Were Hewn: History and the Problem of Identity in the UCC," *Prism* 13 (Fall 1998): 31–46.

60. See, for example, J. Mary Luti and Andrew B. Warner, "Catholics in the United Church of Christ," http://www.ucc.org/writers-group/pdfs/Catholics-in-the-UCC-excerpt.pdf.

61. Borg, *Meeting Jesus Again for the First Time*; Spong, *Why Christianity Must Change or Die*; Oden, *The Rebirth of Orthodoxy*, 9.

62. See, for example, MacIntyre, *After Virtue*; Tickle, *Emergence Christianity*; Bass, *The Practicing Congregation*; McLaren, *Generous Orthodoxy*.

63. Lurhman, *When God Talks Back*, 12, xv; Hunter, *To Change the World*, 26–27.

Bibliography

MANUSCRIPT COLLECTIONS

Congregational Library, Boston, Mass.
   Malcolm Burton Pamphlet Collection
   Commission on Missions Collection
   Congregational Christian Historical Society Records
   Congregationalist Records
   Council for Social Action Collection, 1934–1956
   Dexter, Henry Martyn, Correspondence
   Fagley, Frederick Louis, Papers, 1923–1955
   General Council of the Congregational Christian
      Churches Records, 1965–1961
   Horton, Douglas, Papers, 1915–1942
   Merger Pamphlet Collection
   Park Street Church Collection
   Peabody, Alan Bowe, Papers, 1947–1962
   Small Collections
   Youngs, William Harvey, Papers, 1908–1973
United Church of Christ Archives
   Executive Council Records
   Historical Commission
   Historical Council Minutes
   Robert V. Moss Correspondence
Yale Divinity School
   George Leon Walker Papers
   Williston Walker Papers

PERIODICALS

Advance
Boston Review
Christian Century
Christian Register
Congregational Herald
Congregational Quarterly
Congregationalist
Congregationalist and Christian Herald
Historical Intelligencer
New Englander
Oberlin Evangelist
Outlook

Pacific
Puritan Recorder
Spirit of the Pilgrims
Truth

United Church Herald
Watchman and Reflector
Zion's Herald

MINUTES

National Council of the Congregational Churches, 1870–1930
General Council of the Congregational Christian Churches, 1931–1957
United Church of Christ General Synod, 1960–

BOOKS AND ARTICLES

Adams, Charles Francis. *Massachusetts: Its History and Its Historians.* Boston: Houghton Mifflin, 1894.

Adams, Edward G. *Historical Discourse in Commemoration of the One Hundredth Anniversary of the Formation of the First Congregational Church in Templeton, Massachusetts, with an Appendix, Embracing a Survey of the Municipal Affairs of the Town. By Edward G. Adams, Junior Pastor.* Boston, 1857.

Addresses at the Laying of the Corner Stone of the Theological Hall of the Oberlin Theological Seminary, November 18, 1871. Oberlin, Ohio: Richard Butler, 1871.

American Congregational Association. *Historical Sketch of Its Organization with Addresses at the Dedication of the New Building.* Boston, 1899.

Anderson, Benedict. *Imagined Communities: Reflections on the Origin and Spread of Nationalism.* London: Verso, 1983.

Applegate, Deborah. *The Most Famous Man in America: The Biography of Henry Ward Beecher.* New York: Doubleday, 2006.

Arch, Stephen Carl. *Authorizing the Past: The Rhetoric of History in Seventeenth-Century New England.* DeKalb: Illinois University Press, 1994.

Atkins, Gaius Glen. *An Adventure in Liberty: A Short History of the Congregational Christian Churches.* New York: Missionary Herald, 1947.

Atkins, Gaius Glen, and Frederick Fagley. *History of American Congregationalism.* Boston: Pilgrim Press, 1942.

Atkinson, Henry. *The Tercentenary Program of Social Service for the Churches.* Boston: National Council of the Congregational Churches, 1919.

Babson, Roger W. *Actions and Reactions: An Autobiography of Roger W. Babson.* New York: Harper and Brothers, 1935.

Bacon, Benjamin Wisner. *Theodore Thornton Munger: New England Minister.* New Haven, Conn.: Yale University Press, 1913.

Bacon, Leonard. *Christianity in History; a Discourse Addressed to the Alumni of Yale College, in the Annual Meeting, August 16, 1848.* New Haven, Conn., 1848.

———. *The Genesis of the New England Churches.* New York, 1874.

———. *A Manual for Young Church Members.* New Haven, Conn.: Stephen Cooke, 1833.

Bacon, Leonard Woolsey. *The Congregationalists*. New York: Baker and Taylor, 1904.

Bacon, Theodore Davenport. *Leonard Bacon: A Statesman in the Church*. New Haven, Conn.: Yale University Press, 1931.

Baker, James. *Thanksgiving: The Biography of an American Holiday*. Durham: University of New Hampshire Press, 2009.

Balmer, Randall. *Grant Us Courage: Travels along the Mainline of American Protestantism*. New York: Oxford University Press, 1996.

Bancroft, George. *History of the Colonization of the United States*. Vol. 1. Boston: Charles Little and James Brown, 1841.

Barton, William E. *Congregational Creeds and Covenants*. Chicago: Advance, 1917.

———. *A Congregational Manual of Theory and Practice*. Oak Park, Ill.: Puritan Press, 1916.

———. *The Law of Congregational Usage*. Chicago: Advance, 1916.

Bass, Diana Butler. *The Practicing Congregation: Imagining a New Old Church*. Herndon, Va.: Alban Institute, 2004.

Bates, Esther Willard. *A Pageant of Pilgrims*. Boston: Pilgrim Press, 1920.

Beecher, Thomas. *A Sermon Preached before the Chenango Association, N.Y., February 8th, 1865, by Rev. Thomas K. Beecher, of Elmira*. Congregational Pamphlets, Henry Martyn Dexter Collection, Congregational Library, Boston, Mass.

Bellows, Henry. *Some of the Points of Difference between Unitarian and Orthodox Christians*. Boston: American Unitarian Association, 1844.

Bendroth, Margaret. "New Directions on the Congregational Way." In *American Denominational History: Perspectives on the Past, Prospects for the Future*, edited by Keith Harper, 31–49. Tuscaloosa: University of Alabama Press, 2008.

———. *A School of the Church: Andover Newton at Two Hundred*. Grand Rapids, Mich.: Eerdmans, 2007.

Bercovitch, Sacvan. *The Puritan Origins of the American Self*. New Haven, Conn.: Yale University Press, 1975.

Berman, Marshall. *All That Is Solid Melts into Air: The Experience of Modernity*. New York: Simon and Schuster, 1982.

Bisbee, M. D., ed. *Songs of the Pilgrims: With an Introduction by Henry Martyn Dexter*. Boston: Congregational Sunday-School and Publishing Society, 1887.

Blake, Mortimer. *The First Quarter Century of the Winslow Church: Containing a Historical Discourse, Preached January 12, 1862, and an Appendix*. Taunton, Mass.: Vote of the Congregation, 1862.

Bond, Alvan. *A Historical Discourse, Delivered at the Hundredth Anniversary of the Organization of the Second Congregational Church, Norwich, Conn., July 24, 1860, with an Appendix*. Norwich, 1860.

The Book of the Pilgrimage: A Record of the Congregationalists' Pilgrimage to England and Holland. Boston: Office of the Congregationalist, 1896.

Borg, Marcus. *Meeting Jesus Again for the First Time: The Historical Jesus and the Heart of Contemporary Faith*. San Francisco: HarperSanFrancisco, 1994.

Bozeman, Theodore Dwight. *To Live Ancient Lives: The Primitivist Dimension in Puritanism*. Williamsburg, Va.: Institute of Early American History and Culture, 1988.

Bradford, Amory. *The Pilgrim in Old England: A Review of the History, Present Condition, and Outlook of the Independent (Congregational) Churches in England.* New York, 1893.

Bradford, William. *Bradford's "History of Plimouth Plantation" from the Original Manuscript.* Boston: Wright and Potter, 1899.

Braman, Isaac. *Centennial Discourse, Delivered at the Re-Opening of the Congregational Meeting-House in New-Rowley (Now Georgetown), December 6, 1832, by Isaac Braman.* Haverhill, Mass., 1833.

Brekus, Catherine A. *Sarah Osborn's World: The Rise of Evangelical Christianity in Early America.* New Haven: Yale University Press, 2013.

Brown, Callum. *The Death of Christian Britain: Understanding Secularisation, 1800–2000.* New York: Routledge, 2001.

Brown, Peter. *The Cult of the Saints: Its Rise and Function in Latin Christianity.* Chicago: University of Chicago Press, 1981.

Burrage, Champlin. *The Church Covenant Idea: Its Origin and Development.* Philadelphia: American Baptist Education Society, 1904.

Burton, Malcolm K. *Destiny for Congregationalism.* Oklahoma City: Modern Publishers, 1953.

———. *Disorders in the Kingdom: A History of the Merger of the Congregational Christian Churches and the Evangelical and Reformed Church: Part I. 1942–1949.* Agawam, Mass.: published by author, 1978.

———. *Disorders in the Kingdom: Part II. A History of the Merger of the Congregational Christian Churches and the Evangelical and Reformed Church.* Agawam, Mass.: published by author, 1980.

Bushnell, Horace. *Christian Nurture.* 1861. Cleveland, Ohio: Pilgrim Press, 1994.

———. *The Fathers of New England: An Oration Delivered before the New England Society of New-York, December 21, 1849.* New York: George P. Putnam, 1850.

———. "Living to God in Small Things." In *Sermons for the New Life*, 282–303. New York, 1858.

———. *Nature and the Supernatural, as Together Constituting the One System of God.* New York, 1858.

Cadman Memorial Congregational Society of Brooklyn and the Cadman Memorial Church Suing on Behalf of Themselves, and of Other Congregational Christian Churches Similarly Situated, Plaintiff-Respondents, against Helen Kenyon, as Moderator of the General Council of the Congregational Christian Churches, Defendant-Appellant. New York: New York Supreme Court Appellate Division, 1950.

Carter, Paul. *Decline and Rise of the Social Gospel: Social and Political Liberalism in American Protestant Churches, 1920–1940.* Ithaca, N.Y.: Cornell University Press, 1954.

Cavert, Samuel McCrea. *The American Churches in the Ecumenical Movement, 1900–1968.* New York: Association Press, 1968.

Christensen, Richard, ed. *How Shall We Sing the Lord's Song? An Assessment of the New Century Hymnal.* Centerville, Mass.: Confessing Christ, 1997.

Clark, Elizabeth. *Founding the Fathers: Early Church History and Protestant Professors in Nineteenth-Century America*. Philadelphia: University of Pennsylvania Press, 2011.

Clark, Joseph. *A Historical Sketch of the Congregational Churches in Massachusetts, from 1620 to 1858*. Boston: Congregational Board of Publication, 1858.

Clinchy, Russell. *Faith and Freedom*. New York: Macmillan, 1947.

Cobb, Alvan. *God's Culture of His Vineyard: A Sermon, Delivered in Plymouth before the Robinson Congregation, on the 22nd of December 1831*. Taunton, Mass., 1832.

Coffman, Elesha. *The Christian Century and the Rise of the Protestant Mainline*. New York: Oxford University Press, 2013.

The Commemorative Services of the First Church in Newton Massachusetts on the Occasion of the Two Hundred and Fiftieth Anniversary of Its Foundation. Newton, Mass.: published by the Church, 1915.

Committee for the Continuation of the Congregational Christian Churches in the United States. *Congregationalism B: Replies to the Address of Equality and Persistence in Well Doing, by Dr. Douglas Horton . . . A Study in Essential Congregationalism*. Chicago: published by author, 1950.

Conforti, Joseph. *Imagining New England: Explorations of Regional Identity from the Pilgrims to the Mid-Twentieth Century*. Chapel Hill: University of North Carolina Press, 2001.

Congregational Club of Chicago; Banquet to the Tri-Church Council, March 19, 1907. Pamphlet, Congregational Library.

Congregational Manual for the Iowa Churches, 1870. Davenport, Iowa: Gazette, 1870.

Connerton, Paul. *How Modernity Forgets*. Cambridge: Cambridge University Press, 2009.

——. *How Societies Remember*. Cambridge: Cambridge University Press, 1989.

Constitution and Associate Statutes of the Theological Seminary in Andover; With a Sketch of its Rise and Progress. Boston, 1808.

Cook, Joseph. *Boston Monday Lectures, Preludes, etc., for 1884: Do We Need a New Theology: With a Criticism of the New Congregational Creed*. London, 1885.

Cooper, James F. *Tenacious of Their Liberties: The Congregationalists in Colonial Massachusetts*. New York: Oxford University Press, 1999.

Cramp, J. M. *Baptist History: From the Foundation of the Christian Church to the Close of the Eighteenth Century*. Philadelphia: American Baptist Publication Society, n.d.

Cuckson, John. *The First Church of Plymouth, 1606–1901*. Boston: Beacon Press, 1920.

Davaney, Sheila Greeve. *Historicism: The Once and Future Challenge for Theology*. Minneapolis: Fortress Press, 2006.

Dawson, Jan. *The Unusable Past: America's Puritan Tradition, 1830–1930*. Chico, Calif.: Scholars Press, 1984.

Debates and Proceedings of the National Council of Congregational Churches, Held at Boston, Mass., June 14–24, 1865. From the Phonographic Report by J. M. W. Yerrinton and Henry M. Parkhurst. Boston: American Congregational Association, 1866.

Decision of the Courts in Regard to the Proposed Union of the Congregational Christian and Evangelical and Reformed Communions. New York: New York Court of Appeals, 1953.

Defense before the Council in Reply to Charges of Heretical Teaching by Rev. William Thurston Brown, Pastor First Congregational Church Madison, Conn. Together with the Resolutions Embodying the Decision of the Council and an Address to the Church by Prof. Lewis O. Brastow of Yale Divinity School. Madison, Conn., 1896.

Demerath, N. Jay, III. "Cultural Victory and Organizational Defeat in the Paradoxical Decline of Liberal Protestantism." *Journal for the Scientific Study of Religion* 34 (March 1995): 458–69.

Dexter, Henry Martyn. *As to Roger Williams and His "Banishment" from the Massachusetts Plantation.* Boston: Congregational Publishing Society, 1876.

———. *The Church Polity of the Pilgrims.* Boston: Congregational Publishing Society, 1870.

———. *The Congregationalism of the Last Three Hundred Years, as Seen in Its Literature.* New York: Harper and Brothers, 1880.

———. *Congregationalism: What It Is; Whence It Is; How It Works; Why It Is Better than Any Other Form of Church Government and Its Consequent Demands.* Boston, 1865.

———. *A Hand-book of Congregationalism.* Boston: Congregational Publishing Society, 1880.

———. *Memoranda, Historical, Chronological, &c. Prepared with the Hope to Aid Those Whose Interest in Pilgrim Memorials, and History, Is Freshened by This Jubilee Year, and Who May Not Have a Large Historical Library at Hand. Printed (but Not Published) for the Use of Congregational Ministers.* N.p., 1870.

———. *Street Thoughts.* Boston, 1859.

Dickinson, C. E. *A Century of Church Life: A History of the First Congregational Church of Marietta, Ohio.* Marietta, Ohio, 1896.

Dodge, Joshua. *Sermon Delivered in Haverhill, December 22, 1820 before the Second Centesimal Anniversary of the Landing of the New-England Fathers at Plymouth, by Joshua Dodge.* Haverhill, Mass., 1821.

Dunning, Albert. *Congregationalists in America: A Popular History of Their Origin, Belief, Polity, Growth, and Work.* Boston: Pilgrim Press, 1894.

Durfee, Calvin. *Advantages of Retrospection: A Commemorative Discourse Delivered before the Congregational Church and Society in Great Barrington, May 13, 1866, by Rev. Calvin Durfee.* Boston, 1866.

Eaton, Emma Florence. *Dramatic Studies from the Bible.* Boston: Pilgrim Press, 1906.

Edwards, Bela. "A Puritan Library in New England." *Bibliotheca Sacra* (August 1847): 590–98.

Edwards, Jonathan. *A Faithful Narrative of the Surprising Work of God in the Conversion of Many Hundred Souls in Northampton.* Boston, 1736.

Eire, Carlos. *A Very Brief History of Eternity.* Princeton, N.J.: Princeton University Press, 2010.

Eliade, Mircea. *Myth and Reality.* Translated from the French by Willard R. Trask. New York: Harper and Row, 1963.

Ellingson, Stephen. *Megachurch and the Mainline: Remaking Religious Tradition in the Twenty-First Century*. Chicago: University of Chicago, 2007.

Erickson, Paul D. "Daniel Webster's Myth of the Pilgrims." *New England Quarterly* 57 (March 1984): 44–64.

Fagley, Frederick L. "A Brief Annotated Bibliography of Congregational Manuals and Textbooks on Congregational Polity." *Minister's Quarterly* 7 (1951): 3–9.

———. *The Congregational Churches: An Outline of the History, Beliefs, and the Organization of Congregational Churches in the United States*. Boston: Pilgrim Press, 1925.

Fifield, James W. *The Tall Preacher: Autobiography of Dr. James W. Fifield, Jr. with Bill Youngs*. Los Angeles: Pepperdine University Press, 1977.

Fiftieth Anniversary of the Founding of Pilgrim Congregational Church. St. Louis, Mo., 1916.

Finke, Roger, and Rodney Stark. *The Churching of America, 1776–1990: Winners and Losers in Our Religious Economy*. New Brunswick, N.J.: Rutgers University Press, 1992.

First Congregational Church, Kalamazoo. *Our Church: It's [sic] History, It's Buildings, It's Spirit*. Kalamazoo, Mich., 1928.

Fisher, Nathaniel W. *The Law of Progress as Applied to Morals and Religion: A Sermon Delivered at the Dedication of the First Congregational Church, in Margaretta, at Castalia, Ohio, by Nathaniel W. Fisher*. Sandusky City, Ohio, 1848.

Fiske, D. T. *Historical Discourse Commemorative of the Belleville Congregational Church, Newburyport, Mass., Delivered on Thanksgiving Day, November 25, 1858, by D. T. Fiske, Pastor*. Boston, 1859.

Foster, Frank Hugh. "The Field and Work of a Local Church History Society." In *Papers of the Ohio Church History Society*. Vol. 1:1–30. Oberlin, Ohio, 1899.

Free Congregational Church, Providence. *Pilgrim Jubilee: Celebration in Providence, R.I. of the Two Hundred and Fiftieth Anniversary of Congregationalism in This Country, October 11th 1870, Minutes of Rhode Island Churches in Council; Memorial Address by the Rev. Mark Hopkins, D.D. LL.D., President of Williams College; Festival and Addresses*. Central Falls, R.I., 1870.

Fritzsche, Peter. *Stranded in the Present: Modern Time and the Melancholy of History*. Cambridge, Mass.: Harvard University Press, 2004.

Gay, Peter. *A Loss of Mastery: Puritan Historians in Colonial America*. Berkeley: University of California Press, 1966.

General Association of California. *Hand-Book of the Congregational Churches of California*. San Francisco, 1871.

General Association of Connecticut. *Congregational Order: The Ancient Platforms of the Congregational Churches of New England; with a Digest of Rules and Usages in Connecticut*. Hartford, 1845.

General Association of Iowa. *Minutes of the General Association of Iowa, at Their Session in Grinnell, June 1856*. N.p.

General Association of Illinois. *Historical Papers Prepared for the Quarter Centennial Meeting of the General Association of Illinois, from an Appendix to the Minutes of 1869*. N.p., 1869.

———. *Minutes of the General Association of Illinois, at the Annual Meeting in Bloomington, May 26, 27, 28, & 30.* Ottawa, Ill., 1859.

General Association of Michigan. *Minutes of the General Association of Michigan at Their Meeting in Detroit, May 19, 1859.* Adrian, 1859.

General Association of New York. *Minutes of the General Association of New York at Their Meeting in Madison, August, 1848.* New York, 1849.

Goodall, Norman. *Congregationalism—Plus.* London: Independent Press, 1953.

Gunnemann, Louis. *The Shaping of the United Church of Christ: An Essay in the History of American Christianity.* New York: United Church Press, 1977.

Guyatt, Nicholas. *Providence and the Invention of the United States, 1607–1876.* Cambridge: Cambridge University Press, 2007.

Halbwachs, Maurice. *On Collective Memory.* Edited and translated by Lewis A. Coser. Chicago: University of Chicago Press, 1992.

Hall, David. "Calvin and Calvinism within Congregational and Unitarian Discourse in Nineteenth-Century America." In *John Calvin's American Legacy,* edited by Thomas J. Davis, 147–64. New York: Oxford University Press, 2010.

———. *A Reforming People: Puritanism and the Transformation of Public Life in New England.* New York: Knopf, 2011.

———, ed. *Lived Religion in America: Toward a History of Practice.* Princeton, N.J.: Princeton University Press 1997.

Hand-Book of the Congregational Churches of California. San Francisco: John Carmany, 1871.

Hansen, Karen V. *A Very Social Time: Crafting Community in Antebellum New England.* Berkeley: University of California Press, 1994.

Hatch, Nathan. *The Democratization of American Christianity.* New Haven, Conn.: Yale University Press, 1989.

Harvey, Charles. "Individualism and Ecumenical Thought: The Merger Controversy in Congregationalism, 1937–1961." PhD diss., University of California, Riverside, 1968.

Hawes, Joel. *Tribute to the Memory of the Pilgrims.* 1830. Hartford, Conn., 1836.

Hawley, Z. K. *Congregational Tracts.* New Haven, Conn., 1844.

Hedstrom, Matthew. *The Rise of Liberal Religion: Book Culture and American Spirituality in the Twentieth Century.* New York: Oxford University Press, 2013.

Herring, Hubert. *The Place of Congregationalism in Recent History.* Boston: Pilgrim Press, 1914.

Herzog, Frederick. *Justice Church: The New Function of the Church in North American Christianity.* New York: Orbis Books, 1981.

Hilke, Elsabeth Slaughter, ed. *Growing toward Unity.* Vol. 6 of *The Living Theological Heritage of the United Church of Christ.* Cleveland, Ohio: Pilgrim Press, 2001.

Hill, William. *A History of the Rise, Progress, Genius, and Character of American Presbyterianism.* Washington City, Va., 1839.

Hobsbawm, Eric, and Terence Ranger, eds. *The Invention of Tradition.* Cambridge: Cambridge University Press, 1983.

Hodge, Charles. *The Constitutional History of the Presbyterian Church of the United States of America, Part I, 1705–1741.* Philadelphia, 1839.

Hogan, David. *An Epitome of the Ecclesiastical History of John Lawrence Mosheim, Comprising Extracts of the Principal Matter Contained in the Whole Six Volumes of That Eminent Writer.* Philadelphia: David Hogan, 1812.

Holifield, E. Brooks. *Theology in America: Christian Thought from the Age of the Puritans to the Civil War.* New Haven, Conn.: Yale University Press, 2003.

———. "Toward a History of American Congregations." In *American Congregations.* Vol. 2: *New Perspectives in the Study of Congregations,* edited by James P. Wind and James W. Lewis, 23–53. Chicago: University of Chicago Press 1994.

Hollinger, David. *After Cloven Tongues of Fire: Protestant Liberalism in Modern American History.* Princeton, N.J.: Princeton University Press, 2012.

Hood, E. Lyman. *The National Council of Congregational Churches in the United States.* Boston: Pilgrim Press, 1902.

Horton, Douglas. *Congregationalism: A Study in Church Polity.* London: Independent Press, 1952.

———. *Let Us Not Forget the Mighty William Ames.* Nashville: Abingdon, 1960.

———. *Of Equability and Perseverance in Well Doing* [pamphlet]. Cleveland, Ohio: General Council of the Congregational Christian Churches, 1950.

Howard, Thomas. *Religion and the Rise of Historicism: W. M. L. de Wette, Jacob Burckhardt, and the Theological Origins of Nineteenth-Century Historical Consciousness.* Cambridge: Cambridge University Press, 2000.

Howe, Daniel Walker. *What Hath God Wrought: The Transformation of America, 1815–1848.* New York: Oxford University Press, 2007.

Howes, Frederick G. *History of the Town of Ashfield, Franklin County, Massachusetts.* Published by the town, 1910.

Hughes, Richard T., and C. Leonard Allen. *Illusions of Innocence: Protestant Primitivism in America, 1630–1875.* Chicago: University of Chicago Press, 1988.

Humphrey, Seldon B. "The Union of the Congregational and the Christian Churches." Ph.D. diss., Yale University, 1933.

Hunt, Lynn. *Measuring Time, Making History.* Budapest: Central European University Press, 2008.

Hunter, James Davison. *To Change the World: The Irony, Tragedy, and Possibility of Christianity in the Late Modern World.* New York: Oxford University Press, 2010.

Jones, Landon Y. *Great Expectations: America and the Baby Boom Generation.* New York: Ballantine Books, 1980.

Jubilee of the South Congregational Church, November the Eleventh, Twelfth, Thirteenth and Sixteenth, Nineteen Hundred. Pittsfield, Mass., 1900.

Jubilee Year: Fiftieth Anniversary of the Organization of the First Congregational Church and Society of Detroit, Michigan. Detroit, 1895.

Kammen, Michael. *Mystic Chords of Memory: The Transformation of Tradition in American Culture.* New York: Vintage Books, 1993.

Kelley, Dean M. *Why Conservative Churches Are Growing.* New York: Harper and Row, 1972.

Kennedy, William S. *The Plan of Union; or, A History of the Presbyterian and Congregational Churches of the Western Reserve; with Biographical Sketches of the Early Missionaries.* Hudson, Ohio, 1856.

Kirbye, J. Edward. *History of the First Congregational Church, Medina, Ohio, 1819–1909.* N.p. [1909?]

Landsberg, Alison. *Prosthetic Memory: The Transformation of American Remembrance in the Age of Mass Culture.* New York: Columbia University Press, 2004.

Langworthy, Isaac. "Lessons from Statistics." *Congregational Quarterly* (July 1862): 293–296.

Larkin, Jack. *The Reshaping of Everyday Life, 1790–1840.* San Francisco: Harper Perennial, 1988.

Leach, William. *Land of Desire: Merchants, Power, and the Rise of a New American Culture.* New York: Vintage Books, 1993.

LeGoff, Jacques. *History and Memory.* Translated by Steven Rendall and Elizabeth Claman. New York: Columbia University Press, 1992.

Leonard, Delevan. *The Story of Oberlin: The Institution, the Community, the Idea, the Movement.* Boston: Pilgrim Press, 1898.

Lofton, Kathryn. "The Methodology of the Modernists: Process in American Protestantism." *Church History* 75 (June 2006): 374–402.

Lundy, John Patterson. *Review of Bishop Hopkins' Bible View of Slavery by a Presbyter of the Church in Philadelphia.* Philadelphia, 1863.

Lunt, William P. *Two Discourses, Delivered September 29, 1839, on Occasion of the Two Hundredth Anniversary of the Gathering of the First Congregational Church, Quincy, by William P. Lunt.* Boston, 1840.

Lurhman, Tanya. *When God Talks Back: Understanding the Evangelical Relationship with God.* New York: Knopf, 2012.

Machen, J. Gresham. "History and Faith." *Princeton Theological Review* 13 (July 1915): 337–51.

MacIntyre, Alasdair. *After Virtue: A Study in Moral Theology.* Notre Dame, Ind.: University of Notre Dame Press, 1981.

MacLeod, Hugh. *The Religious Crisis of the 1960s.* New York: Oxford University Press, 2007.

Maddox, Randy, ed. *Aldersgate Reconsidered.* Nashville: Kingswood Books, 1990.

Manual of Church Polity, Prepared by a Committee of the General Congregational Association of Iowa. Burlington, Iowa, 1850.

Manual of the Principles, Doctrines and Usages of Congregational Churches, Compiled for Use in the Organization of Churches in Missouri. 2nd ed. St. Louis, Mo., 1868.

Marble, Annie Russell. *The Women Who Came in the Mayflower.* Boston: Pilgrim Press, 1920.

Marini, Steven. *Sacred Song in America: Religion, Music, and Public Culture.* Champaign-Urbana: University of Illinois Press, 2003.

Marsden, George. *The Evangelical Mind and the New School Presbyterian Experience.* New Haven, Conn.: Yale University Press, 1970.

———. *Fundamentalism and American Culture: The Shaping of Twentieth-Century Evangelicalism, 1870–1925.* New York: Oxford University Press, 1980.

———. *Reforming Fundamentalism: Fuller Seminary and the New Evangelicalism.* Grand Rapids, Mich.: Eerdmans, 1995.

———. *The Soul of the American University: From Protestant Establishment to Established Nonbelief.* New York: Oxford University Press, 1994.

May, Samuel. *Letters to the Rev. Joel Hawes, D.D., in Review of His "Tribute to the Memory of the Pilgrims."* Hartford, Conn., 1831.

McElvaine, Robert S. *The Great Depression: America, 1929–1941.* New York: Times Books, 1993.

McLaren, Brian. *A Generous Orthodoxy.* Grand Rapids, Mich.: Zondervan, 2006.

McLeod, Hugh. *The Religious Crisis of the 1960s.* Oxford, England: Oxford University Press, 2007.

Mead, Sydney. *The Lively Experiment: The Shaping of Christianity in America.* New York: Harper and Row, 1963.

Meehan, Seth. "Denominating a People: Congregational Laity, Church Disestablishment, and the Struggles of Denominationalism in Massachusetts, 1780–1865." Ph.D. diss., Boston University, 2014.

Memorial of the Twenty-Fifth Anniversary of the Settlement of Rev. Joshua Emery, Pastor of the First Congregational Church, Weymouth, Massachusetts. Boston, 1851.

Micklem, John. *Congregationalism To-Day.* London: Hodder and Stoughton, 1937.

Miller, Glenn. *Piety and Intellect: The Aims and Purposes of Ante-Bellum Theological Education.* Atlanta, Ga.: Scholars Press, 1990.

Miller, Moses. *Historical Discourse: Delivered by Rev. Moses Miller, Former Pastor of the First Congregational Church in Heath, at the Request of Said Church, October 13, 1852.* Shelburne Falls, Mass., 1853.

Miller, Perry. *Orthodoxy in Massachusetts, 1630–1650: A Genetic Study.* Cambridge, Mass.: Harvard University Press, 1933.

Miller, Robert Moats. *American Protestantism and Social Issues, 1919–1939.* Chapel Hill: University of North Carolina Press, 1958.

Miller, Samuel. *Presbyterianism: The Truly Primitive and Apostolical Constitution of the Church of Christ.* Philadelphia: Presbyterian Tract and Sunday School Society, 1836.

Minear, Paul, ed. *The Old and New in the Church: Faith and Order Studies.* Minneapolis: Augsburg, 1961.

Minutes of the National Council of the Congregational Churches of the United States of America, at the First Session, Held in Oberlin, Ohio, November 15–21, 1871. Boston: Congregational Publishing Society, 1871.

Minutes of the Western Congregational Convention, Held in Michigan City, Indiana July 30–August 3, 1846. New York, 1878.

Mitchell, John. *Guide to the Principles and Practices of the Congregational Churches of New England; with a Brief History of the Denomination.* Northampton, Mass., 1838.

Murphy, Andrew. *Prodigal Nation: Moral Decline and Divine Punishment from New England to 9/11.* New York: Oxford University Press, 2009.

National Council of Congregational Churches. *Ecclesiastical Polity: The Government and Communion Practised by the Congregational Churches in the United States of America, Which Were Represented by Elders and Messengers in a National Council at Boston, A.D. 1865.* Boston: Congregational Publishing Society, 1872.

———. *Pilgrim Deeds and Duties: A Handbook of Congregational History and Outlook.* Boston: Pilgrim Press, 1916.

Noll, Mark. *America's God: From Jonathan Edwards to Abraham Lincoln.* New York: Oxford University Press, 2002.

Novick, Peter. *That Noble Dream: The "Objectivity Question" and the American Historical Profession.* Cambridge: Cambridge University Press, 1988.

Oden, Thomas. *The Rebirth of Orthodoxy.* San Francisco: HarperSanFrancisco, 2003.

Outler, Albert. *The Christian Tradition and the Unity We Seek.* New York: Oxford University Press, 1957.

Parker, Theodore. *Discourse on the Transient and Permanent in Christianity; Preached at the Ordination of Mr. Charles C. Shackford.* Boston, 1841.

Patton, William. "An Account of the National Council at Boston, Mass." MS sermon, 1865, Small Collections, RG 160, Congregational Library, Boston, Mass.

Payne, John. "Tradition in Ecumenical Perspective." *Prism* 4 (Spring 1989): 4–24.

Peabody, Alan Bowe. "A Study of the Controversy in Congregationalism over Merger with the Evangelical and Reformed Church." Ph.D. diss., Syracuse University, 1964.

Pease, Jane H. "On Interpreting Puritan History: Williston Walker and the Limitations of the Nineteenth-Century View." *New England Quarterly* 42 (June 1969): 232–234.

Peel, Albert. *Inevitable Congregationalism.* London: Independent Press, 1937.

Peel, Albert, and Douglas Horton. *International Congregationalism.* London: Independent Press, 1949.

Pelikan, Jaroslav. *The Vindication of Tradition.* New Haven, Conn.: Yale University Press, 1986.

Perkins, Frank. *Handbook of Old Burial Hill.* Plymouth, Mass.: A. S. Burbank, 1902.

Piper, John F., Jr. *The American Churches in World War I.* Athens: Ohio University Press, 1985.

Pond, Enoch. *The Church.* Boston, 1837.

———. *A History of God's Church from its Origin to the Present Time.* Hartford, Conn., 1871.

Proceedings of the Board of Managers of the Western Methodist Historical Society. Cincinnati: Methodist Book House, 1893.

Proceedings of the General Convention of Congregational Ministers and Delegates in the United States, Held at Albany, N.Y., on the 5th, 6th, 7th, and 8th of October, 1852. New York, 1852.

Progressive Orthodoxy; A Christian Contribution to the Christian Interpretation of New Doctrines. Boston, 1892.

Punchard, George. *A View of Congregationalism.* New York, 1840.

Putnam, Robert, and David Campbell. *American Grace: How Religion Divides and Unites Us.* New York: Simon and Schuster, 2010.

Reasons Why I Am a Congregationalist. Hartford, Conn., 1843.

"The Renewal of the Christian Tradition: The Report of the North American Section." In *Faith and Order Findings: The Final Report of the Theological Commissions of the Fourth World Conference on Faith and Order, Montreal 1963.* London: SCM Press, 1963.

Report of the Convention of Unitarian Churches Held in New York, on the 5th and 6th of April 1865 and of the Organization of the National Conference. Boston, 1866.

Rhinesmith, Deborah F. "The League to Uphold Congregational Principles." *International Congregational Journal* 92 (Winter 2010): 40–41.

Rich, A. Judson. *Historical Discourse Delivered on Occasion of the One Hundred and Twenty-Fifth Anniversary of the Congregational Church and the Fiftieth Anniversary of the Sunday School, in Westminster, Mass., September 9, 1868, by A. Judson Rich (The Pastor).* Springfield, Mass., 1869.

Richards, Charles H. *The Improvement of Worship: A Report Read at the National Council of Congregational Churches, at Worcester, Mass., October 12, 1889.* Boston: Congregational Publishing Society, 1889.

Richards, George. *The Nature of the Church according to the Teaching of Congregationalists.* New York: Commission on Interchurch Relations and Christian Unity, 1939.

Roe, Azel Stevens. *History of the First Ecclesiastical Society in East Windsor, from its Formation in 1852, to the Death of its Second Pastor, Rev. Shubael Bartlett in 1854, with a Sketch of the Life of Rev. Mr. Bartlett, and His Farewell Discourse, Prepared for the Fiftieth Anniversary of His Settlement.* Hartford, Conn., 1857.

Rohrer, James. *Keepers of the Covenant: Frontier Missions and the Decline of Congregationalism, 1774–1818.* New York: Oxford University Press, 1995.

Roof, Wade Clark. *Spiritual Marketplace: Baby Boomers and the Remaking of American Religion.* Princeton, N.J.: Princeton University Press, 1999.

Ross, A. Hastings. *A Pocket Manual of Congregationalism.* 1883. Oberlin, Ohio, 1889.

Rouse, Thomas H. *Fiftieth Anniversary of the Organization of the First Congregational Church of Jamestown, N.Y.* Jamestown, N.Y., 1866.

Roy, J. E. *A Manual of the Principles, Doctrines and Usages of Congregational Churches.* Chicago, 1869.

Sandeen, Ernest R. *The Roots of Fundamentalism: British and American Millenarianism, 1800–1930.* Chicago: University of Chicago Press, 1970.

Sandhurst, Philip. *The Great Centennial Exhibition Critically Described and Illustrated.* Philadelphia: P. W. Ziegler, 1876.

Sanford, John E. "Memoir of Rev. Henry Martyn Dexter, D.D., LL.D." *Proceedings of the Massachusetts Historical Society* 7 (November 1891): 90–103.

Schiffman, Zachary Sayre. *The Birth of the Past.* Baltimore, Md.: Johns Hopkins University Press, 2011.

Schmidt, Leigh Eric, and Sally Promey, eds. *American Religious Liberalism*. Bloomington: Indiana University Press, 2012.

Schneider, Carl E. *A History of the Evangelical and Reformed Church*. New York: Pilgrim Press, 1990. Originally published in 1960 by Christian Education Press.

Schneider, Robert A. "Voice of Many Waters: Church Federation in the Twentieth Century." In *Between the Times: The Travail of the Protestant Establishment in America, 1900–1960*, edited by William R. Hutchison, 95–121. Cambridge, Mass.: Harvard University Press, 1989.

Second Church in Newton. *Our Church: Its History, Its Buildings, Its Spirit*. West Newton, Mass., 1926.

Seelye, John. *Memory's Nation: The Place of Plymouth Rock*. Chapel Hill: University of North Carolina Press, 1998.

Shedd, William G. T. *Lectures upon the Philosophy of History*. Andover, Mass., 1856.

———. *The Nature and Influence of the Historic Spirit: An Inaugural Discourse*. Andover, Mass., 1854.

A Silver Jubilee Celebration: The Twenty-Fifth Anniversary of the First Congregational Church Montclair, New Jersey, and the Pastorate of Amory Howe Bradford, Its First and Only Minister, 1870–1895. New York, 1895.

Silverman, Kenneth. *The Life and Times of Cotton Mather*. New York: Harper and Row, 1984.

Smith, Christian. *American Evangelicals: Embattled and Thriving*. Chicago: University of Chicago Press, 1998.

Smith, H. Shelton. *Changing Conceptions of Original Sin*. New York: Charles Scribner's Sons, 1955.

Smith, Timothy L. "Congregation, State, and Denomination: The Forming of American Religious Structure." *William and Mary Quarterly* 25 (April 1968): 155–76.

———. *Revivalism and Social Reform in Mid-Nineteenth-Century America*. New York: Abingdon Press, 1957.

Snow, Stephen Eddy. *Performing the Pilgrims: A Study of Ethnohistorical Role-Playing at Plimoth Plantation*. Jackson: University of Mississippi Press, 1993.

Somers, Margaret. "The Narrative Construction of Identity: A Relational and Network Approach." *Theory and Society* 23 (October 1994): 605–49.

Spong, Shelby. *Why Christianity Must Change or Die*. San Francisco: HarperSanFrancisco, 1998.

Stearns, George Warren. *Two Hundredth Anniversary of the First Congregational Church in Middleboro, Mass., Historical Discourse*. Middleboro, Mass.: published by the Church, 1895.

Stebbins, Rufus P. *A Centennial Discourse Delivered to the First Congregational Church and Society in Leominster, September 24, 1843*. Boston, 1843.

Stephens, Randall, and Karl Giberson. *The Anointed: Evangelical Truth in a Secular Age*. Cambridge, Mass.: Harvard University Press, 2011.

Storrs, Richard. *A Discourse Delivered at Stoughton, Mass., at the Funeral of Rev. Calvin Park, D.D. on Friday January 8, 1857*. Andover, Mass., 1847.

Stout, Harry S. *The New England Soul: Preaching and Religious Culture in Colonial New England*. New York: Oxford University Press, 1986.

Stowe, Harriet Beecher. *The Minister's Wooing*. New York: Penguin Press, 1999.

Sturtevant, J. M., Jr., ed. *Julian M. Sturtevant: An Autobiography*. New York: Fleming H. Revell, 1896.

Taves, Ann. *Fits, Trances, and Visions: Experiencing Religion and Explaining Experience from Wesley to James*. Princeton, N.J.: Princeton University Press, 1999.

Taylor, Charles. *A Secular Age*. Cambridge, Mass.: Harvard University Press, 2007.

Taylor, Sharon. "That Obnoxious Doctrine: Future Probation and the Struggle to Construct an American Congregationalist Identity." Ph.D. diss., Boston College, 2004.

Taylor, Richard. *Congregational and Plan of Union Churches in the Great Lake States*. Providence, R.I.: Published by author, 2009.

Thompson, Augustus C. *Better Land; or, The Believer's Journey and Future Home*. Boston, 1859.

———. *Future Probation and Foreign Missions*. Boston, 1886.

Thuesen, Peter. *In Discordance with the Scriptures: American Protestant Battles over Translating the Bible*. New York: Oxford University Press, 1999.

Tickle, Phyllis. *The Great Emergence: How Christianity Is Changing and Why*. Grand Rapids, Mich.: Baker Books, 2012.

Townsend, Robert B. *History's Babel: Scholarship, Professionalization, and the Historical Enterprise in the United States, 1880–1940*. Chicago: University of Chicago Press, 2013.

Trost, Theodore. *Douglas Horton and the Ecumenical Impulse in American Religion*. Cambridge, Mass.: distributed by Harvard University Press for Harvard Theological Studies, 2002.

Tucker, Bruce. "The Reinterpretation of Puritan History in Provincial New England." *New England Quarterly* 54 (December 1981): 481–498.

Tucker, Mark. *The Centennial Sermon, Preached before the Beneficent Congregational Church and Society in Providence, R.I., March 19, a.d. 1843, by Rev. Mark Tucker*. Providence, R.I., 1845.

Tucker, William Jewett. *My Generation: An Autobiographical Interpretation*. Boston: Houghton Mifflin, 1919.

Turner, James. *Without God, without Creed: The Origins of Unbelief in America*. Baltimore, Md.: Johns Hopkins University Press, 1985.

Upham, Thomas. *Ratio Disciplinae or the Constitution of the Congregational Churches*. Portland, Maine, 1829.

Von Rohr, John. *The Shaping of American Congregationalism, 1620–1957*. Cleveland, Ohio: Pilgrim Press, 1992.

Wacker, Grant. *Augustus H. Strong and the Dilemma of Historical Consciousness*. Macon, Ga.: Mercer University Press, 1985.

———. "Second Thoughts on the Great Commission: Liberal Protestants and Foreign Missions, 1890–1940." In *Earthen Vessels: American Evangelicals and Foreign Missions, 1880–1980*, edited by Joel Carpenter and Wilbert Shenk, 281–300. Grand Rapids, Mich.: Eerdmans, 1990.

Walker, Williston. *Creeds and Platforms of Congregationalism*. 1893. Cleveland, Ohio: Pilgrim Press, 1991.

————. *A History of the Congregational Churches of the United States.* New York: Christian Literature, 1894.

————. *Ten New England Leaders.* 1901. New York: Arno Press, 1969.

Weir, David. *Early New England: A Covenanted Society.* Grand Rapids, Mich.: Eerdmans, 2005.

Wellman, J. W. *The Church Polity of the Pilgrims. A Sermon by Rev. J .W. Wellman, Pastor of the Eliot Church, Newton, MA. With an Appendix.* Boston: Congregational Board of Publication, 1857.

Weston, David. *The Baptist Movement of a Hundred Years Ago, and Its Vindication. A Discourse Delivered at the One Hundred and Twelfth Anniversary of the First Baptist Church, Middleborough, Mass., January 16, 1868.* Boston, 1868.

White, Ronald C., Jr. *Liberty and Justice for All: Racial Reform and the Social Gospel, 1877–1925.* Louisville: Westminster/John Knox Press, 1990.

Wigger, John. *Taking Heaven by Storm: Methodism and the Rise of Popular Christianity in America.* Urbana: University of Illinois Press, 2001.

Winship, Michael P. *Godly Republicanism: Puritans, Pilgrims, and a City on a Hill.* Cambridge, Mass.: Harvard University Press, 2012.

Wood, Joseph F. *The New England Village.* Baltimore, Md.: Johns Hopkins University Press, 1997.

Woods, Leonard. *The Heaven of Christians: A Sermon Delivered at the Funeral of Mrs. Phebe Farrar, Wife of Samuel Farrar, Esq., Andover, Mass., January 26, 1848.* Andover, Mass., 1848.

————, comp. *Report on Congregationalism, Including a Manual of Church Discipline, Together with the Cambridge Platform, Adopted in 1648, and the Confession of Faith, Adopted in 1680.* Boston, 1846.

Wright, Conrad. *Congregational Polity: A Historical Survey of Unitarian and Universalist Practice.* Boston: Skinner House, 1997.

————. "The Growth of Denominational Bureaucracies: A Neglected Aspect of American Church History." *Harvard Theological Review* 77 (1984): 184–85.

————. *The Unitarian Controversy: Essays on American Unitarian History.* Boston: Skinner House Books, 1994.

Wuthnow, Robert. *The Restructuring of American Religion: Society and Faith Since World War II.* Princeton, N.J.: Princeton University Press, 1988.

Wuthnow, Robert, and John H. Evans, eds. *The Quiet Hand of God: Faith-Based Activism and the Public Role of Mainline Protestantism.* Berkeley: University of California Press, 2002.

Yearbook of the American Congregational Union for the Year 1854. New York: American Congregational Union, 1854.

Zakai, Avihu. *Exile and Kingdom: History and Apocalypse in the Puritan Migration to America.* Cambridge: Cambridge University Press, 1992.

————. *Jonathan Edwards' Philosophy of History: The Re-Enchantment of the World in the Age of Enlightenment.* Princeton, N.J.: Princeton University Press, 2003.

Zikmund, Barbara Brown. *Hidden Histories in the United Church of Christ.* 2 vols. Cleveland, Ohio: United Church Press, 1987.

Index